ELIAS SIME

EREGATA

እረገታ

Edited by Gemma Brace

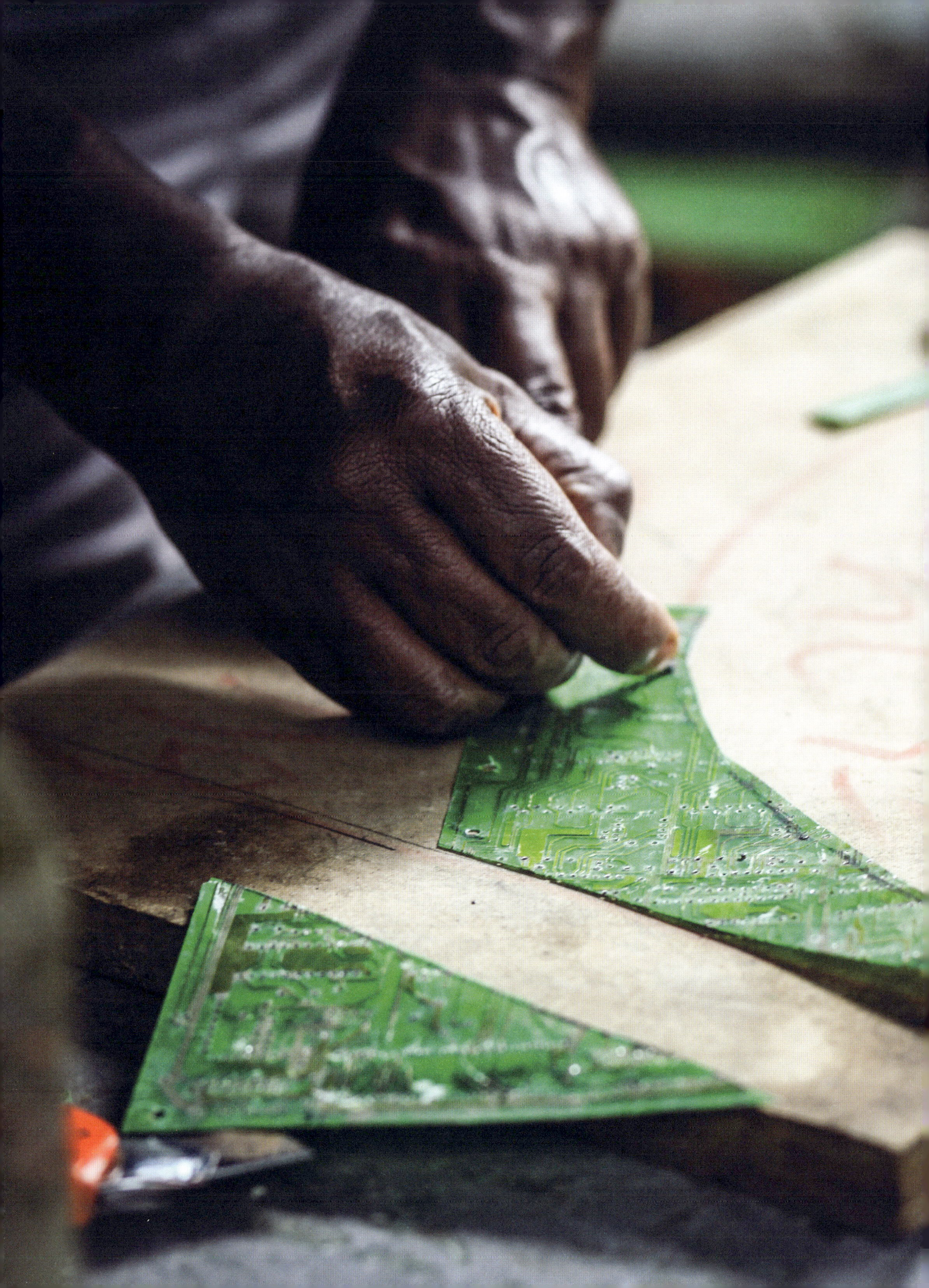

CONTENTS

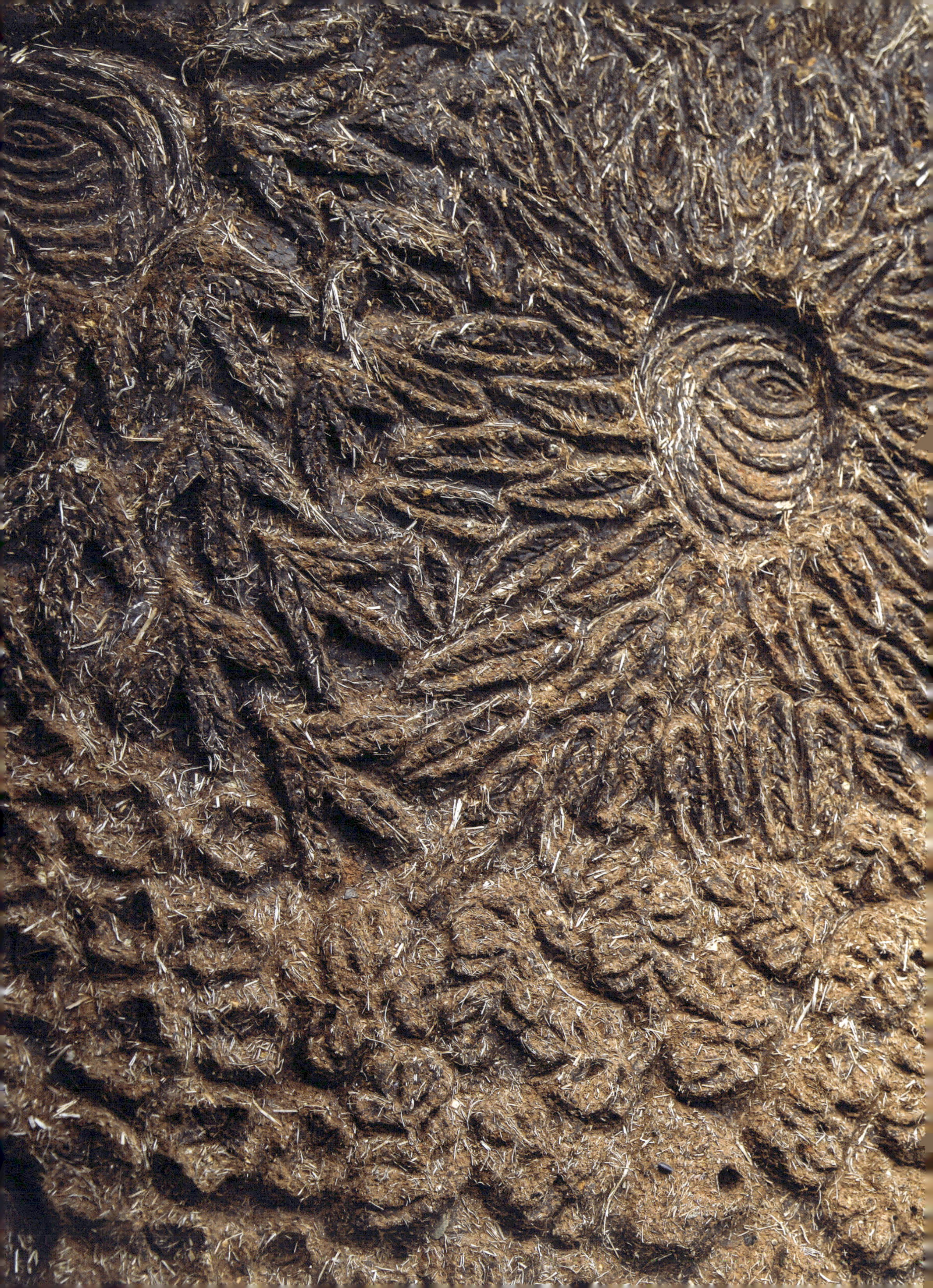

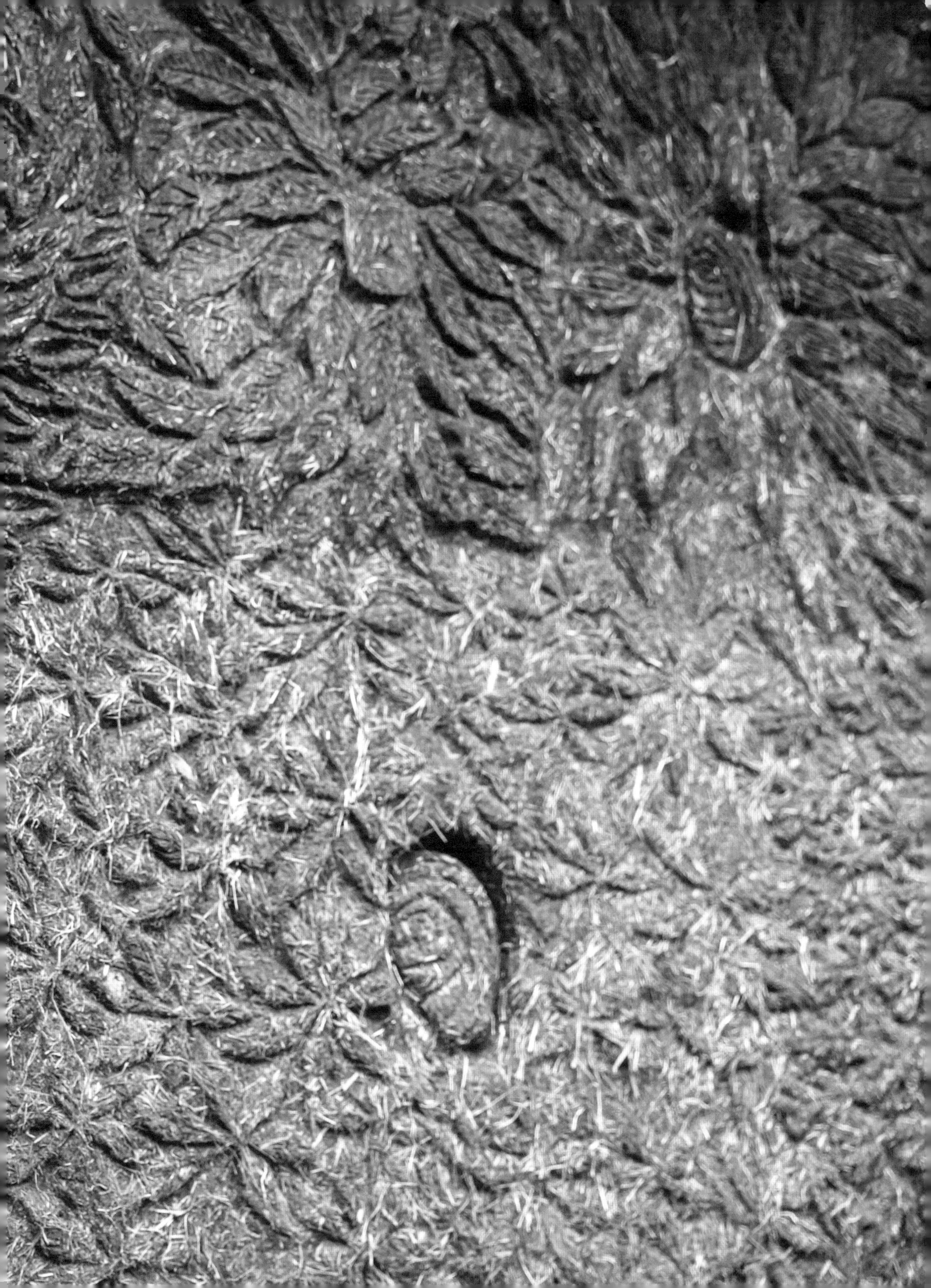

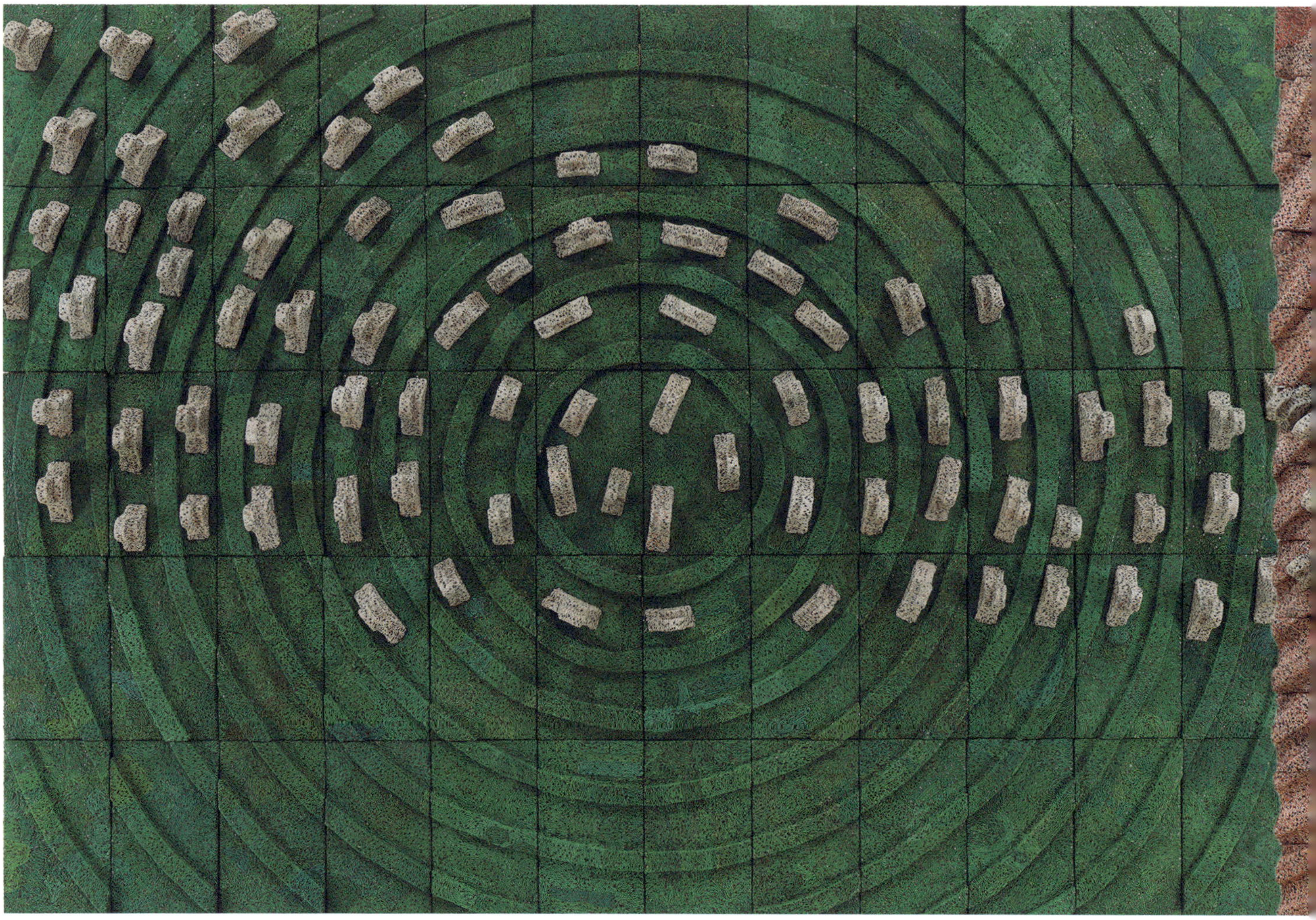

FOREWORD

It's always hot in Venice in August as the Biennale casts its magic and complexity into the world. The Arsenale space feels too big to hold on to and then you find yourself standing in front of work that orientates your day in a new way. Elias Sime's *Red Leaves*, and its partner piece *Veiled Whispers*, provided the perfect example of this kind of encounter. With the repetitive staccato of the three-dimensional bright red leaves against a green background in the former giving way to the stuttering rhythm and drifting space of the latter. Both works stretched out along the wall with enough scale to overcome the vast space before you walk towards them and closely examine the detail and intricacy, with each fold of the coloured wires matched by the perfect placement of the nails that hold it all together: jewel like and enchanting, mixing the ancient and the modern, permanent and fleeting.

I am excited to bring *Veiled Whispers* to the Arnolfini this autumn as part of *Eregata* — Elias's first major public show in the UK. As if the artworks themselves were not already enough to share with our audiences and communities, any project with Elias quickly brings into focus the equally astonishing project that is the Zoma Museum and the indomitable creativity and vision of his co-founder, Meskerem Assegued.

Veiled Whispers
2022, three-dimensional wall piece with woven electrical wires and other components on wood panels, 200.7 × 571.5 × 20.3 cm

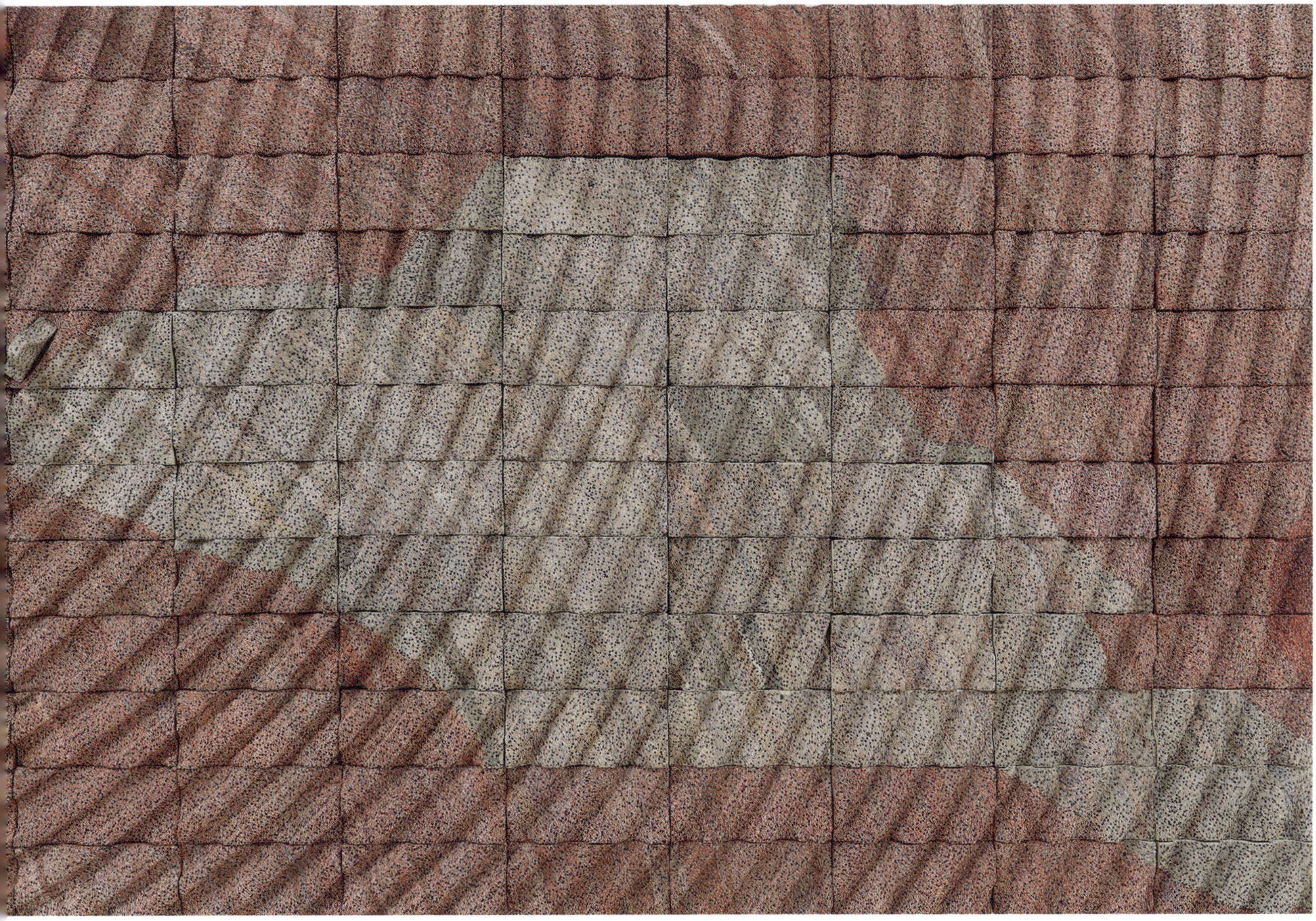

The Zoma Museum, in Addis Ababa, immediately reveals itself as one of the most contemporary manifestations of a cultural centre anywhere in the world. It is literally 'made out of its place' (in materials, vision and tradition) and incorporates a school, gardens, food production, architectural brilliance and clear creativity in everything it does and thinks. All of these qualities speak to the Arnolfini's own determination to be a civic space with many different values, communities and purposes at its heart. I am very clear that Zoma can lead us on our own organisational journey.

Eregata is happening because of the work, insight and determination of many people. My deep thanks to Elias and Meskerem for trusting us, to Jim and Annie at James Cohan, New York, for your tireless support and vision (we are following in your footsteps on this one). Thanks also to Southern & Partners who have worked with us to share Elias's work across Europe, and to our colleagues in Düsseldorf who will pick up the baton as the tour continues. Our Bristol partners have been central to the project as always: Black South West Network, Bridges for Communities and Let's Make Art. Thanks also to our colleagues at UWE Bristol and the other funders listed in this book.

Thank you, as always, to my colleagues in the Arnolfini team and to Gemma (who led the charge) and Keiko (for taking a team of colleagues to Zoma). And to the entire Arnolfini team for making it happen — *Eregata* exists because of all your commitment and skill.

Gary Topp
Director, Arnolfini

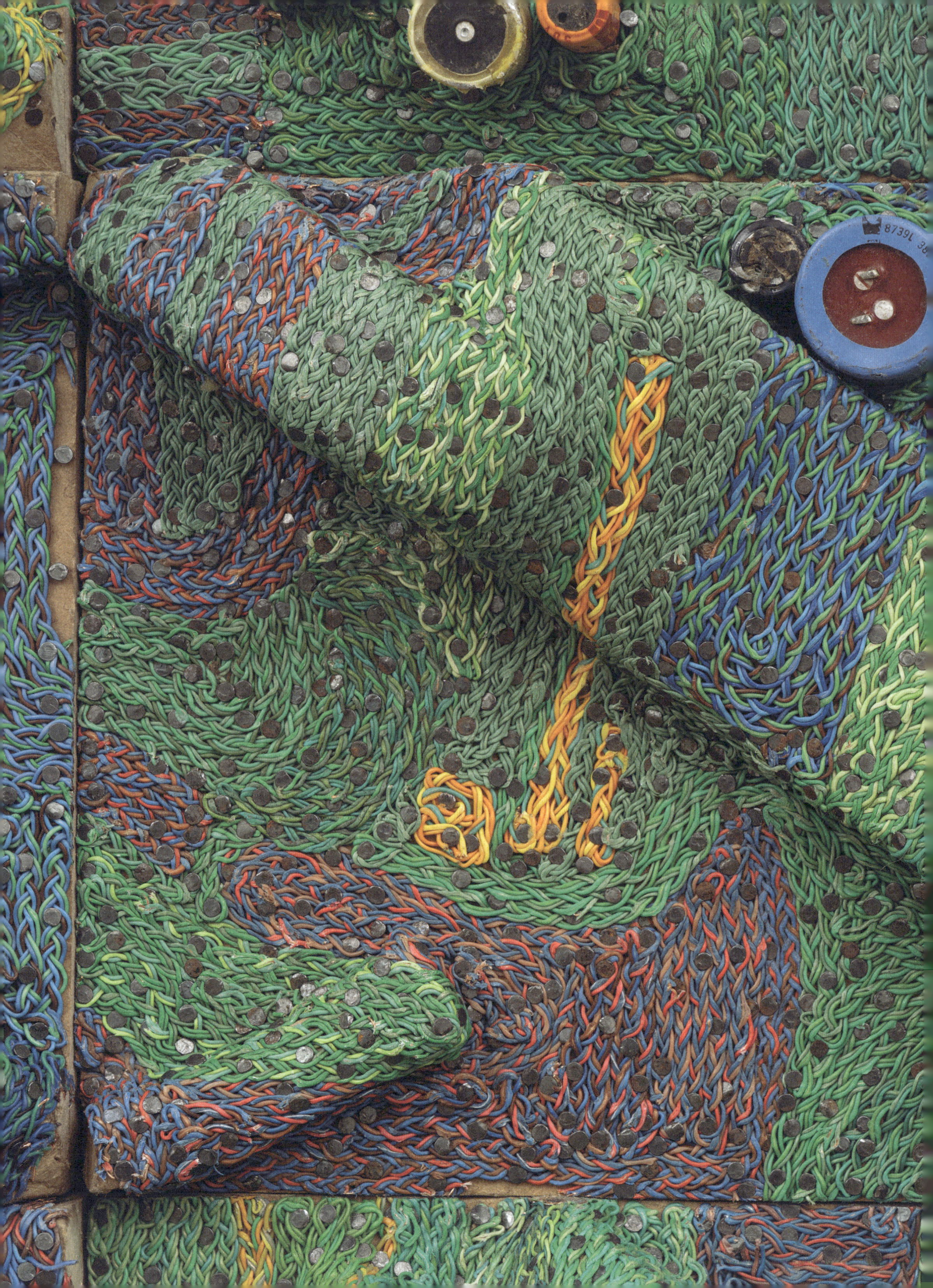

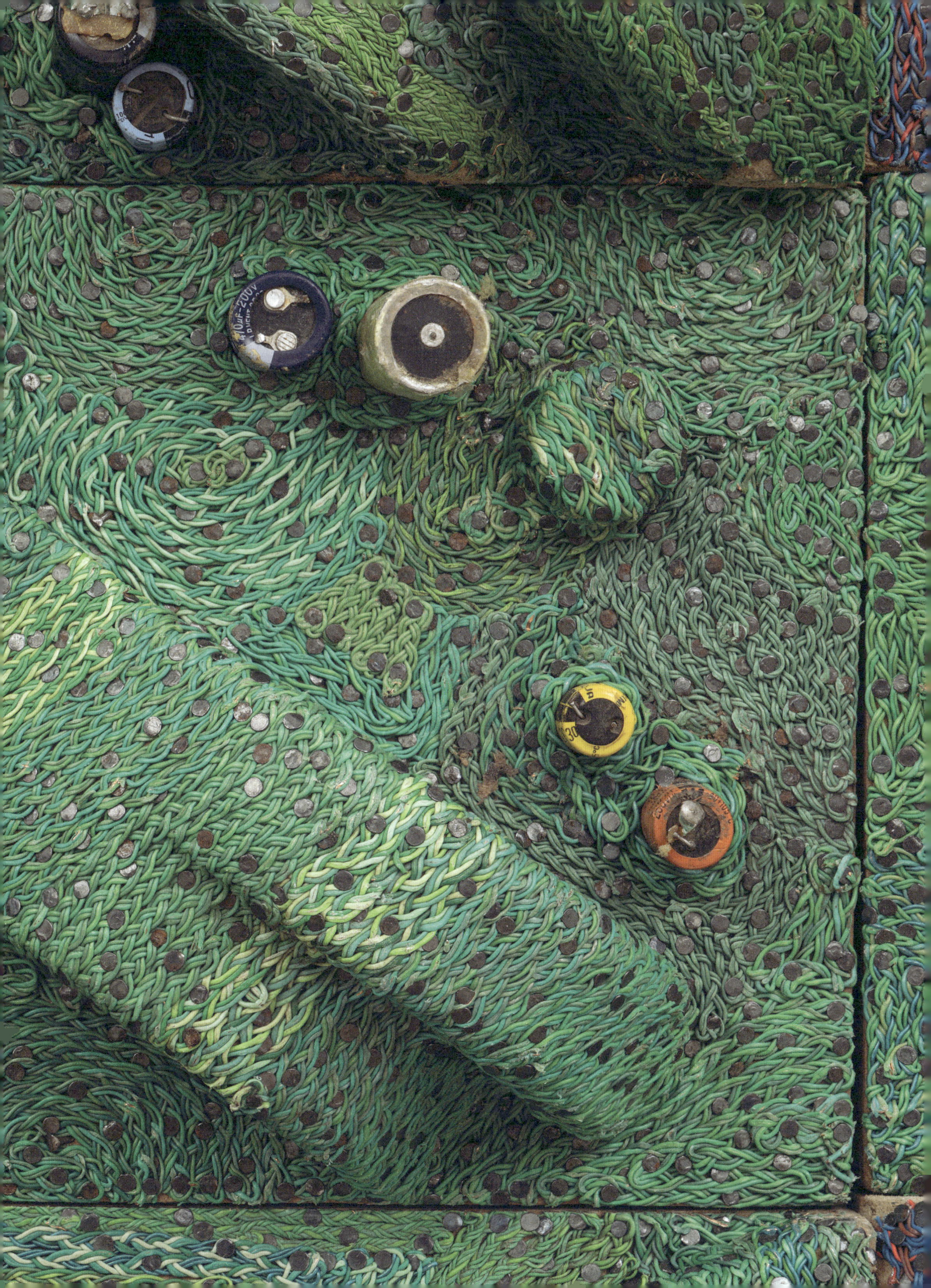

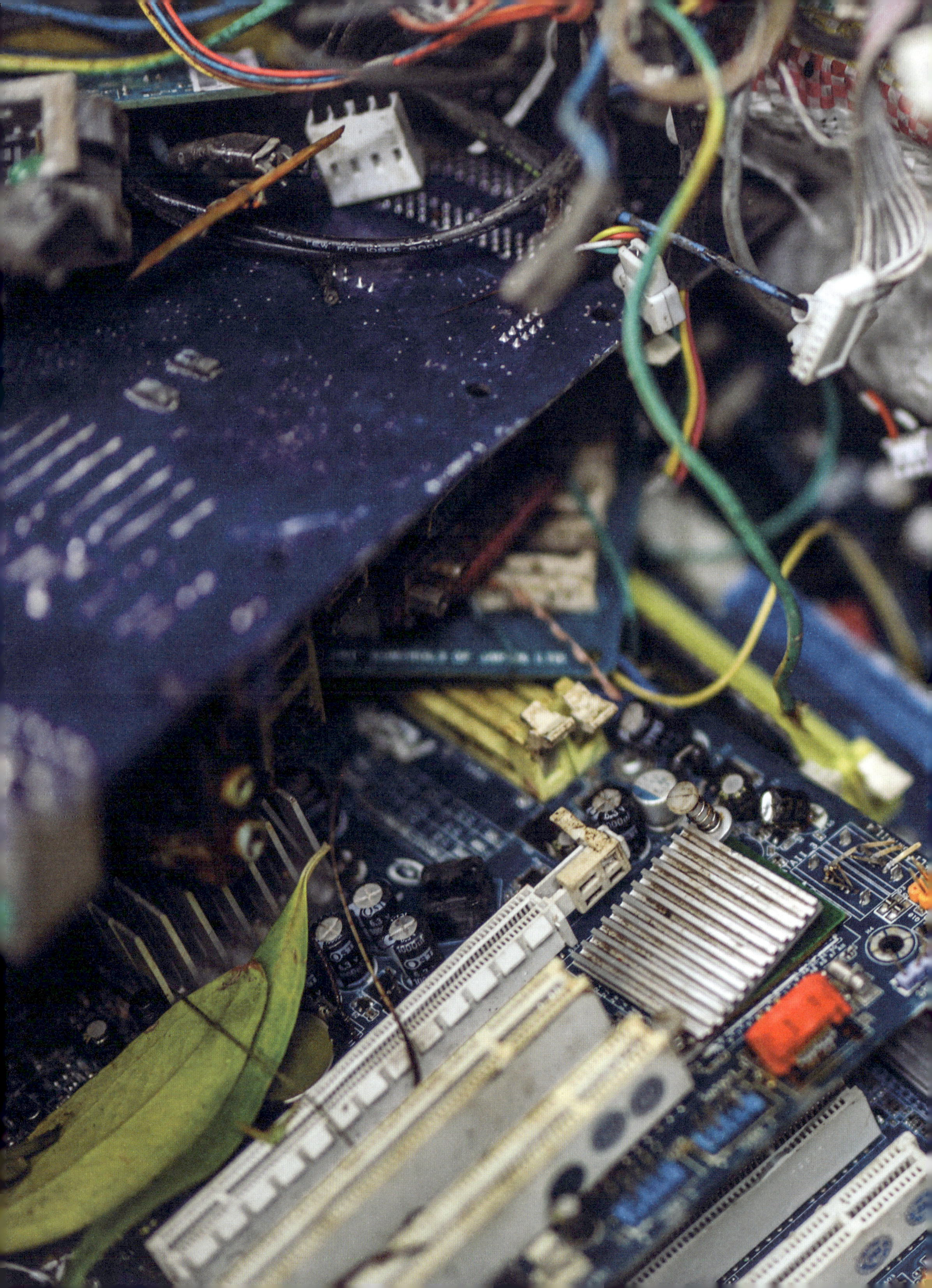

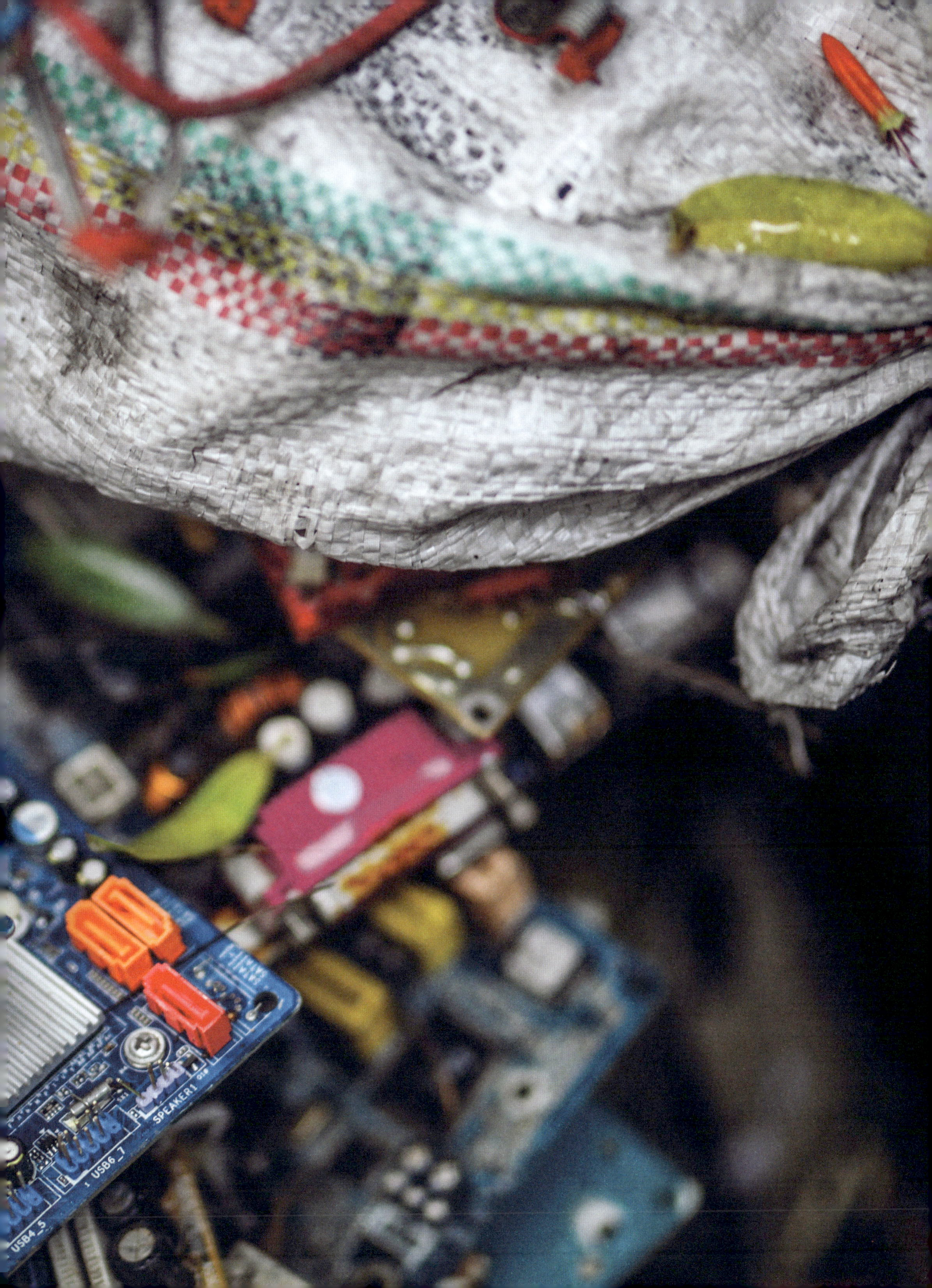
SPEAKER1
USB6_7
USB4_5

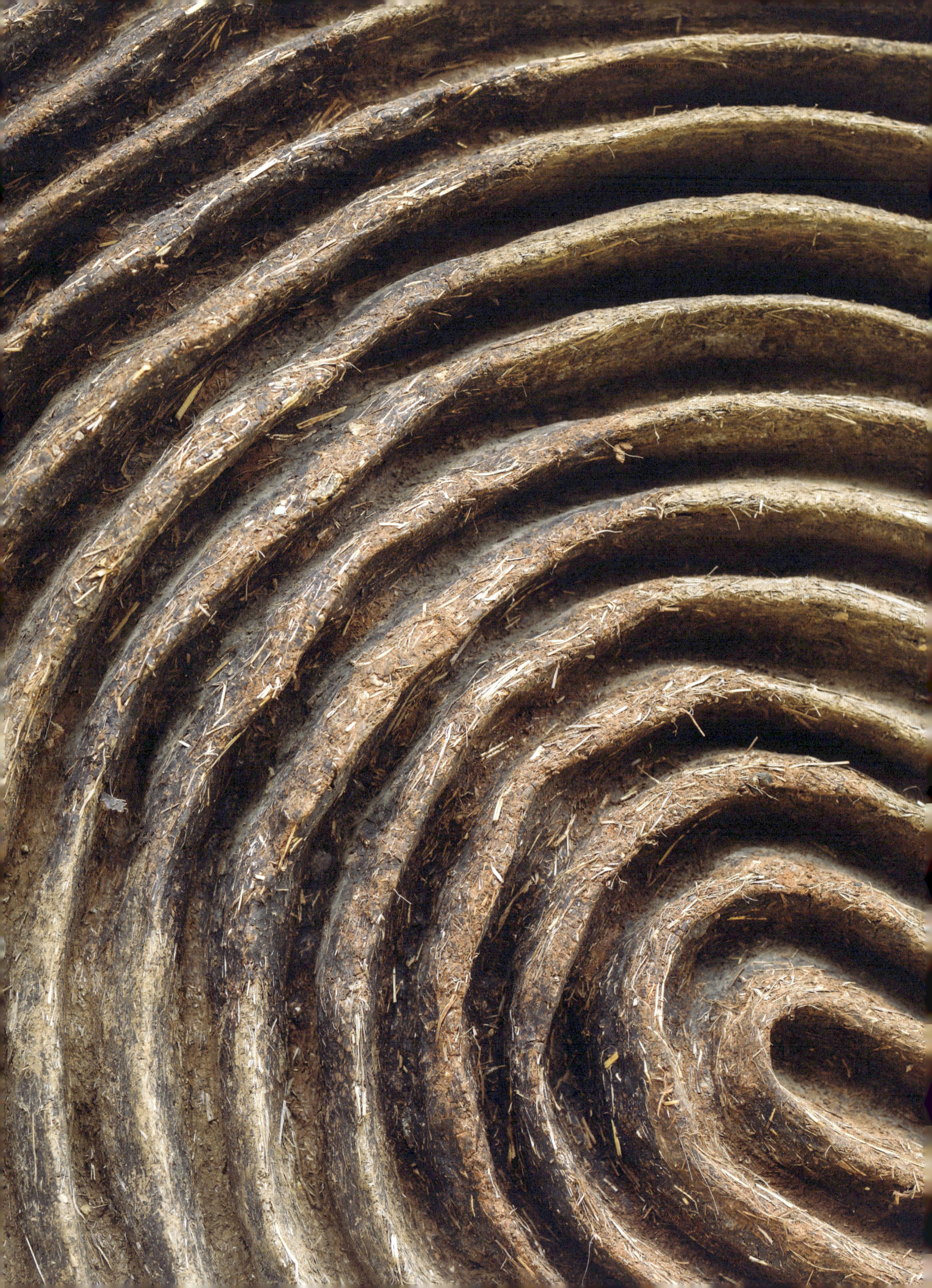

Gemma Brace

—

My art is slowing it down. The work *forces* me to slow down.

— Elias Sime[1]

LOOKING SLOWLY

The idea of a 'moment in time' often comes up in conversation with Elias Sime, an artist who has carved out a space for his work amongst the perpetual motion of the modern world.

This relationship to time is multifaceted. There is technological time, ever-present in the materiality of his ongoing *Tightrope* series (2009–); the time it physically takes to make his labour-intensive compositions, which has led to many describing his work as an act of 'patience'; the time that the artist asks of audiences in experiencing the work; and then the deep sense of cultural time seen in the transition in his choice of materials and subject matter from his early yarn, stitch and button works to his current braided relief constructions.

Eregata — the title of Sime's exhibition at Arnolfini and his first major solo 'museum' exhibition in Europe — reveals the artist's relationship to a body of work that spans 22 years of practice (2001–2023). The closest translation of eregata from Amharic to English (or certainly that which rings most true for Sime) is the word *serene*. Yet, for all its connotations of calmness and tranquillity, for Sime eregata encapsulates a recognition that our minds are never truly still or silent: 'We struggle to stop and sleep because our brains are constantly stimulated by technology. We are constantly moving faster, not slower.'[2] *Eregata* encompasses Sime's ability to identify both the constant march of progress and the stilled moment. In this way *Eregata* cradles multiple notions of time in one moment, inviting us to explore a world (and a view of humanity) in which both future and past, fast and slow are allowed to exist simultaneously.

Sime's own attempts to explain this notion of temporality can seemingly tie us in knots with what at first feel like contradictory explanations. He says, 'My art is slowing it down' (in reference to technology), yet his relationship to the work is the opposite of slowness, embracing movement and the continual hum of progress. Sime himself is at ease with acknowledging the difficulty this conundrum presents: 'Slowness is the opposite of what I am trying to do. I recognise that technology has gone beyond us and has in many ways become part of us, therefore we struggle to separate ourselves from it, even when we experience art.'[3]

Mud and straw wall, Zoma Museum

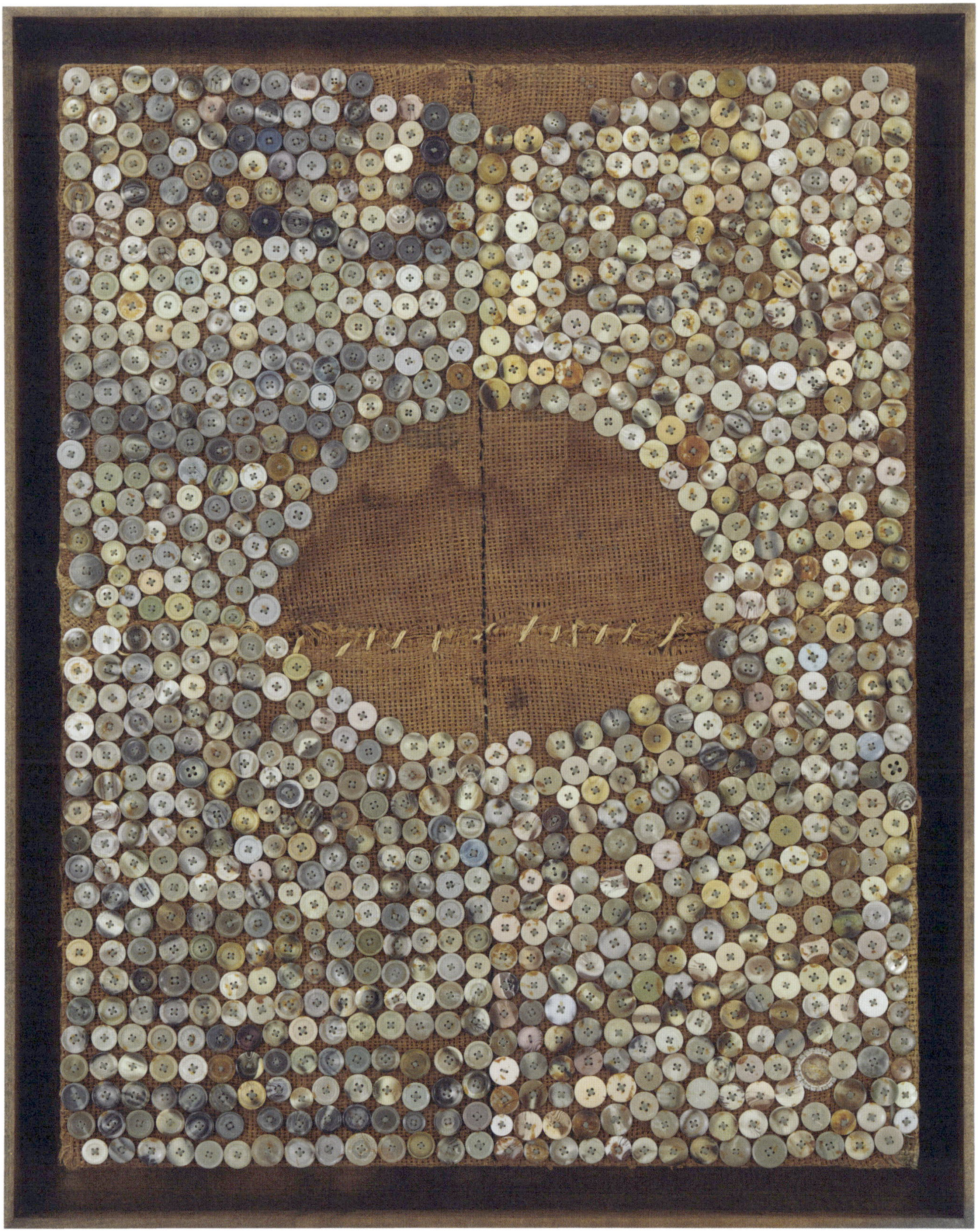

Messil 3 (self portrait)
2004, buttons on hessian, 96 × 76 cm

It is this experience — the dual time in which an artwork exists for both artist and audience — that is so well understood and acknowledged by Sime. And it is this shared, yet often at odds, moment in time that he is interested in capturing within the exhibition's title, which is (as with all Sime's titles) never intended as a finite instruction. Rather, it is an invitation, a prompt or a jumping-off point. For Sime this point, or moment, is one of serenity (eregata); for us it is an opportunity to slow down, and to look slowly.

This slow looking is something Sime, who was born in Addis Ababa, Ethiopia, has incorporated into his process from childhood, when he first began collecting objects and materials. Although the majority of works in *Eregata* were made in the last six years, featuring intricately braided abstract topographies, protruding megaphones and organic reliefs, audiences are also introduced to a small selection of key early works, made with buttons, metal objects, and yarn stitched on canvas supports made from organic muslin. These works are described by Meskerem Assegued — Sime's longstanding curatorial partner and co-founder of the equally 'patient' project the Zoma Museum (explored by Nana Biamah-Ofosu later in the book) — as marking a significant break with the wood carvings and collage Sime made in the period after graduating in 1990 from the School of Fine Arts and Design at Addis Ababa University.

Sime grew up in Chirqos (where he remained living during art school), a neighbourhood of the city known for its bustling market. Visiting at the end of the day as traders packed away their wares, Sime would scour through the multitude of objects on offer, searching out specific materials with a curiosity that has served him throughout his career. This included 'piles of old silver keychains, coins, untouched banknotes from different eras, buttons, musical instruments, toys, books, medals and of course mountains of electronic components.'[4] Many of these items remained in Sime's personal possession as objects of interest, whilst others have become part of his work: 'I collected anything I found interesting and made art with it.'[5]

Continuing this childhood pursuit, for the last 14 years Sime's work has been made from materials originating from all over the world that have found their way to the city he calls home. Much has been made of his affection for the Menyalesh Tera ('what do you have?') section of the Merkato market in Addis Ababa, the largest open-air market in Africa, however, Sime sources material from many corners of the city. Collating pile upon pile of electrical wires, computer keyboards and circuit boards, he patiently hoards these resources until he has assembled enough material to commence a new body of work. As discussed in greater detail by Andria Hickey in 'A tapestry for humanity', objects are often stripped down into individual components, such as wire 'threads', which are subsequently 'braided, layered and reassembled' into abstract forms. Although Sime has always worked with a mix of old and new materials — buying bundles of yarn, shop-shined buttons or electrical wire in bulk — more recently some of the electronic components Sime works with have become obsolete or hard to find, creating 'a marker of time' as 'inevitably, what he collects becomes extinct'.[6]

Collecting, for Sime, informs his relationship to time. This is perhaps most clearly seen in the earliest works in *Eregata*, in which it is not only materials that are collected, but human and cultural traditions and stories. In 2003 Sime began accompanying Assegued (a curator and anthropologist as well as co-founder of Zoma) on research trips across Ethiopia, in which she documented the ancient religious rituals and cultural practices of different ethnic groups. One trip to south-central Ethiopia, visiting the Gurage region, resulted in the exhibition *Min Neber* at the Italian Cultural Institute in 2004. Many of the works in this exhibition were stitched canvases, such as *Migueb 1*, *Min Neber (what is it)* (2004), and *Felega 1*, *2* and *9* (2004), which document the thunder ritual that forms part of the yearly

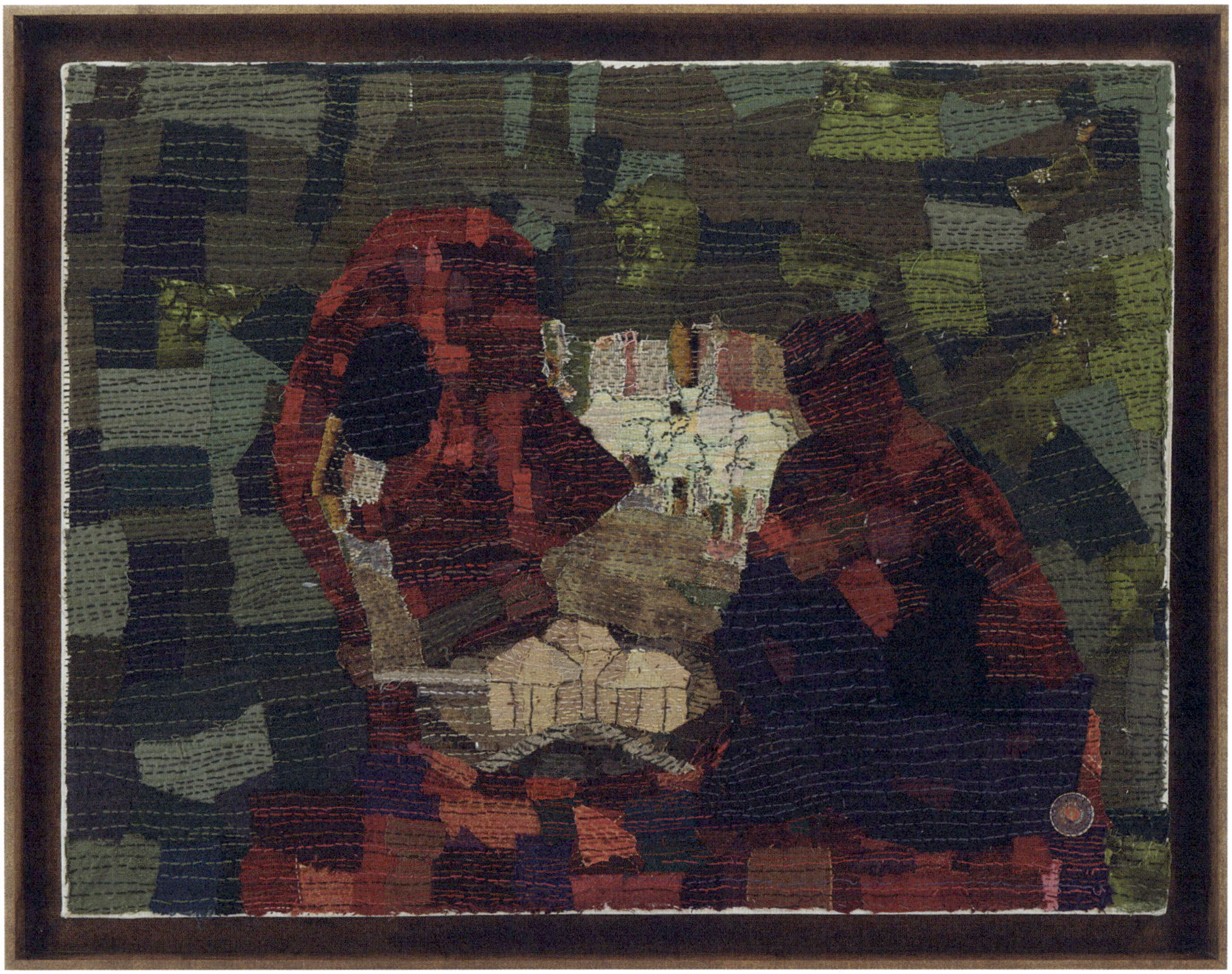

Bojje ceremony, worshipping the forests, thunder and water, as well as a myriad of inspirations from other seminal visits. Following the trip, Sime said: 'I just could not stop stitching. I was overwhelmed by how little I knew about my own culture. I was very excited. I felt like a baby learning how to walk for the first time ... More importantly, everything I was seeing was confronting my own belief systems and values about what was right and wrong.'[7]

Similar trips, such as those to see ceramicists across Ethiopia, including the Gambela region of western Ethiopia on the border of Sudan, have also simultaneously provided inspiration for Assegued's research and Sime's artwork. Such as the fragile monumentality of *Bareness* (2014), which was made with the help of a community of ceramicists working alongside Sime. He suggests that the work 'reflect[s] those moments of vulnerability, of feeling naked, exposed, unprotected, and fragile. They are also about how we will all end up being fragments of the Earth, regardless of our status in life.'[8] These traditions, rituals and crafts each have their own deep-rooted relationship to *another* moment in time, one that both Sime and Assegued are keen to re-explore as part of the present day, as they do with the ancient architectural techniques they have used to bring the holistic world of Zoma to life through mud and straw.

Migueb 1, Min Neber (what is it)
2004, textile and yarn stitch, 74.6 × 96.2 cm

Bareness
2014, ceramics, installation, dimensions variable

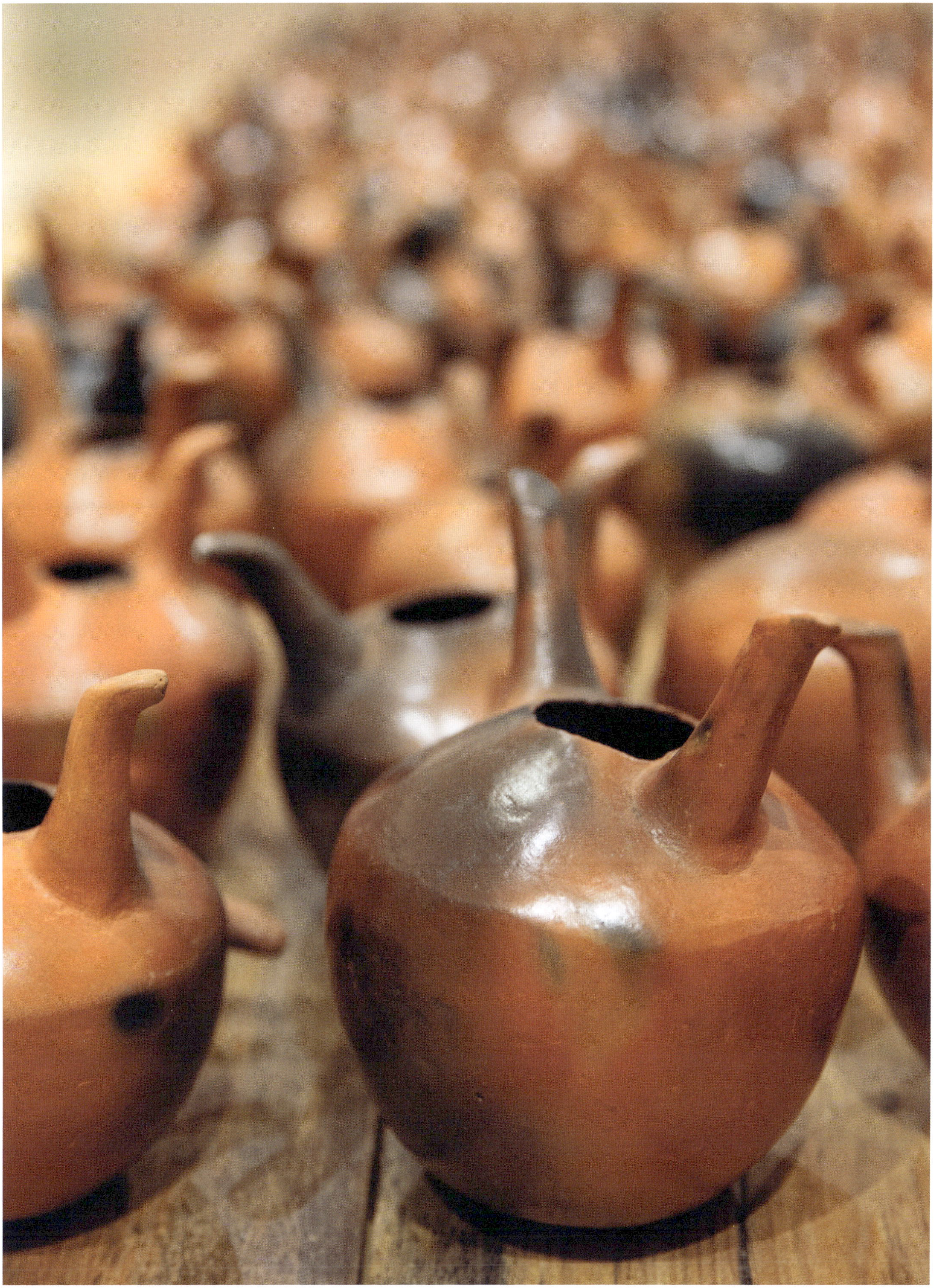

Time, or the passing of it, also takes on new meanings when we think about the acts of collecting and telling stories. The notion of Sime the storyteller is not a new idea. The title *Täarät-Täarät* (meaning storytelling in Amharic) was chosen for an exhibition in 2009 and is a reference to Sime's retelling of the stories witnessed throughout his travels. Perhaps more telling is the explanation attached to another exhibition title *GOTA Täarät-Täarät*. Curated by Assegued in 2006, it featured a vast grain silo made of mud and straw alongside anthropomorphic creatures in the work *Monkeys, Frogs and Televisions* (2004). Assegued explains that 'täarät-täarät' is what storytellers say before beginning a tale, likening it to the phrase 'once upon a time'.[9]

This sense of 'once upon a time' feels implicit throughout Sime's work, whether we are remembering cultural histories and craftsmanship, reflecting upon the many hands through which a mobile phone has passed, or considering the speed of technological progress in which once futuristic and sought-after material components have now become redundant. It is these stories and layers of time that Sime prompts us to consider by looking slowly. This idea is also explored by Tracy L. Adler, director of the Wellin Museum of Art and curator of the 2019 North American touring exhibition *Elias Sime: Tightrope*. She suggests that 'slow looking is integral to Sime's approach … as he reminds us that we must take the time to observe closely, to follow each thread'[10] — of which there are many to pursue within the interwoven crisscrossing passages that flow across the individual wooden blocks that make up the expansive surfaces of Sime's work.

These winding 'threads' physically prompt us to look slowly. However, when it comes to the traditional and metaphorical connotations of 'once upon a time', Sime is quick to add caution: 'I don't focus on tradition; I focus on being in the moment. Tradition is part of other people's assumptions. I see the same thing wherever I go. The same lifestyle, the same emotions, the same personalities, everything. Even the traditions. That's not what I try to do with my art. My art is often a reaction to what I see in that moment. My art could fit in anywhere.'[11]

This idea of Sime's work fitting in 'anywhere' is also not without its need for consideration. His early work appears to be deeply embedded within Ethiopian culture, and his practice is one that emerged under the Derg regime of 1974 to 1991, with his artistic education governed by strict parameters rooted in the socialist realist art sanctioned by the dictatorship. Much has already been written about Sime's relationship to time and place within this context, unpicking the complexities of applying a Western-centred lens to our understanding. Yet it is also important to recognise that his is a practice informed by the universality of human stories, an aspect that Assegued has attributed to the growing internationalism of Addis Ababa in recent years (and no doubt also influenced by Sime's own travels). In this respect his work often transcends a static sense of time and place, allowing for multiple interpretations to co-exist within different cultural contexts.

This openness to interpretation is also expressed through the dichotomy conjured up by a title such as *Tightrope*, which emphasises the tension that exists between two moments — the fine line between holding on and falling off. The series, which Sime began working on in 2009, allows for multiple meanings, including: an exploration of the tensions existing between society, technology and communication; 'configurations (topographical, aerial, and structural) of the modern city'[12]; a technological 'archive' or 'timeline'[13]; and a metaphorical image of something that could break if pulled too tight.[14] Spread across four sites in Addis Ababa — the British Council, Goethe-Institut, Istituto Italiano di Cultura and Alliance Ethio-française — the work itself took over five years to make. However, although the work was slow in its making, Sime has described the techniques he used, such as braiding, as reflecting a sense of speed and 'our need to get somewhere faster'.[15]

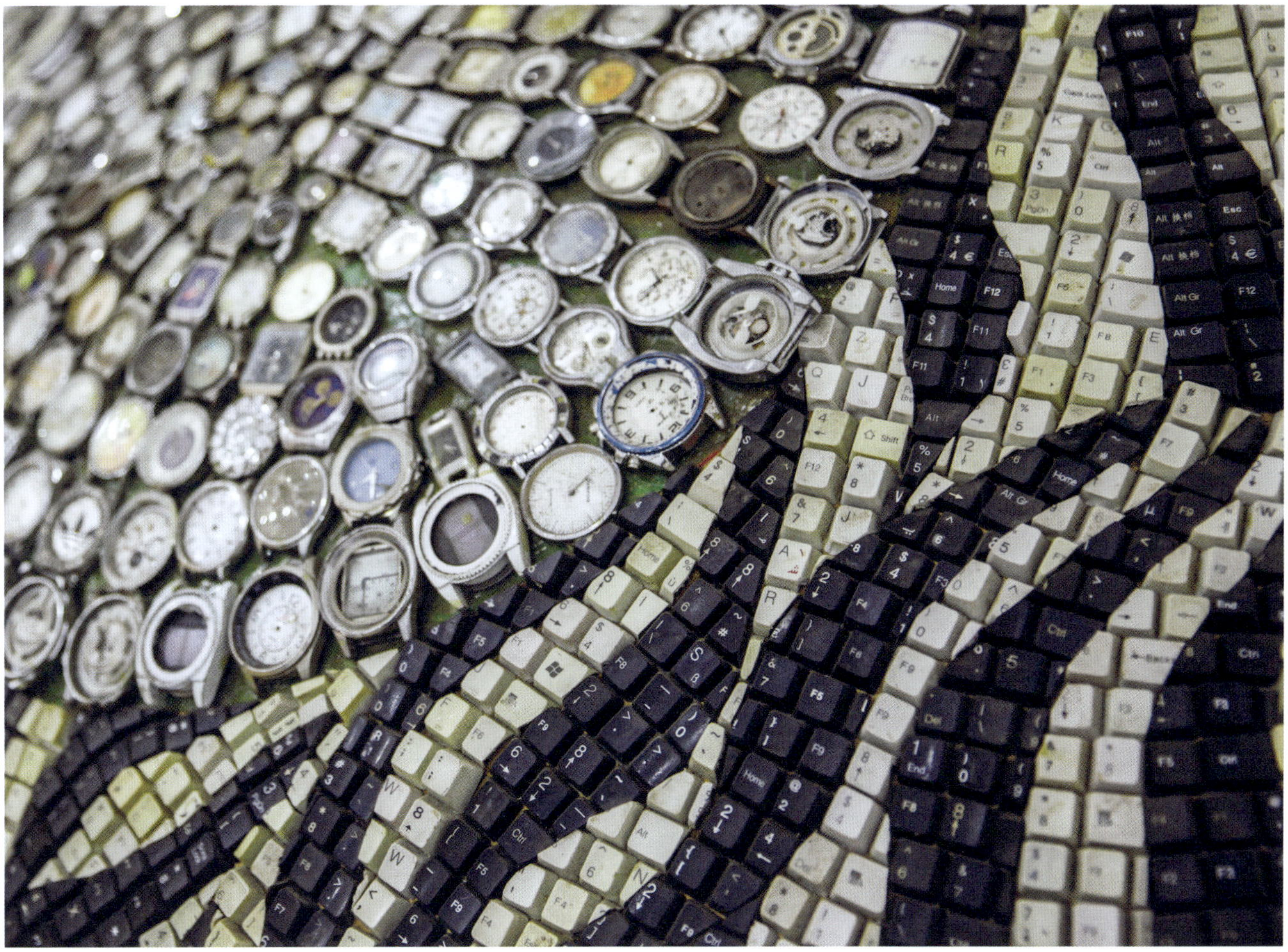

Concave Triangle artwork in Elias Sime's studio

However, it is the sense of time passing that feels most important in these works, which contain a history of computer manufacturing, as this richly detailed description in Kate Cowcher's review of the first *Tightrope* exhibition suggests: 'Here were stripped-down motherboards from the 1970s, TV circuit boards with their traces indicating the former presence of a tube, a pre-LED lighting system known as NIXI tubes, and the remnants of processors from obsolete manufacturers such as Zilog. Here, 1960s colour-coded resistors and early read-only memory appeared alongside an Intel I486 processor from 1991, and components marked as being manufactured in Japan, Malaysia, Singapore, Portugal, Brazil, Germany, and Russia.'[16] The redundancy of materials once considered technologically exciting and new is underlined by Sime's own reminder that much of his material is not 'recycled' waste but new components bought for the very purpose of creating an artwork. Therefore in their obsolescence time has literally caught up with his way of working.

Here, however, the passing of time is not simply technological but human: intimately connected to the development of humanity as it 'changes information, it changes the way you think.'[17] This human time in Sime's work is expressed through the tactility of his materials. Just as buttons carry imprints from the many hands that have touched them before, so too do the computer keys, circuit boards and stripped wires, rich in 'human traces and emotions'.[18] These traces have been a feature of Sime's practice from the beginning, and within this context the age of his tactile material is not important: 'New and old, *everything* carries fingerprints.'[19] These fingerprints for Sime are the link that unlocks stories. As Sime's own hands rest upon these invisible marks, he adds new stories, spiralling outwards like the concentric growth rings of a tree. In this way Sime creates *more* time within the work.

In the same sense that Sime considers his art to be or to fit in anywhere, these new stories are also not confined to the specificities of time and place, pointing firmly towards the future: 'Sometimes you tell a story and the story stops. I'm waiting for the story to end. It is a world history. It's not about Ethiopia. It's not about Africa. Globalization is everywhere.'[20]

This image of Sime's stories stretching out beyond the studio walls to reach a global audience leads us to a final consideration of time, that which is contained within the time of storytelling; between 'once upon a time…' and the edges of his monumental works, where wires appear to weave between wooden blocks with the sinuous ease of waterways making a path across the landscape. How long it takes these stories to be told and the means of telling them is intimately linked. Interestingly, Sime's chosen materials within *Tightrope* are inherently tied to acts of communication—wires that voices travel down, keyboards used to tap out a thousand emails, and the circuit boards that store and dictate these means of interaction.

In a number of works, each titled *Tightrope: Echo!?*, embellished megaphones protrude from wooden blocks. Sime has suggested that their role is to question which, or whose, voices are amplified. He suggests that it is 'the sound and the frequency' of the speaker's words that are most important, dictating how far the echo 'expands' or travels.[21] The very idea of an echo is bound up in an understanding of time, creating a distance between the spoken word or sound and the multiple moments in which it is heard. Yet sometimes these words are silenced, as explored in a number of works titled *Tightrope: Noiseless*. Adler suggests that these noiseless works ask us to consider the power of silence, pointing to a quote from Sime in which he says: 'Noise is often associated with unpleasant sounds. Noise can… seem to create words, or words can be part of noise. Words channel our thinking along familiar paths toward realistic images. The absence of noise allows our minds to create unfamiliar and abstract images.'[22]

It is to this absence that we return. The dual time in which an artwork exists for both artist and audience, in which noise and noiselessness share a similar relationship to that of stillness and movement, two ends of the tightrope, between 'slow' looking and 'fast' materials, between time and timelessness, space for storytelling, for interpretation, serenity: *Eregata*.

Tightrope: Echo!? (detail)
2021, reclaimed electrical wires and components on panel with two megaphones, 114.9 × 120 × 15.2 cm

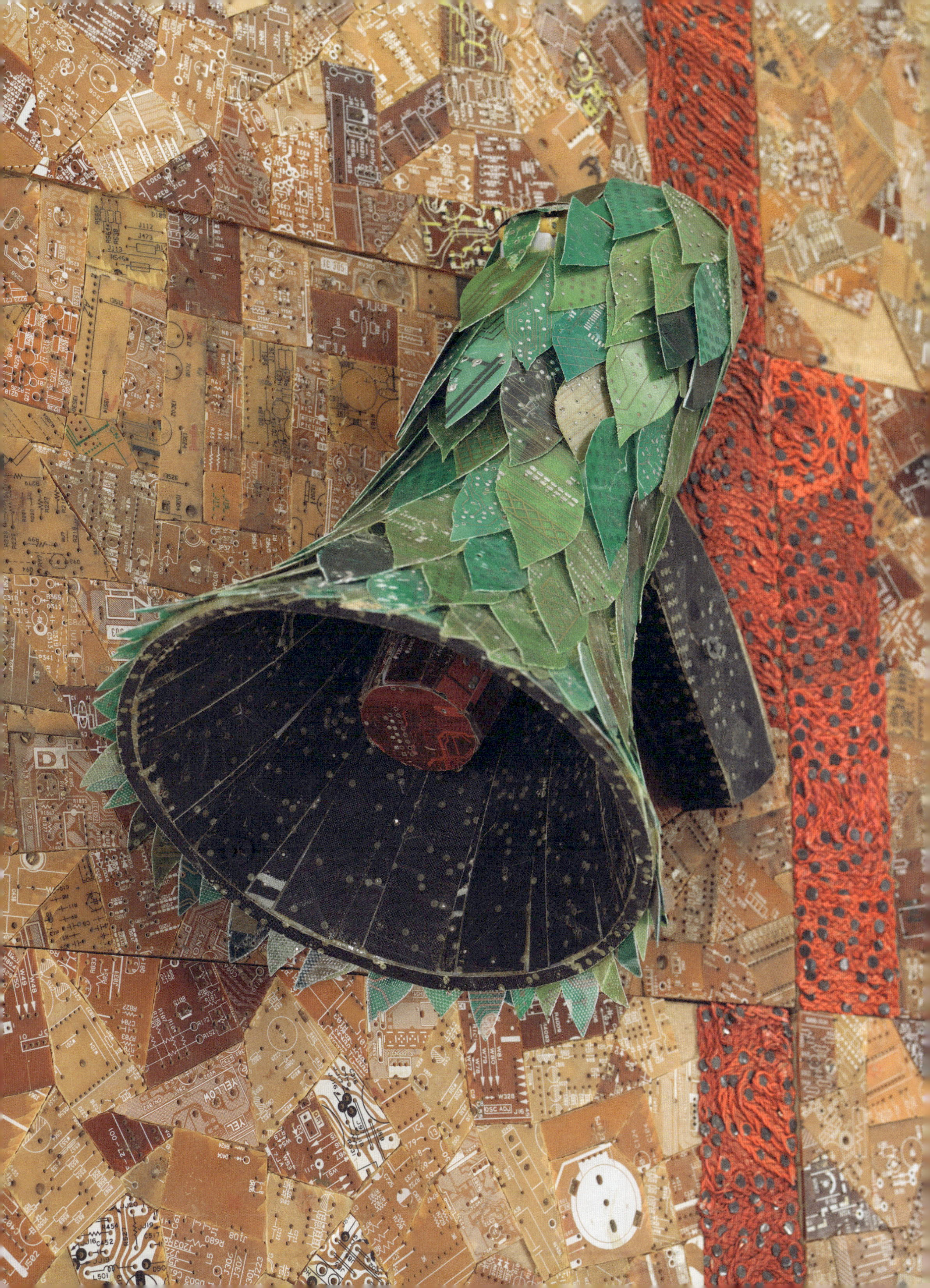

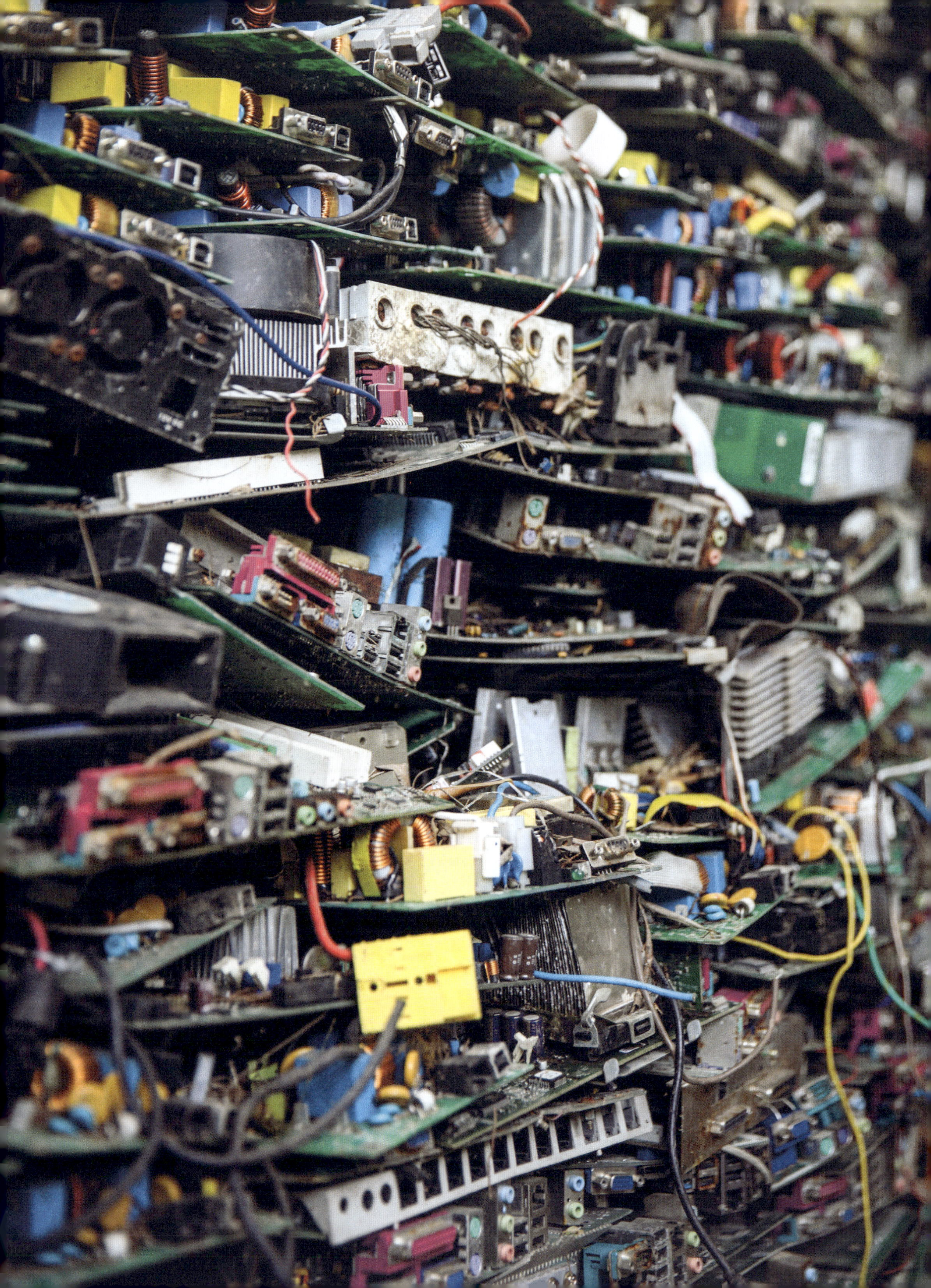

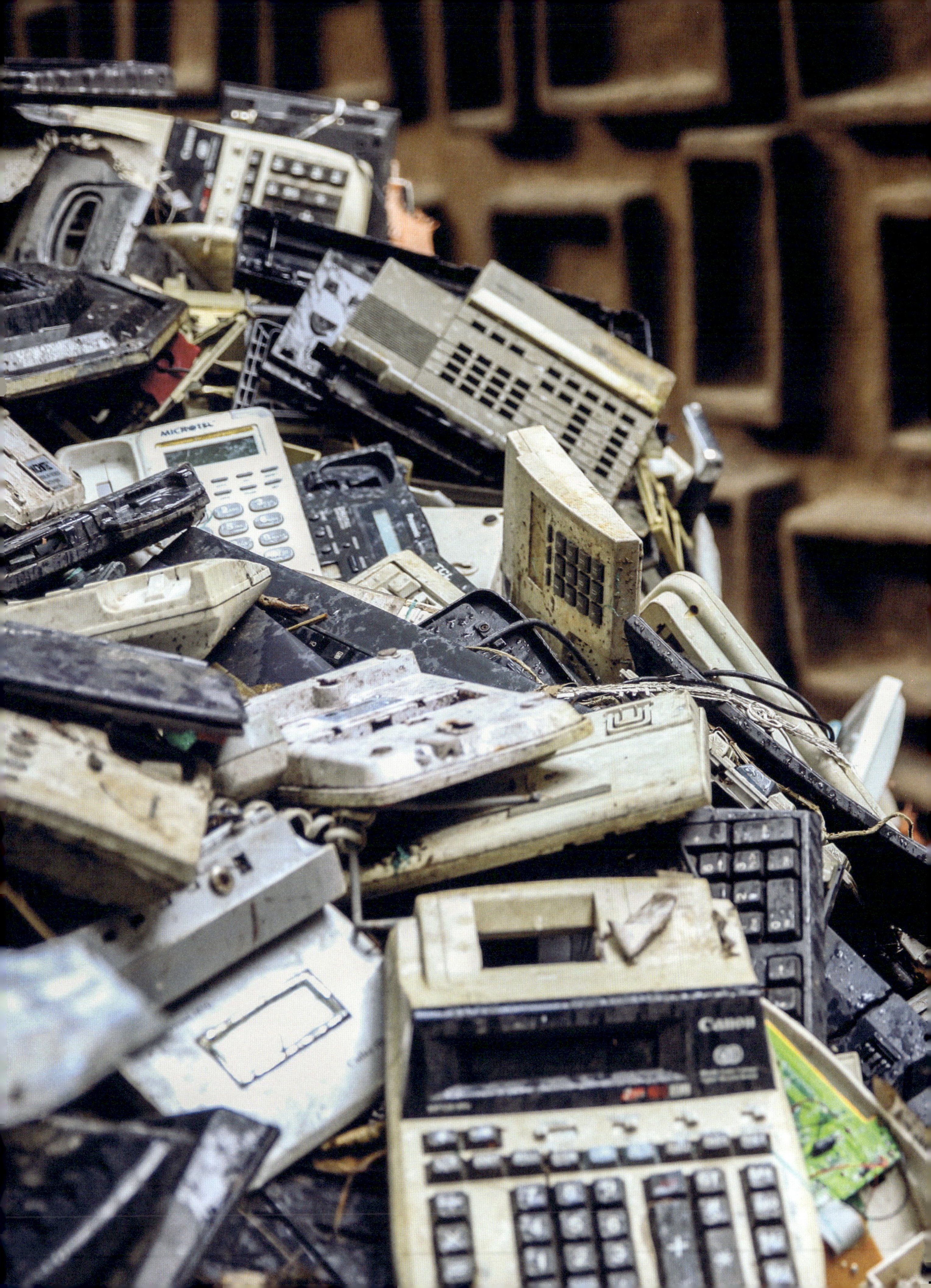
MICROTEL
Canon

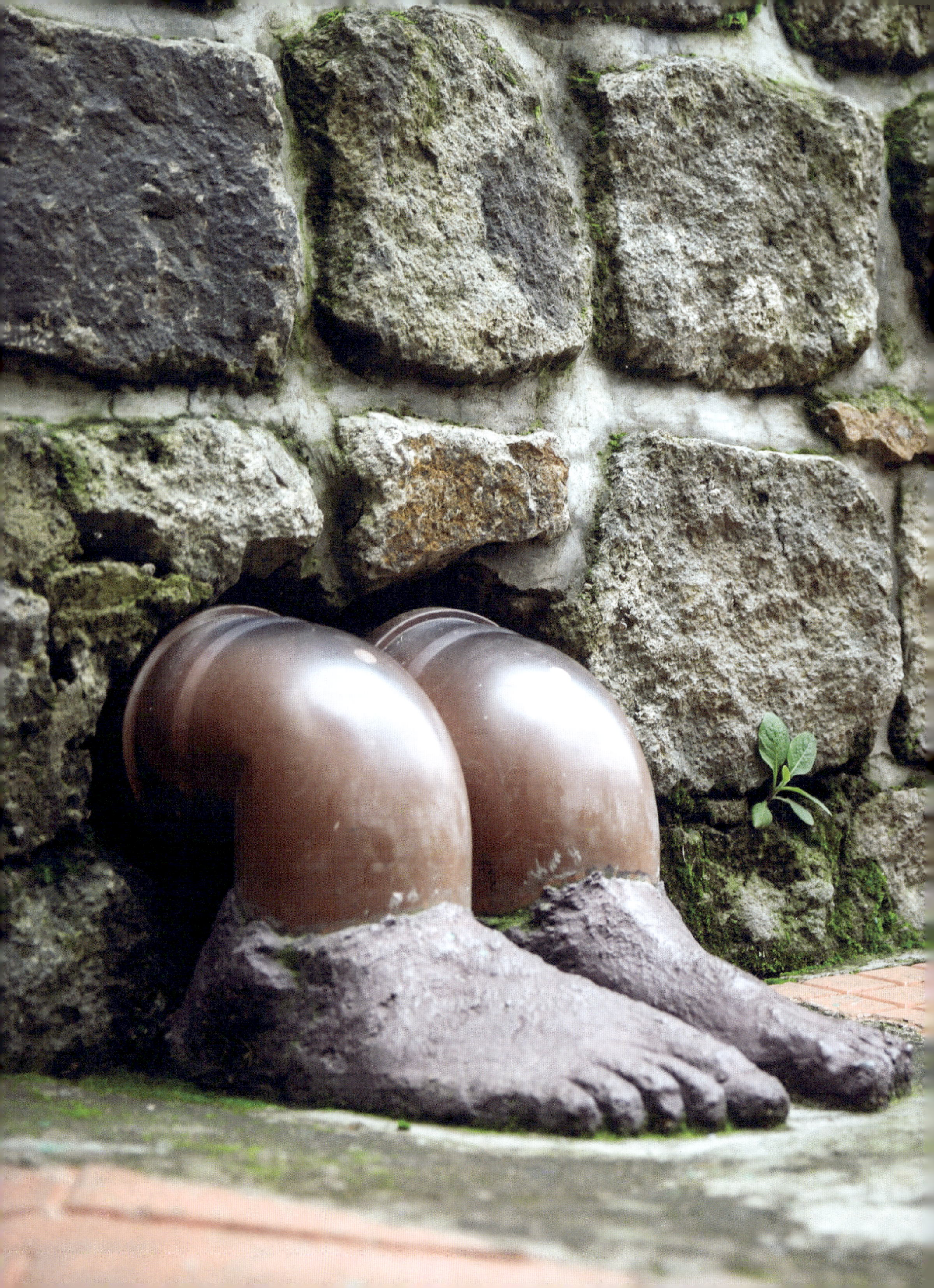

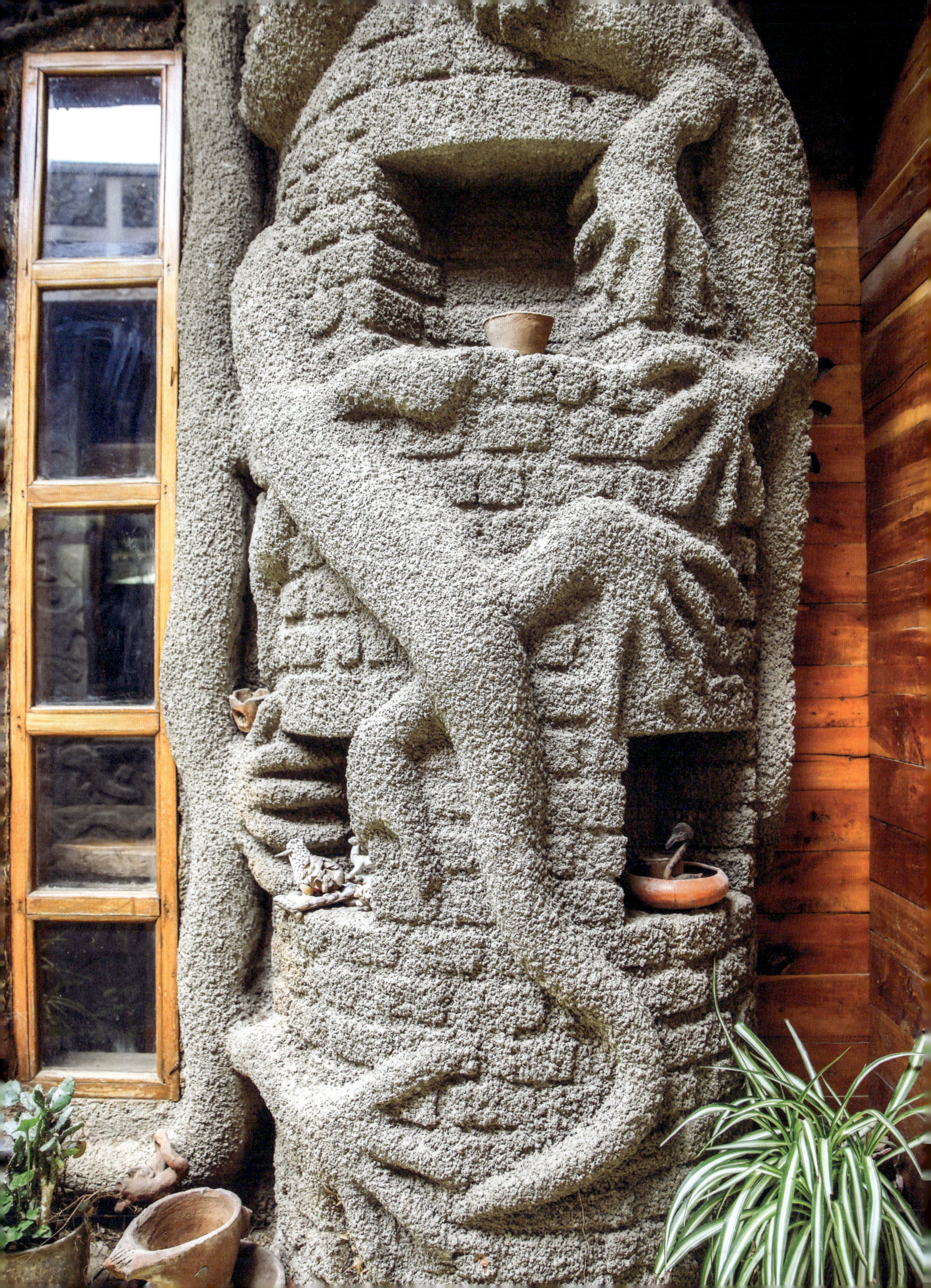

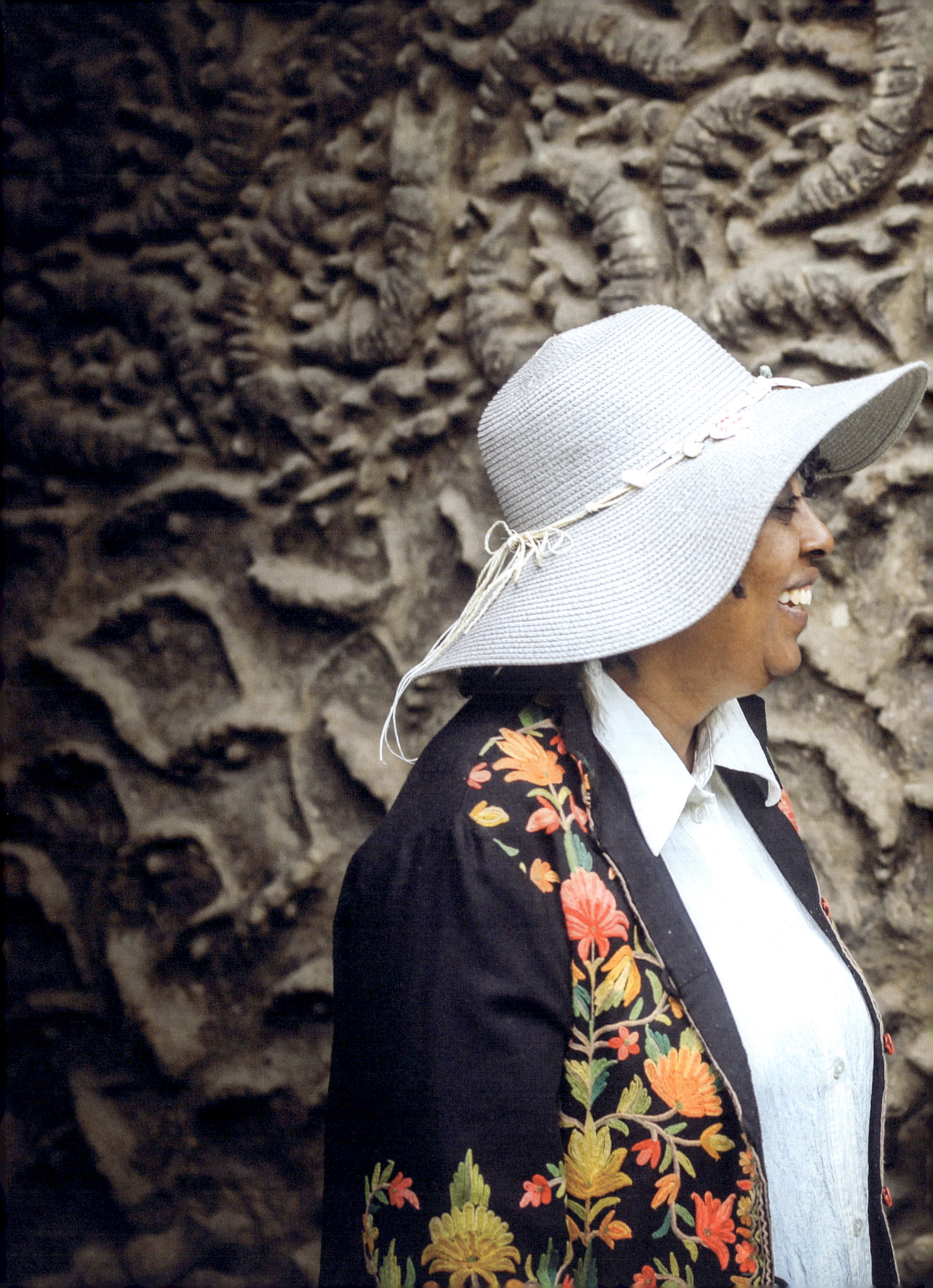

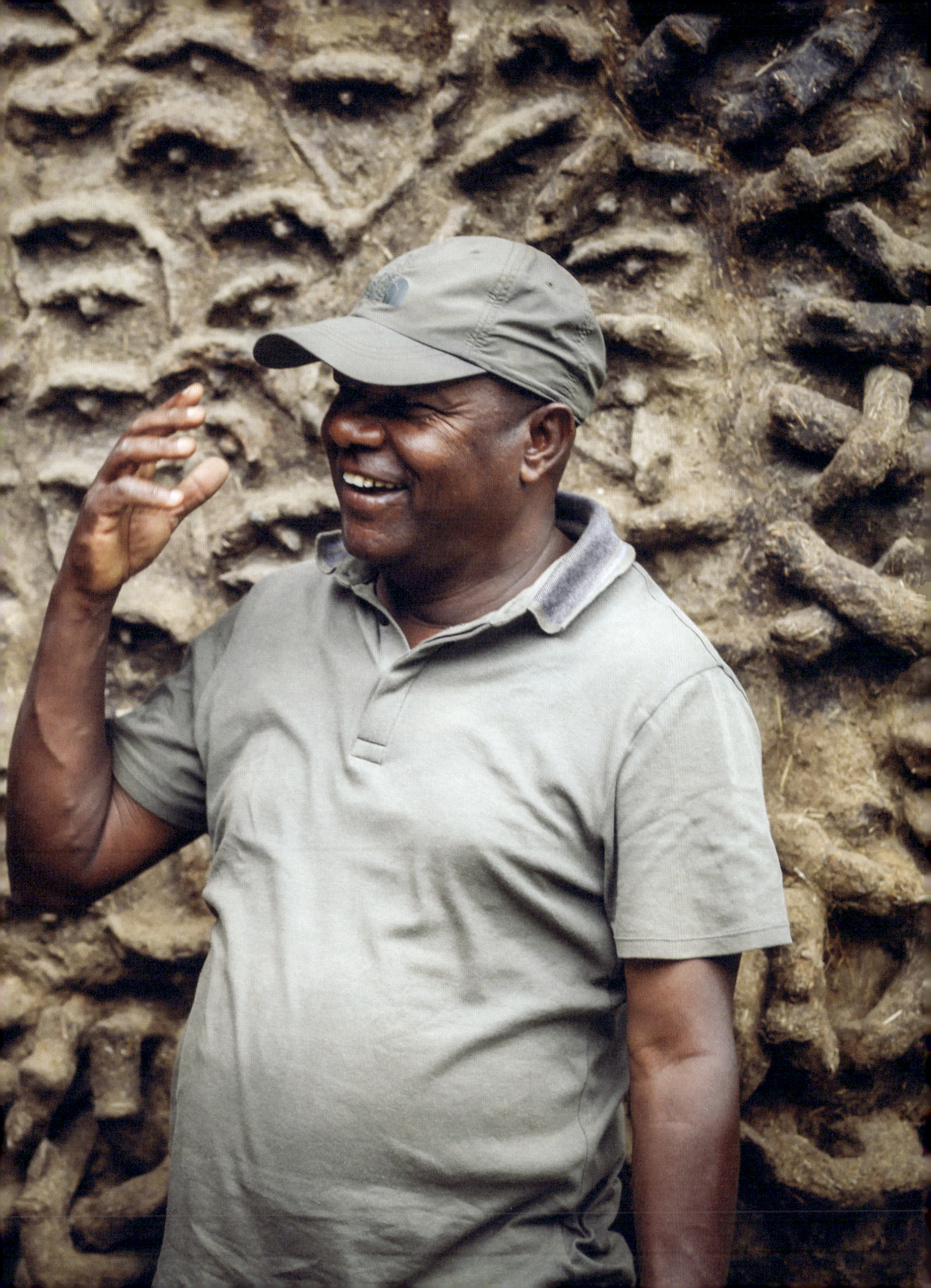

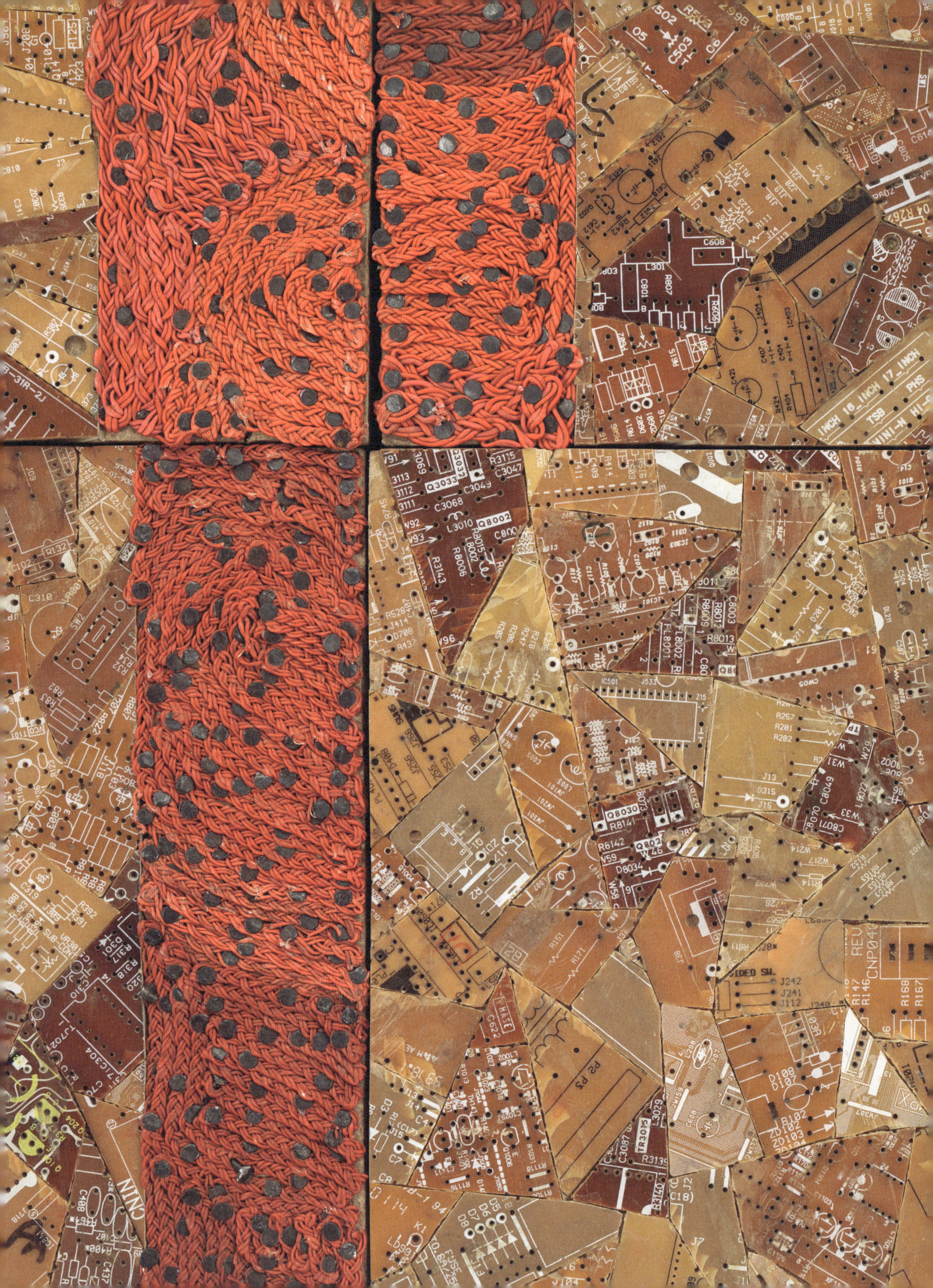

A conversation between Elias Sime, Meskerem Assegued & Gemma Brace

—

Ideas can flow from either one of us, but executing them requires trust, hard labour and, more importantly, love.

— Elias Sime & Meskerem Assegued

COLLABORATION AND CARE

The following interview with Elias Sime and Meskerem Assegued took place over Zoom and email between 26 May and 30 June in 2023. Sime's responses are kindly translated by Assegued.

GB *Time feels like such an important component of your process and I want to begin with a quote from you, Elias, in which you say that: 'my art is about slowing it down. The work forces me to slow down'. Can you expand on this?*

ES The process of making my art can be tedious and takes a great deal of patience and time to finish. This is probably why I said that 'my work *forces* me to slow down'. It is impossible to rush when you are sorting out different colours of electrical wires, braiding them and nailing them on individual small panels that will eventually connect to make one large piece.

GB *You have also spoken about the idea of creating 'snapshots' or 'moments in time'. What do you mean by this when working simultaneously on a group or series of works over a long period?*

ES Ideas are like 'flashes' that can come to mind anywhere and anytime. I tend to capture them as soon as they appear by drawing simple sketches with short notes. These sketches help me jog my memories from the time I made them. When I am ready to transform them into works of art, I go from one studio to another and lay out the panels according to the size I want, then I transfer the small sketches to the large panels. This helps me extract the ideas from my mind. Finishing the art may take a long time depending on the availability of the materials. As soon as I finish a piece, I store it away because I want to move on to the next artwork. This process may take months or years.

GB *This way of working over years and decades on the same series —* Tightrope*, for example — suggests that you see these works as being part of the same story. Does this affect the way you title them?*

MA Normally, before Elias and I title a piece of art, I ask Elias to tell me the stories and the concepts that inspired the artwork. I want to have a clear

Tightrope: Echo!? (detail)
2021, reclaimed electrical wires and components on panel with two megaphones, 114.9 × 120 × 15.2 cm

understanding of the work because the title must express these ideas in the best way possible. Once we agree, we share the title publicly. Who comes up with the title is irrelevant for either one of us. What is relevant is how the title relates to the artwork.

GB *Elias and Meskerem, you agreed upon an Amharic word,* Eregata, *as the title of this exhibition which encompasses several different bodies of work, and you also incorporated an Amharic translation into the title with the recent show at James Cohan. What led you to reprise this approach?*

MA We chose to use the Amharic word written in the ancient Ethiopian script, Ge'ez, which has stood the test of time. Many ancient written languages, such as the Egyptian hieroglyph in Africa or the Mayan hieroglyph from Mesoamerican civilisations, are no longer in use although they have been deciphered. The majority of newspapers in Ethiopia are printed in Amharic with very few in English or other languages. There have been other exhibitions and artworks in the past where we have used the Ge'ez scripts, such as ምን ነበር (Min Neber), which translates to *What Was It*; ጉንዳኖች እና ሸክላ ሰሪዎች (Gundanoch ena Shekla Seriwoch), which means *Ants and Ceramicists*; and የተሰጠረ ገመድ (Yetewetere Gemed), which translates to *Tightrope*.

GB *Talking about the title* Tightrope, *which has been used for a large body of work spanning over a decade of practice, what is the story behind this series?*

ES *Tightrope* is about my observations and reaction to how humans have struggled to find different survival skills as they navigate through life. In 2013 Meskerem curated *Tightrope* at four different European cultural institutes in Addis Ababa. The exhibition explored how humans use both their minds and bodies to stay balanced, just like a tightrope walker who carefully walks on a stretched string from one end of a pole to another without falling. The speedy advancement of technology may have eased communications and production, but it has not replaced our natural instincts, emotions and love, essential to our survival. The *Tightrope* exhibitions are about sharing and questioning both the benefits and the damage that computers have contributed to our lives as humans.

GB *The idea of sharing people's stories has been implicit in your work for a long time, and you even named an exhibition* Täarät-Täarät *(at Haunch of Venison, London, in 2009), meaning storytelling in Amharic. Do you consider yourself a storyteller?*

ES Storytelling is human nature. My art is about my observations of the world around me regardless of where I am. When two or three individuals sit together, they share stories. The hardware and software of computers are full of stories, so I express them in my art the way I perceived and understood them. I also enjoy listening to stories. In this context, yes, I am a visual storyteller.

GB *You have also likened the idea of storytelling to collecting, which you started doing as a child living in Chirqos. Where does the impulse or desire to collect originate?*

ES There are stories and histories behind all the items I collect. For instance, when I look at one button, I think about when and where it was made. I try to imagine how the person who first bought the clothes [on which the button is found] felt as he or she was touching the buttons. These and all the different stories related to the material move me. I then transform these reactions into art. I don't know where my impulse or desire to collect comes from. All I know is that I have enjoyed collecting a variety of material since my childhood.

GB *When you talk about collecting, it sounds as if you take real joy in the experience. Can you recall your first memory of finding and holding onto objects in this way?*

Elias Sime in his studio

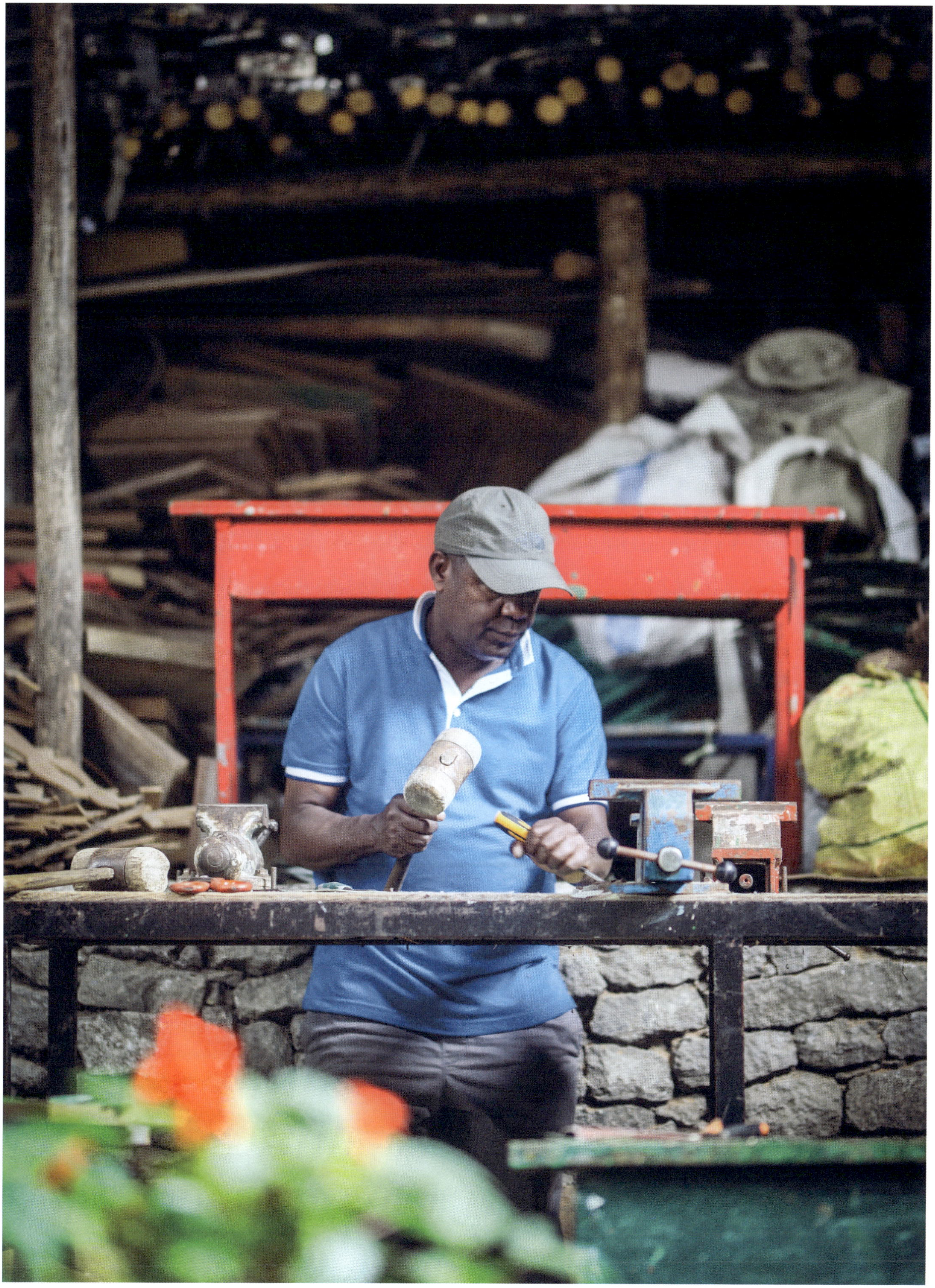

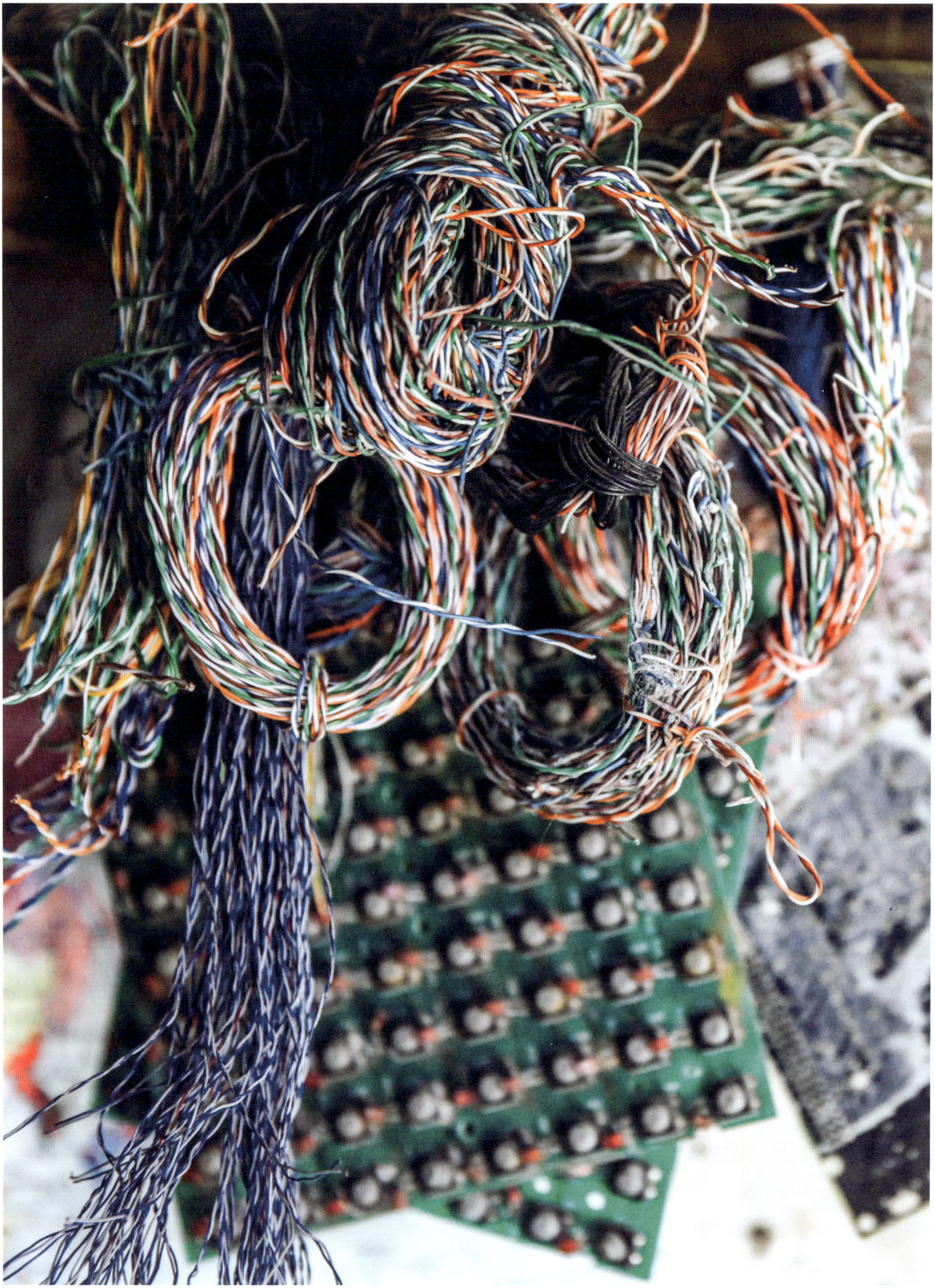

ES I don't remember why or when I started collecting. When I was a kid, I used to enjoy keeping hold of materials that I found interesting, but I never thought that what I was doing was collecting. I just enjoyed playing with different types of materials and objects. The first time I realised that the objects I had been piling up were 'collections' was most probably about 30 years ago, when they ended up being incorporated into my art.

GB *A lot of the objects that you collected have come from markets, such as in Chirqos as a child, and then from the Merkato. Do you need to have a relationship with the place where an object comes from, or are you more interested in the journey it has been on?*

ES All the objects I collect for my art come from different places including the Merkato. When I find interesting objects that I think I can use in my art, I collect them in large amounts. Now, there is a group of people who collect the material I need and bring it to my studio. I don't need to have a relationship with the place where an object for my artworks comes from, but I do enjoy learning about their origins and the history of the material, and Meskerem helps me with researching these material stories and histories.

GB *When you talk about this origin or the history of an object, human touch is often woven into your retelling of this story. How important is this tactile element to you?*

ES Well, one example right now is this computer that you and I are using to communicate. The laptop at my end belongs to Meskerem and contains all of her anger and joy. As she constantly touches it, it becomes part of who she is. It is also like lovers sitting in cafes and spending most of their time communicating with others through their smartphones rather than with the human being who is sat next to them.

GB *Can you expand upon these material stories that are collected?*

MA Sometimes people give Elias gifts. When they find things in their storage they call him to see if he is interested in buying them. Recently, someone showed him thousands of little beautifully carved wooden pieces. I Googled them and found out that they were parts of wooden spinners used in textile factories. The carvings on the wood and their history fascinated him and he ended up buying all of them. I am sure we will see them soon in one of his artworks.

GB *Has this always been the way you've worked together, combining your curiosity, Elias, with Meskerem's research methodology to add to or 'further' a story?*

ES Meskerem and I have been working together for a long time. There is a tendency to read each other's minds when you spend a great deal of time together for many years. You share ideas and build on them. We were born and raised in the same city but in different neighbourhoods with different social norms. We have different experiences in life and our problem-solving capacities vary. Yet, we also share core social norms such as language, music, ritualistic ceremonies and more. This is why our collaboration works. When I look at any material, I feel it and react to it, eagerly trying to understand its history. What Meskerem does is go deeper and dig out what it is, where it comes from and how it was made. This collaboration enriches the artwork.

MA Soon after we met, we started travelling to different parts of the country. Driving long distances gave us time to talk and share a variety of ideas. As much as Elias's art fascinated me, he was also fascinated by how I analysed it, or built upon his stories. One example is the field research we did in Gojam in Northern Ethiopia. There, we visited women who were building Gotas (traditional silos)

Electrical wires and materials in Sime's studio

made from mud and straw. The exhibition *GOTA Täarät-Täarät* (ጎታ ተረት፣ተረት) was a product of this collaboration. As I documented and researched the lives of the silo makers, Elias was sketching. In the end, he produced ten provocative sculptures of Gota made from mud and straw which were shown alongside my short films at the Italian Cultural Institute in Addis Ababa. The other aspect of our collaboration is the trust and respect we have for each other's differences.

GB *Elias, these traditional crafts and building methods appear to have been part of your practice for a long time now, influencing your way of working. Did the ceramic installation* Bareness *also come from this collaborative way of working to draw out stories?*

ES I don't consider that traditional crafts and building methods have been part of my practice for that long. On the contrary, I used to make collages using a variety of materials. I consider what I do contemporary because I incorporate materials that I find interesting into what I have composed in my mind. Even when I used to transform wooden objects into a form of art, I used to simply add different materials on to them to express stories about what I had felt at the time they were found. It could be stories about the people who owned them, or an event that moved me.

Building with mud and straw, which is a worldwide practice, is something I developed after meeting Meskerem. In 2006 I went to Vienna, Austria, to build three Gotas on site using mud and straw at the *Green Flame* exhibition which Meskerem curated for Peter Sellars's New Crowned Hope Festival. There, we visited old breweries made from mud and straw. Then I learned about various mud and straw buildings located all over Europe, Asia and both North and South America. What I found interesting about these buildings is that they are environmentally sound, recyclable, and can withstand weathering for many years. Meskerem also shared detailed photos and stories of highrise buildings (which were over a thousand years old) that she had visited in Sana, Yemen, made from mud, straw, stone, wood and stained glass. We also undertook extended research into the lives of traditional artisans including ceramicists. The mud and straw buildings and the ceramicists I met have influenced me to tell a very contemporary story of humanity through *Bareness*, which is a hand-moulded and traditionally fired ceramic work. I made an artistic decision to fire the ceramics outdoors with traditional techniques instead of a kiln, which was readily available to me. I wanted to express our bareness and fragility as human beings, regardless of who we are, by exposing the most sensitive parts of our bodies.

MA I have been researching artisans for many years. I think of them as artists who have been misunderstood or undervalued. Meeting Elias brought these ideas to light. The long drives and walks to get to where the artisans lived gave us ample time to share ideas and stories. Observing them as they collect various soil types, mix, shape and finally fire, gave us a better understanding of their techniques and lives. *Bareness* is a compilation of all these stories.

GB *Elias, these early research trips took place in Ethiopia and the stories that were told appear to be rooted in Ethiopian culture, yet you have said that 'my art could fit in anywhere'. How do you reconcile these two elements?*

ES My research trips with Meskerem have never been limited to Ethiopia. Since we first met we have been travelling across the world. In fact, our first international travel was in 2004 to Dakar, Senegal, when she was a member of the selection committee for the Dak'Art Biennale. When I returned, I made art about my observations of Dakar and its history. I was born, raised and still live in Addis Ababa, known as the political capital of Africa, where the African Union, Economic

Mud and straw wall, 'little Zoma'

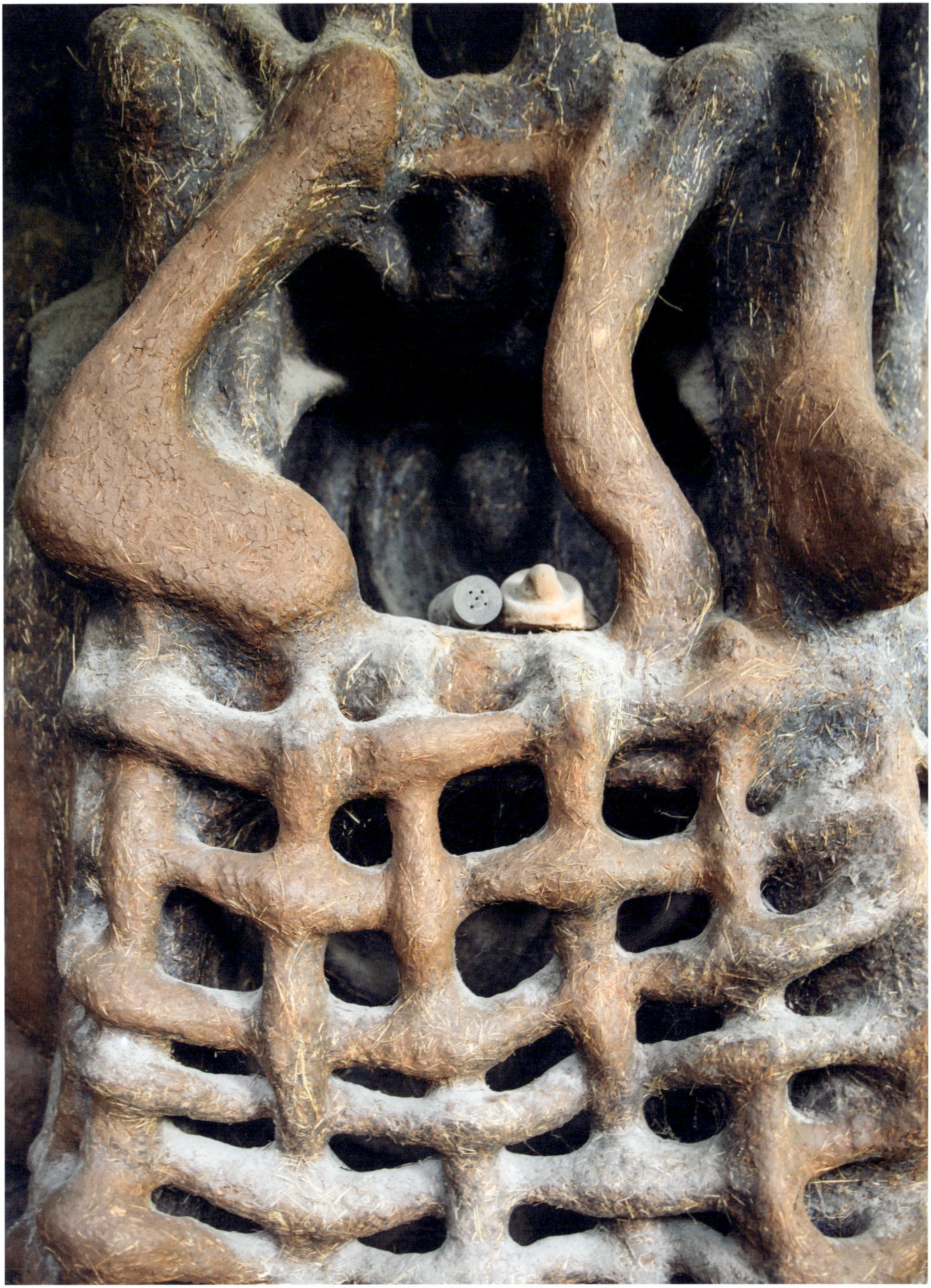

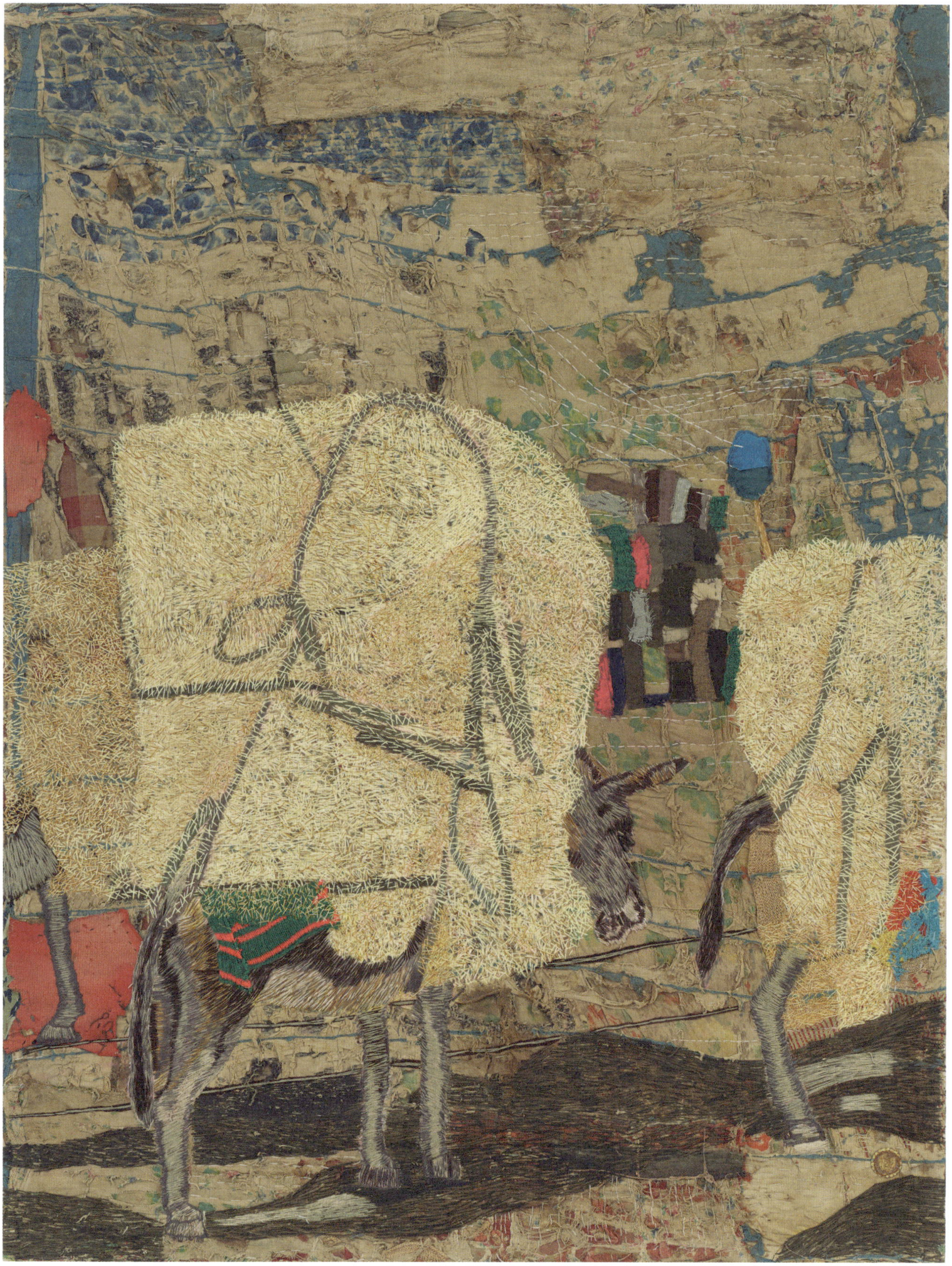

Chenet
2007, clothes, yarn and stitch on canvas, 160 × 119 cm

Commission for Africa and the United Nations are housed. It is also home to one of the largest embassies in the world. The fact that I grew up in a city, where I was exposed to all types of people, gave me the opportunity to have a deeper understanding of humans, regardless of their background. The research I have done with Meskerem has taught me how humans historically have used rituals to create awareness about the importance of co-existing with nature. I have also learned that rituals exist in various forms all over the world, including Europe, Asia and elsewhere. Sometimes I make art about lovers I observe on the streets as I walk in New York or another big city. Other times I make art about dung beetles and their stories. I tend to mute the audience from my mind when I make art and focus on how I can transfer what I have envisioned onto the wooden panels. The audience is then free to interpret what they see and relate it to their own experiences. I make art because I am an artist with a curious mind.

GB *Whilst we are discussing these influential journeys, I would also like to revisit some of your earlier works — of which examples can be seen in* Eregata*, such as* What is Love? (1), Chenet *and* Yemegnot Alem*. Was embroidery something you learnt as a child?*

ES When I was a child I used to enjoy watching weavers embroidering on the clothes they made. I rarely do embroidery myself; what I do is stitching. I also grew up in a neighbourhood where everyone carried needles and threads in their pockets. The stitched artworks I made may have been influenced by these experiences. I used to buy different coloured yarns from the market because they were readily available. I then used them like oil, acrylic or watercolour paint on canvases.

GB *Can you see a relationship between these stitch and yarn works and your later way of working with electronic components?*

ES The processes of sewing buttons, stitching yarns and working with electronics are very similar. Dissecting motherboards, pulling out the wires, sorting them into colours, braiding them and nailing them onto wooden panels is simply an extension of the sewing and stitching that I have done for many years. The last stitched work I made was *Splash of A Pebble In Muddy Water* (2006), which I felt was one of my best works. I made tiny stitches on a huge canvas; it was as if it wasn't produced by a human hand. I wanted to truly express the endurance it had taken me and Meskerem when we walked through the mountains, crossing rivers to find a specific ritual about making peace and co-existing with the thunder and the rain. What I stitched represented what it had taken to interview, photograph, write, sketch, sleep on the floor and be woken up by a rooster spreading dust on everyone's faces as it flew over us. The long walks and the breathtaking landscapes left unforgettable memories of things I had never expected to see. I wanted to express the intensity of this journey within these small stitches.

GB *The braiding technique you use with electrical wires, was this something you learnt later in life?*

ES Braiding hair or bracelets for jewellery are common practices in many parts of the world, including Ethiopia. Some braids are made with three strings and others with four or five. My assistants and I learned braiding from our families, friends and neighbours.

GB *As your work has developed from working with yarn and buttons to working with electronic materials, it has also become more abstract, leading to the suggestion that the title* Tightrope *might also be understood as referring to the 'tension' between figuration and abstraction in your work. How do you feel about this interpretation?*

ES My work represents both figuration and abstraction, this is true. I worked with both yarn

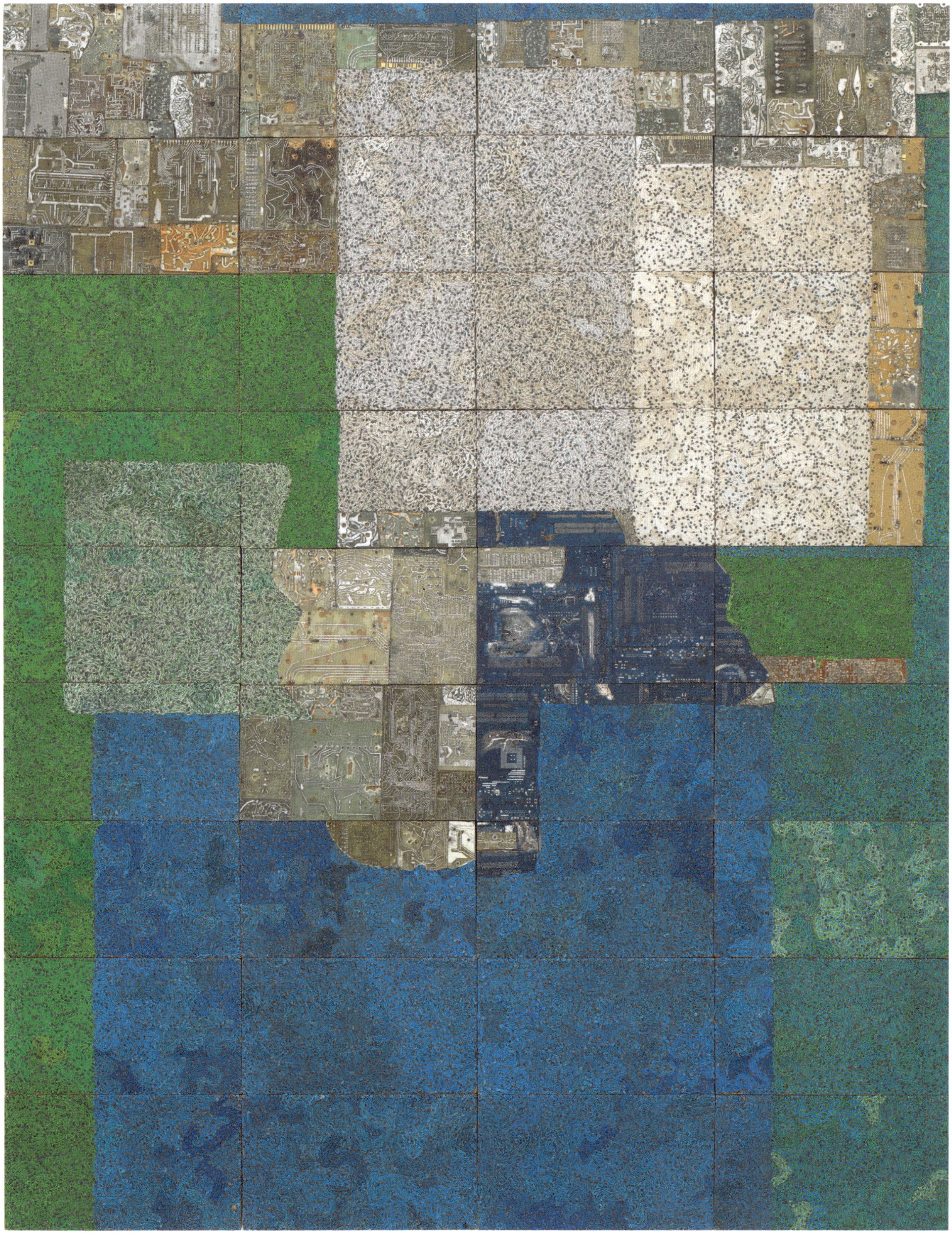

Tightrope: Noiseless 20
2019, reclaimed electrical wires and components on panel, 208.9 × 160 cm

and buttons at the same time. Eventually I stopped making art using needles because my eyes got tired and I moved to electronic components. I don't worry about how my art is interpreted because people are free to make their own interpretations. If I read what is written about my work, or about me as an artist, I am worried that I may stop working. It may influence my art, so why take a chance? I also know that they don't write it for me. They write it for themselves and their audience.

GB *Some of the early works in* Tightrope *have been referred to as resembling cityscapes or landscapes. Can you see a relationship between these images and the works, even if it was not a conscious consideration?*

ES Yes, occasionally I think about landscapes, other times I think about love, interesting forms and history. I also enjoy imagining the future. Humans for the most part tend to mimic one another. If someone describes my work in a certain way, then others repeat it. I decided long ago to be free from this, and not to worry about viewers', writers' or interviewers' references. As much as I protect my freedom to express my art from my point of view, they are also free to make their own references and interpretations.

GB *These interpretations have often been made in direct relation to urbanisation and technological developments within society. What changes have taken place in Addis Ababa since you first started dreaming of Zoma?*

MA Addis Ababa has changed dramatically in the last five years. It is greener, cleaner, richer and busier. Twenty-five years ago, when I was dreaming about Zoma, the idea of art was mostly enclaved amongst a few people. Most of the exhibitions took place at the European cultural institutes and a handful of locally owned galleries. Now, new galleries have opened, and new museums are built such as the Science Museum with a gallery for contemporary art, the Art School Museum in Entoto and Zoma Museum, all attracting large audiences.

GB *Returning to the notion of time, some of the materials you work with Elias have started to become obsolete and you have needed to buy them 'new' rather than sourcing them second-hand. Are you interested in the longevity of the materials you use in terms of their lifespan? Is the survival of materials or the technology they represent important to you?*

ES Yes, some of the materials have become obsolete but I have always bought them. I never found them for free. The only change between my early process and now is that the price has gone up and is ten times higher. I used to go to the Merkato to buy them from people. The number of materials I use for each artwork is immense, so it is impossible to source them myself. I have always needed to buy old and new materials depending on my compositions. However, the survival of the material is still important to me. One of the reasons it takes me a long time to finish some of my works is that I wait a long time until I find the specific material I need for certain compositions.

GB *Many of the materials you use are part of our daily lives and readily available to us (albeit not in large quantities), from buttons to computer keyboards, suggesting a certain democratisation within the process of making. When we were talking during your visit to Bristol (in June 2023), I wrote down something you said: 'Anyone can do art'. Can you expand on what you meant by this?*

ES Art can be expressed verbally, physically or materially. The materials I select for my art are always part of my compositions. Some artists express their art through performance, writing poetry or designing buildings. Diaries can also be a form of art. Art can be a survival tool where we sometimes find ourselves being creative to get out of trouble. Therefore, I believe that humans, in general, are artists.

GB *You have been collaborating for a number of years, since your early trips around Ethiopia, curating exhibitions and creating the Zoma Museum. What does collaboration mean to you both?*

MA & ES We come from two different backgrounds and these different upbringings have been instrumental to the way we exchange and support our knowledge and ideas. I [Meskerem] was born and raised by a well-to-do family in an affluent neighbourhood and attended private schools. Our neighbours lived in fenced-in villas where we met by appointment. I [Elias] was born in a diverse neighbourhood with rows of houses sharing walls, where our front door opened directly on to a shared walkway. This proximity made the entire neighbourhood one family. Because we shared everything, we had no choice but to show love and respect for one another.

For us, collaboration is sharing ideas, labour and, more importantly, respecting our differences. Ideas can flow from either one of us, but executing them requires trust, hard labour and, more importantly, love. We both believe that competition is dangerous, so we use our differences as leverage to bind our ideas.

GB *This exchange of knowledge and ideas seems to have come together seamlessly in the Zoma Museum, which curator Hans Ulrich Obrist has described aptly as both a 'collage' and an embodiment of the idea of Gesamtkunstwerk (a 'total work of art').[1] What do you feel about these descriptions?*

MA & ES We think Hans Ulrich Obrist is right. When Hans interviewed us, Zoma Museum was under construction, so he did the interview at 'little Zoma' (which used to be known as Zoma Contemporary Art Center). Collage is a good analogy because Zoma is based upon layers and layers of ideas.

MA The idea of building a modern museum using vernacular construction techniques was something we introduced to the public. It is about aesthetics, sustainability, caring, daring and loving. The beauty is that Elias and I put all our efforts into realising it. It is an example of how collaboration with respect, care and love can have a beautiful outcome.

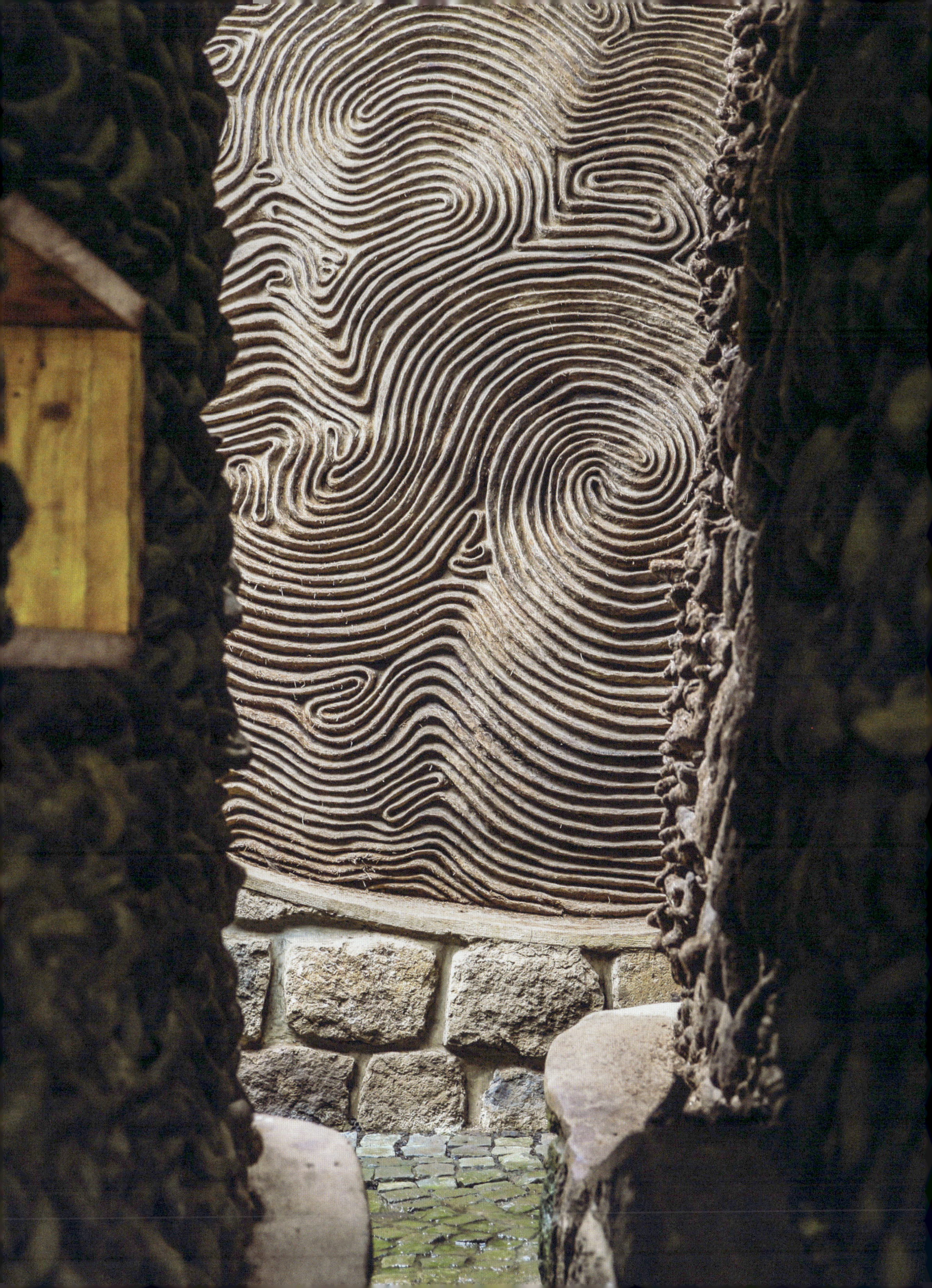

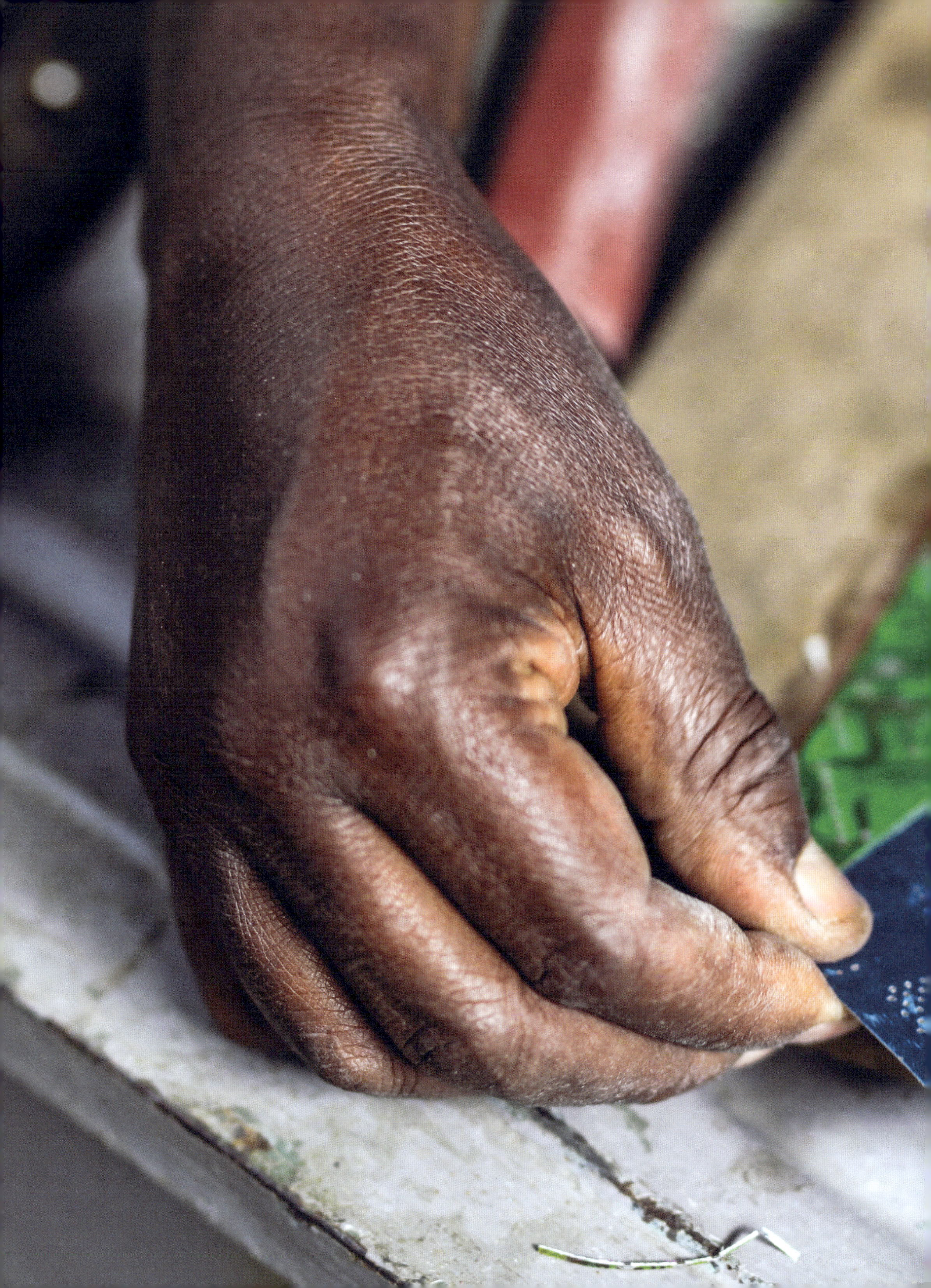

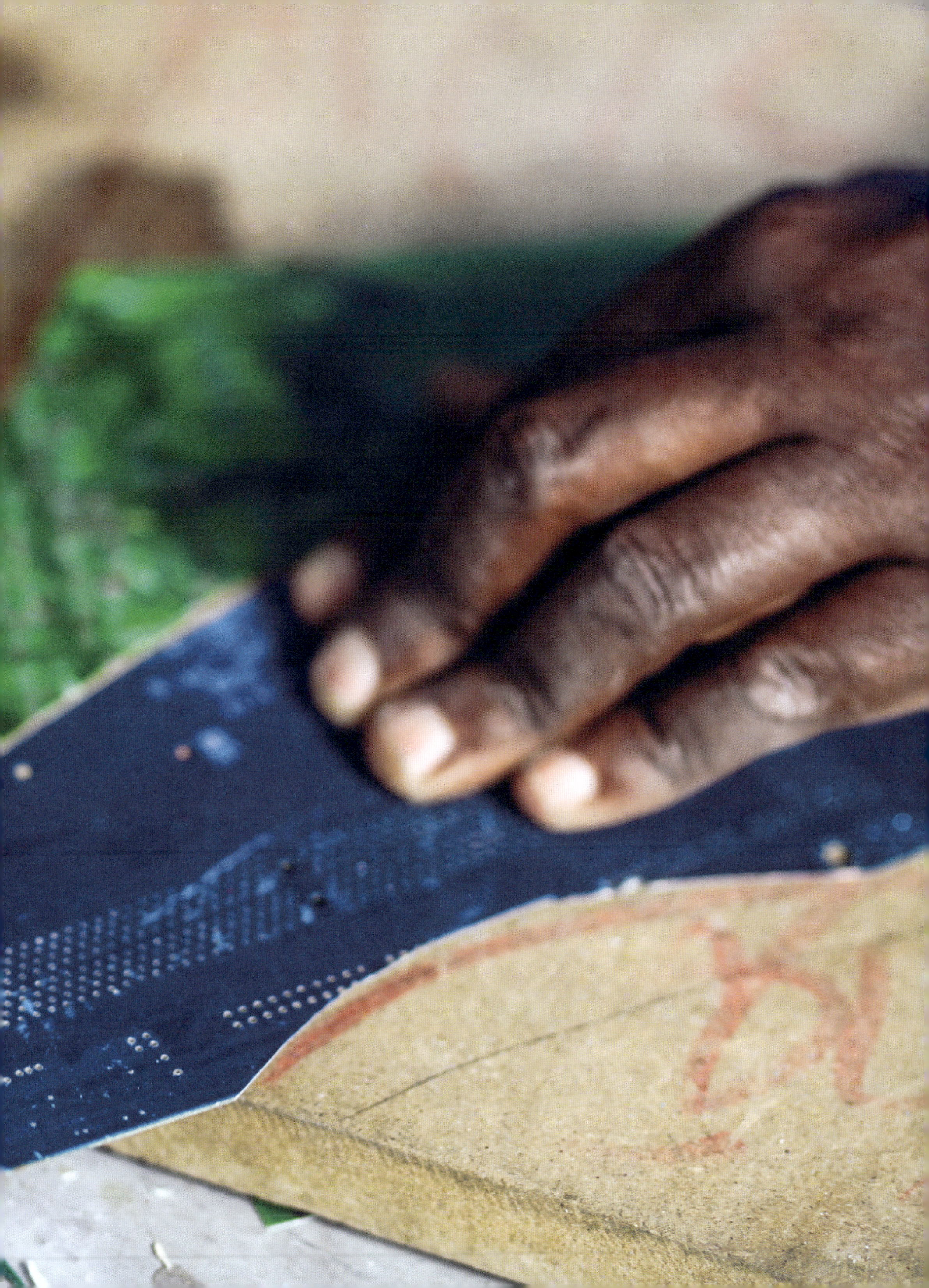

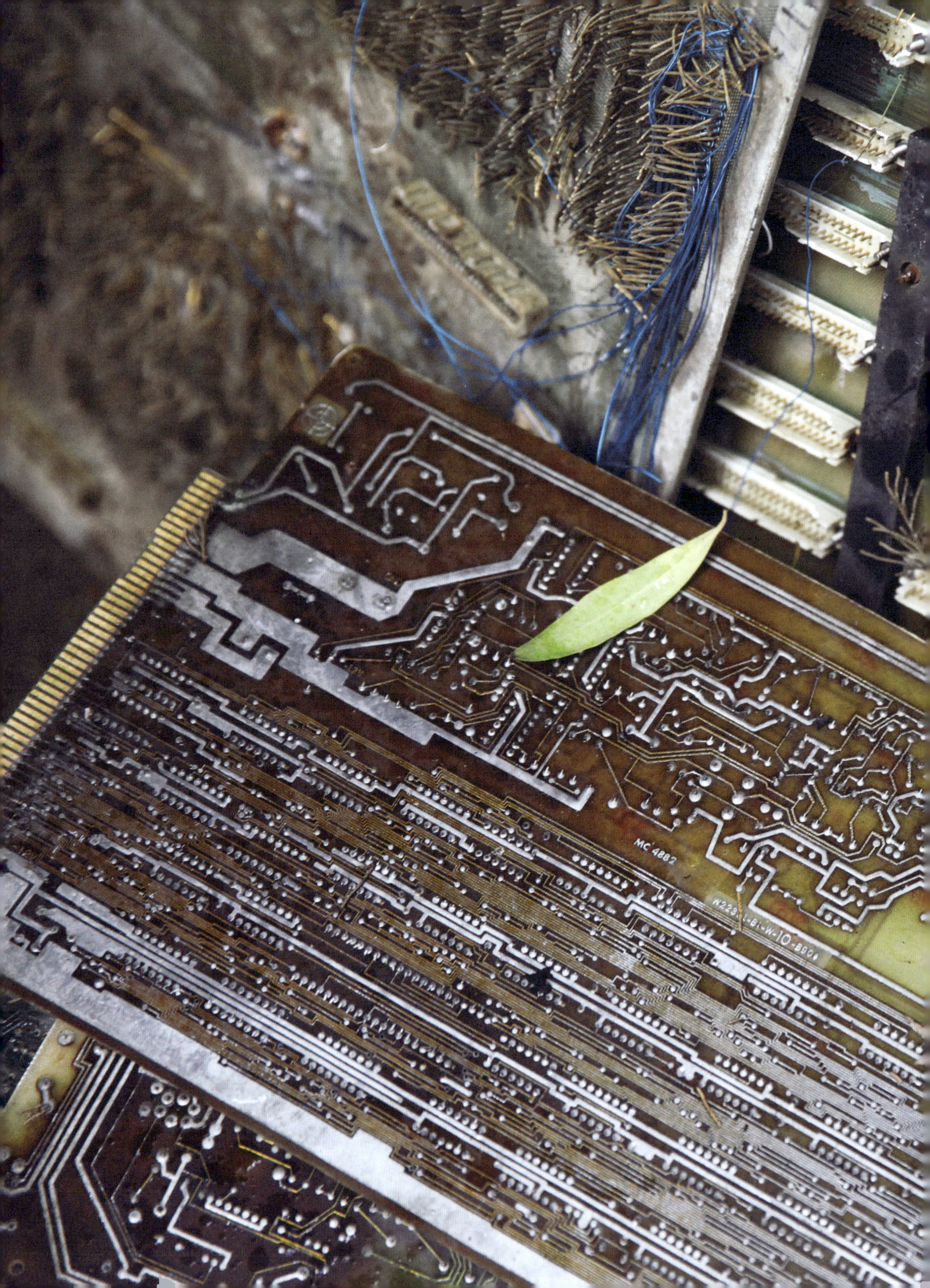

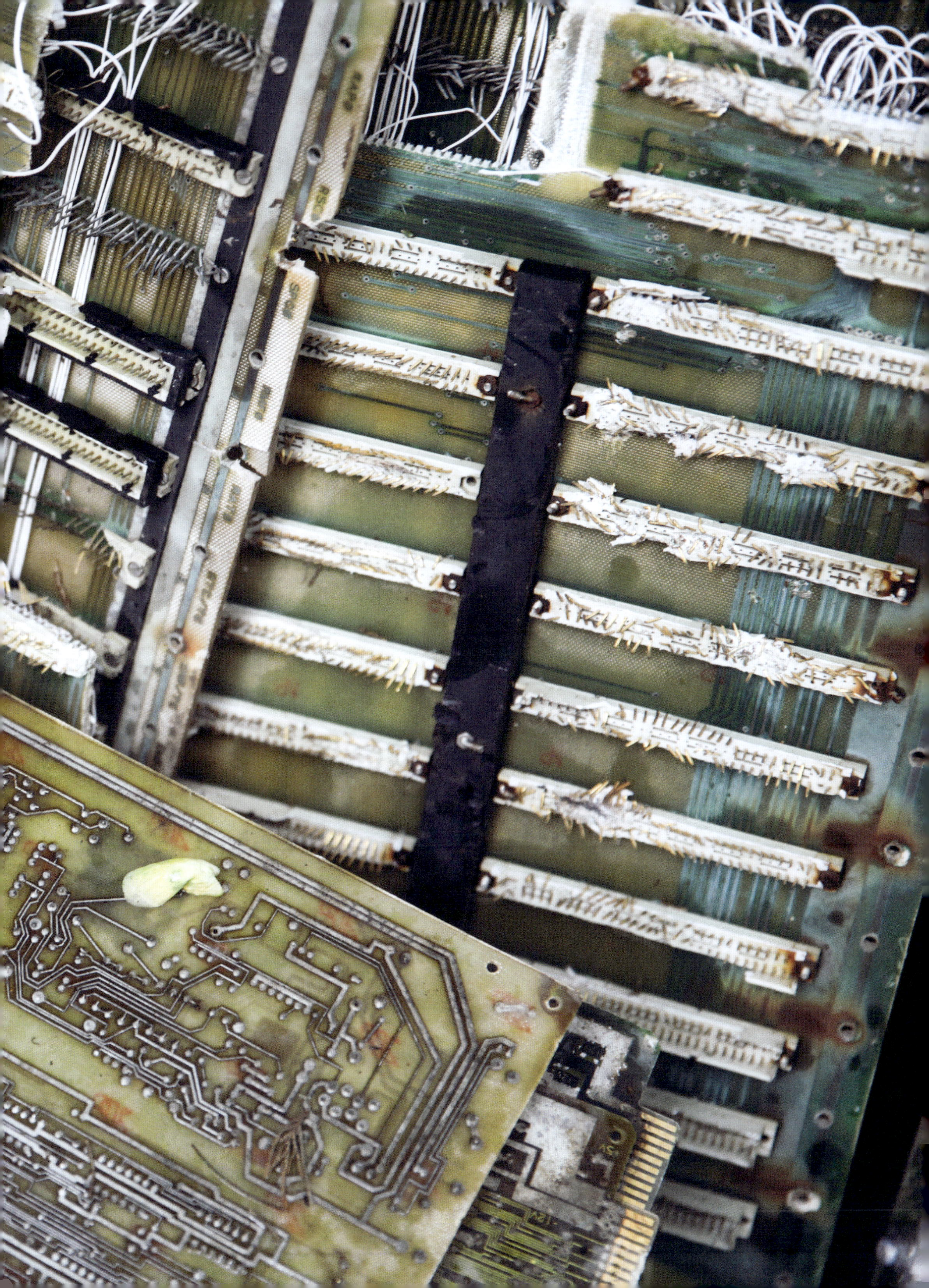

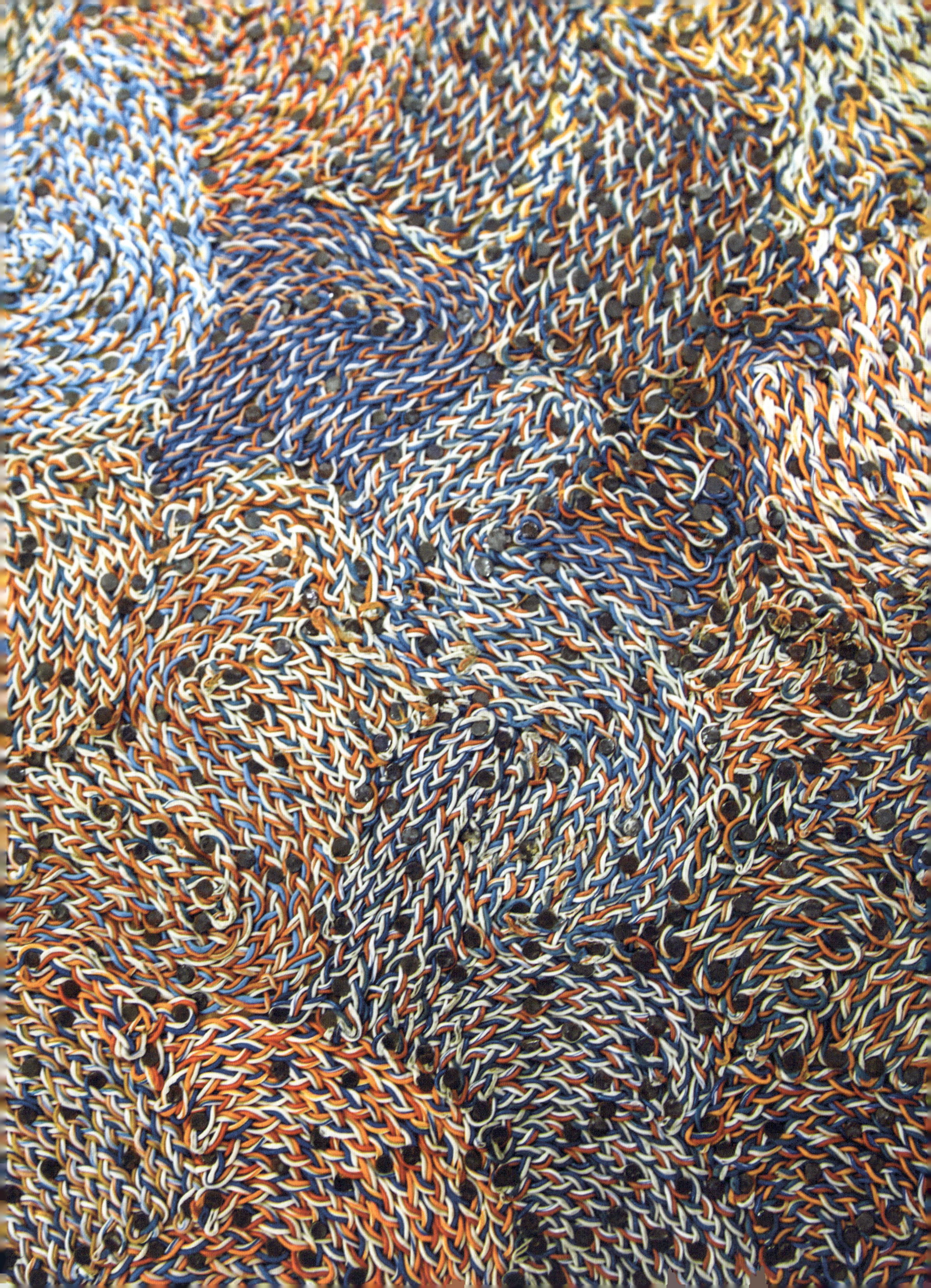

Andria Hickey
—

Each material I collect has its own story. It has its own language.
— Elias Sime

A TAPESTRY FOR HUMANITY

'If it is a human thing to do to put something you want, because it's useful, edible or beautiful, into a bag, or a basket, or a bit of rolled bark or leaf, or a net woven of your hair, or what have you, and then take it home with you, home being another larger kind of pouch or bag, a container for people, and then later on you take it out and eat it or share it or store it up for the winter in a solider container or put it in the medicine bundle or the shrine or the museum, the holy place, the areas that contain what is sacred, and then next day you probably do much the same again — if to do that is human, if that's what it takes, then I am a human being after all.' [1]

In her essay 'The Carrier Bag Theory of Fiction', science fiction writer Ursula K. Le Guin proposes an alternative approach to storytelling to help us to understand the complexity of human existence. She looks to the origins of our heroes and suggests that the carrier bag, the tool of the gatherer, rather than the spear of the heroic hunter, is a more fitting symbol for the narrative arc of stories. The carrier bag, in Le Guin's view, can hold a collection of unexpected elements, divergent perspectives and multifaceted experiences, each with equal weight. While Le Guin speaks of novels and storytelling, this framework is also useful when considering the function of art, of its making, its materials and its meaning.

With this in mind, we might consider Elias Sime's meticulous compositions as a kind of carrier bag where materials take on the role of narrators, whispering stories of human labour, connections, systems, cultural traditions and their intertwined impact on our environment. His carrier bag becomes an infinite weaving of human histories, embedded with personal and collective memories gathered from repurposed objects. In his work, materials are both literally and metaphorically braided together, creating a carrier bag that holds the potential for renewed human connection.

To make the meticulous patterns and texture in his wall works and sculptures, Sime gathers electrical wires, computer keyboards, broken cell phones and circuit boards over decades, and dismantles his findings into individual material components that are then reassembled and transformed into colourful shapes, patterns and

Example of electrical wire braiding

textures that move between abstraction and figuration. Threads of wire, for instance, are intricately braided, layered and reassembled. Each type of wire is specifically chosen to be reimagined into wall panels and sculptures that evoke a myriad of narratives, selected for their metaphorical potency. For example, in 2018, when Sime was commissioned to create a monumental work for Facebook's headquarters in Menlo Park, he was inspired by a visit to the nearby National Park's redwood trees. In considering what materials would be the most fitting, Sime stated: 'Because I'm already working with electronic material, I started thinking that this could actually tell a story. I felt that the electronics, the computer, the designs, the material — all of those things — could express what I wanted to say ... The way life is moving — the speed, the complications, the woven world we're living in. I felt I could tell the background of the trees' stories, the current and the future of the story.' [2]

Sime began working with electronic components as early as 2009, presenting new work in the exhibition *Ants and Ceramicists* (2011). However, it is his *Tightrope* series (2009–) that is most well-known for its use of repurposed material components gleaned from electronics and technological devices — computers, cell phones, hard drives — that evoke stories of our past, present and future. For the past 14 years, Sime has sourced the vast majority of his materials from the Menyalesh Tera section of the Merkato market in Addis Ababa. Computers, televisions, radios and telephones that are new, used and in parts, are available for purchase. Initially, Sime bought used objects to dissect for special parts and electrical components, but today Sime sources material from many different places — purchasers who buy in bulk, government office auctions, international sources like eBay, or directly from manufacturing companies. As the work has evolved, he has begun to purchase electronic objects that are new, ensuring consistency across his use of materials for specific pieces — the colour, texture and pattern of his materials are vital to the composition of each work. As such, the colour-coded wires, circuit boards and microchips Sime finds conjure a history of our contemporary moment that spans vast distances, geographies and cultural contexts.

As Sime explains 'Each material I collect has its own story. It has its own language. Every story has a beginning.' [3] The beginning of the story of the material production of the digital devices that permeate our everyday lives is infinitely complex. The most important parts of our cell phones start out as raw extracted materials, processed into specialised components to be assembled and packaged into consumer goods — all at multiple factories in different parts of the world — to be shipped to other locations once again for distribution and sales. They arrive in our hands, on our desks, in our homes and become beloved; we cannot seem to look away from their screens and the stories and people they connect us with. Nevertheless, they are eventually discarded — broken, obsolete, outdated — and sent away from our homes to unknown landfills, recycling plants and material markets.

This cycle entangles the countless stories of people whose hands have played a part in the making and movement of these objects around the world: copper and cobalt miners in Chile and Rwanda, microchip factory workers in Shenzhen, sea captains from everywhere on shipping containers, retailers at multinational companies around the world. These are some of the many individuals who play a part in the production of these seemingly innocuous and cherished items. Each part of this process has a story that inspires Sime and leads him to the materials he sources. As he states: 'The materials I select, by the time they get into my hands, they've been touched by so many people, and now they're in my hands. Even though it may not be visible, when you're working on your personal computer, you leave a part of you on that. Then, when it breaks, there is somebody else who goes inside it and touches it; there's that fingerprint.' [4]

Elias Sime in his studio

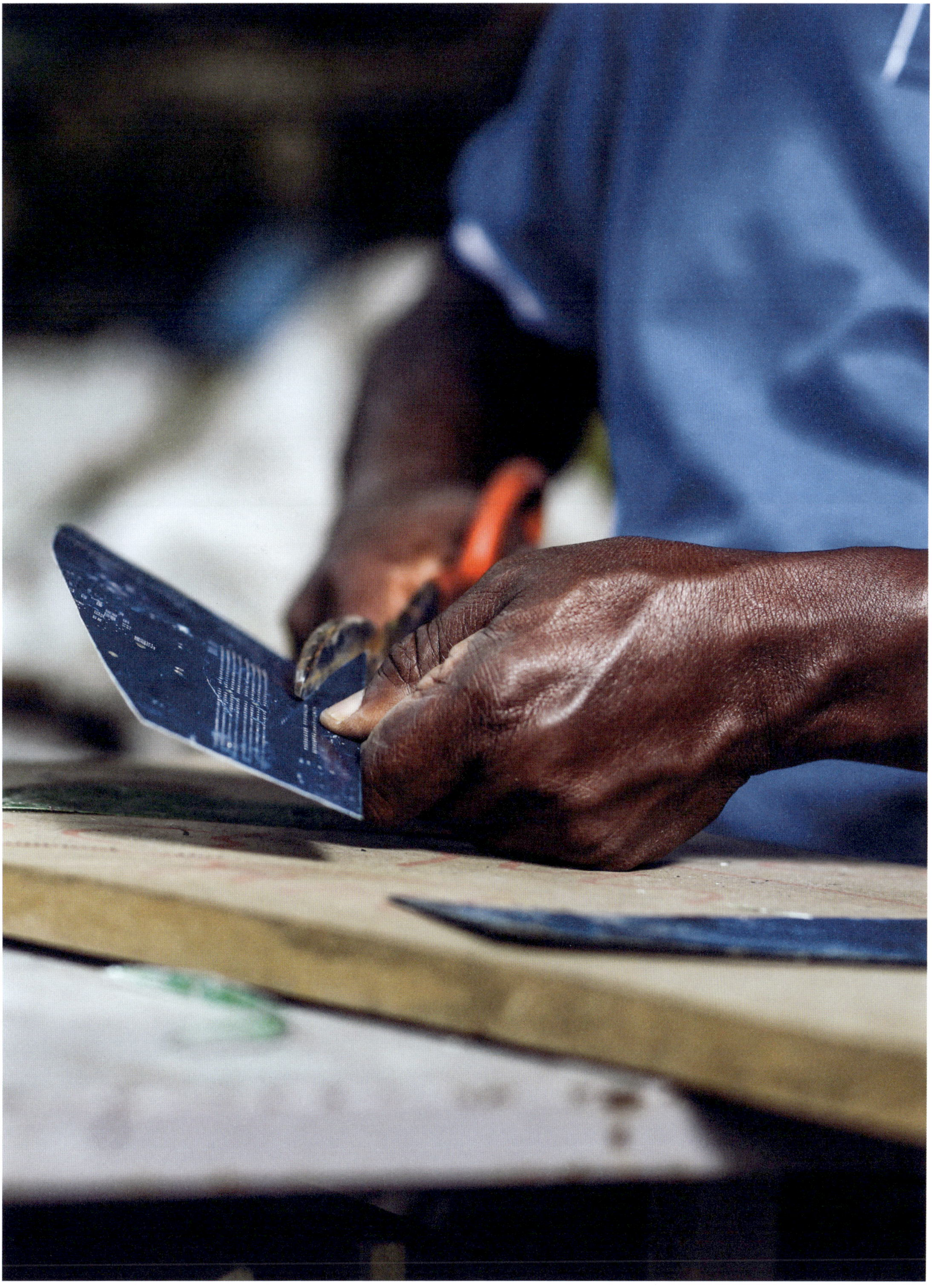

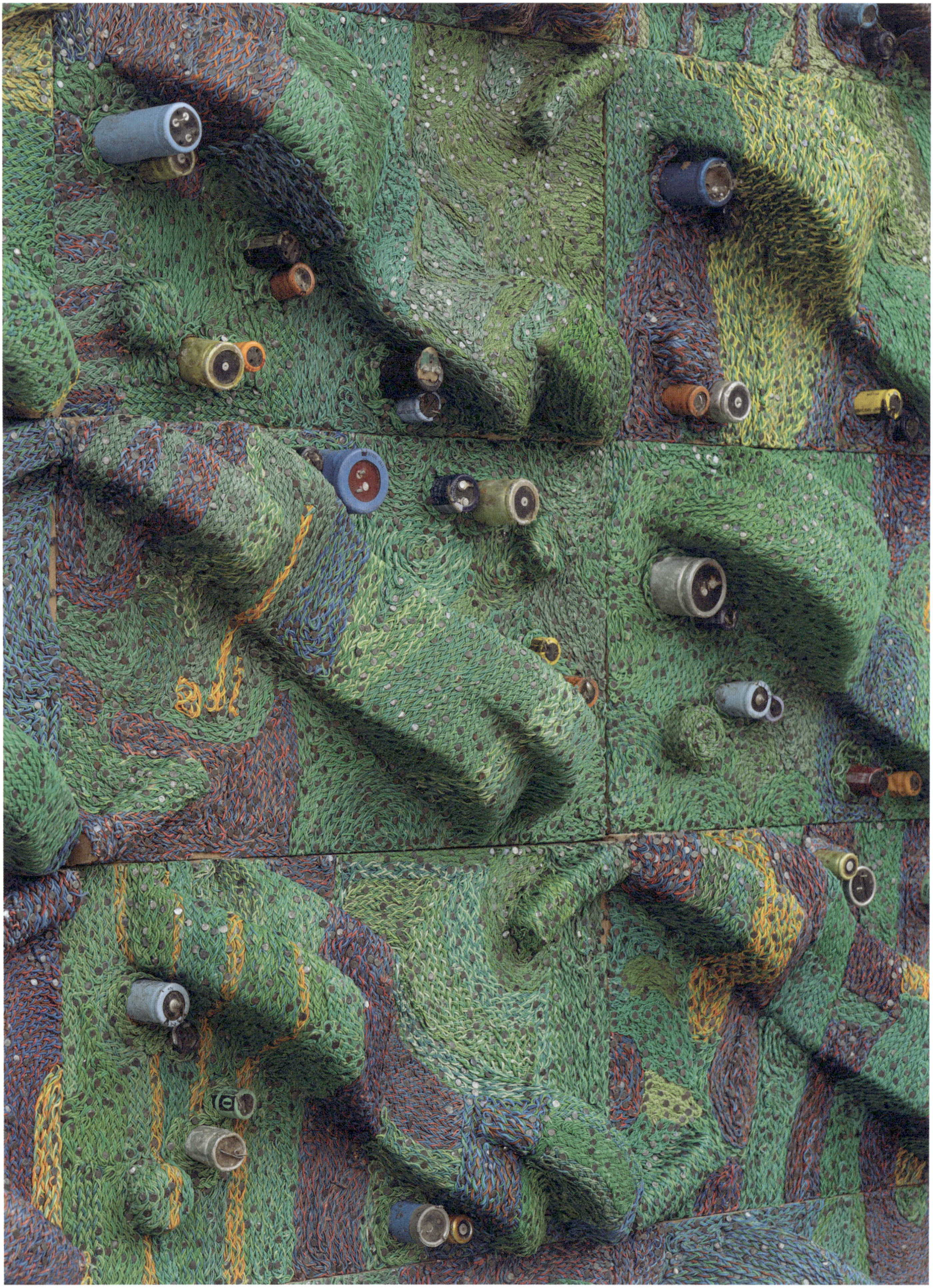

Addis Ababa, where Sime lives and works, shares global characteristics with places like Hsinchu, Taiwan, or Sulawesi, Indonesia, or Fort McMurray, Canada — all places where the impact of natural resource extraction and processing increasingly collides with daily life in ways that are enmeshed with other places, systems and people around the world. This is ever more apparent as we witness the increasing effects of climate change. For Sime, understanding this is an essential part of what it means to be human in the twenty-first century: 'Sometimes you tell a story and the story stops. I'm waiting for the story to end. It is a world history. It's not about Ethiopia. It's not about Africa. Globalization is everywhere. Whether we like it or not, it's in every one of our lives. If you didn't know my name, if you didn't know who I was, if you looked at the art, you will know where it came from. It's about human life. Just as is.' [5]

Sime's exploration of the tension between the pleasures of technological advancement and the simultaneous loss of shared embodied human experiences is deeply connected to the specific electronic materials he selects, which include an array of items that once played a role in digital communications — reclaimed electrical wires and components, circuitry, motherboards, wood panels and even megaphones. As forms of conduit and components of connectivity, they contain narratives of production and tell the stories of their consumer use, making visible the past lives of these materials and the impact of globalised systems on our collective consciousness.

Collaboration is at the heart of Sime's response to our loss of human connection in globalised life today. Each of his works — some taking years to complete — possess a tactile quality that connects to the hands that have directly shaped the piece. The techniques Sime employs are dependent on the shared labour of many people. Throughout the *Tightrope* series, for example, Sime utilises a range of braiding techniques to weave together complex webs of coated copper electrical wire in alternating colour patterns, held in place by glinting steel nails embedded within the surface. Braiding is more than a meticulous formal approach to the vinyl and copper threads; it is also a collective experience. In Sime's studio, many hands come together to fold metres of wire over wire, forming three-, four- and five-thread braids into lines, shapes and textures. As Sime explains: 'Braiding is a skill that a lot of people know how to do. It's like braiding your hair. It's not only Ethiopian, but it is a mobilised knowledge of braiding around the world that has been happening for centuries. It's just human nature to want to braid something, to bring them together. Some of the braids are braided with five strings. Some are with four, some are with three. That is intentional. That is what makes it human. It's about you and me braiding right now. You and me talking. We're braided. We're sharing ideas. We're braiding our ideas together.' [6] There is an intimacy between the hands of the makers and a tactility to the material that is interwoven in the shared space of working together. Braiding here is a conceptual gesture as much as a formal technique.

Often constructed in pieces, Sime's works come together on the floor of his large studio, with a team working across wooden blocks assembled to form a cohesive whole. Sime works in and with the community throughout this process, bringing people together to source materials, discuss ideas and work alongside one another to meticulously craft his often monumental compositions. The sublime dexterity required to realise the intricate patterns and textures, particularly in large-scale works like *Tightrope: Behind the Processor No.6* (2022), means that they become both a record of collective labour and a signature of shared time. As Tracy L. Adler has stated, 'This temporal element in both the making and the viewing of Sime's works cannot be overstated: a braid of wire appears to wend endlessly, or, at least, the implication of the infinite is there. The meshed strands point to a continuum and connectedness that takes time to unfold.' [7]

Importantly, Sime has worked closely with long-time collaborator Meskerem Assegued,

Tightrope: Behind the Processor No.6 (detail)
2022, three-dimensional wall piece with woven electrical wires and other components on wood panels, 253 × 400 × 12 cm

a curator and anthropologist also based in Addis Ababa, for over three decades, developing projects, exhibitions and new bodies of work. Together Assegued and Sime co-founded ZCAC (Zoma Contemporary Art Center), an ambitious civic architectural work in Addis Ababa and Harla, a small village south of Dire Dawa, Ethiopia, that speaks to Sime's deep commitment to community. As described elsewhere in this publication, Zoma encompasses various elements, including a school, farm, garden, library and exhibition and project space, presenting a comprehensive perspective on how community, sustainability and art converge into a cohesive vision, echoing Sime's interest in human connectivity in his sculptures and wall works.

Building community and collaboration is also an important part of Sime's site-responsive commissions. For example, to make *Flowers & Roots* (2019) — a commissioned public sculpture for his 2019 exhibition *Elias Sime: Tightrope*, at the Ruth and Elmer Wellin Museum of Art, Hamilton College, in Clinton, NY — Sime worked in close collaboration with students from the college, building the piece together over several weeks onsite. Likewise, when invited by Peter Sellars to develop the exhibition *Eye of the Needle, Eye of the Heart* (2009) at the Santa Monica Museum of Art, Assegued and Sime brought together a community of artists and artisans, including well-known contemporary artists like Julie Mehretu and El Anatsui, as well as a group of Mayan weavers from Mexico. Similarly, when invited to create a major work as part of the New Crowned Hope Festival in Vienna, Sime and Assegued worked with festival participants — many of whom were staying in the same apartment complex. In this case, the collaboration took place across languages and cultures, with an organic community finding themselves stitched together through the making of Sime's work.

Throughout his work, Sime is interested in the community and human connection that begin to be formed in tandem with the objects he is making, so much so that he chooses not to sign his name on his work, in recognition of the many hands that participate in its creation. As he explains: 'I feel very humbled when I talk about my art, because it's actually a combination of other people's art. I feel like it has a lot of people's hands in it. The people around me, the forces who help me make this art, come through. The final product of the work is not just me. It's a lot of people's work. I'm very lucky I'm sitting here talking to you, but I do want to recognise everybody. Meskerem Assegued and I have worked together for many, many years. It's been many years of building step by step. And when you look at the work, I never sign my name. I want to say that. Nobody has ever asked me that question, but that's why I don't sign... There are so many people who are unnamed here. Their product is what I created into this art, so I don't like to take the acclaim for myself. They influenced me, because their work is what I transformed.' [8]

Along with students, his studio team, artisans and other collaborators that he encounters in different locations, Sime's work is also in dialogue with a global movement of artists working with mass-produced, commercially available materials. Sime's techniques and approach to material resonate with the work of artists like Tara Donovan, Brian Jungen, Subodh Gupta and El Anatsui, who similarly embrace the transformative power of repurposed materials. While their artistic approaches, subject matter and cultural contexts differ significantly, they share an impulse to recontextualise and transform mass-produced objects, revealing the extraordinary capacity of our everyday material world to be reworked and reimagined.

Some artists, such as Donovan, draw attention to the potential of ordinary materials to create a sense of wonder and discovery. Utilising mundane objects such as plastic cups and straws, Donovan creates immersive installations and sculptures that completely transform our expectations and evoke awe at the capacity of the material itself. Others, like Jungen, dissect consumer goods,

Electronic materials collected by Sime

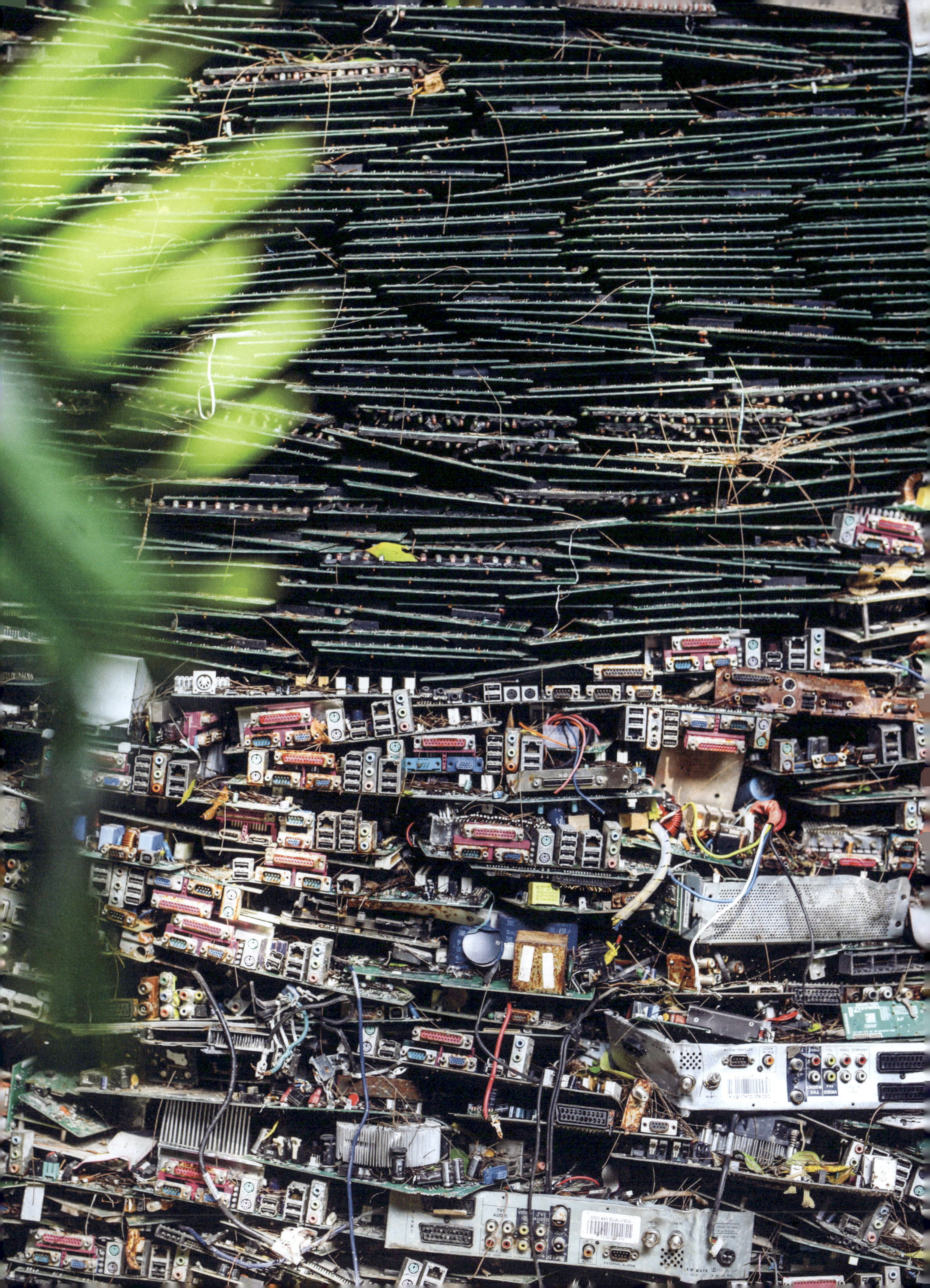

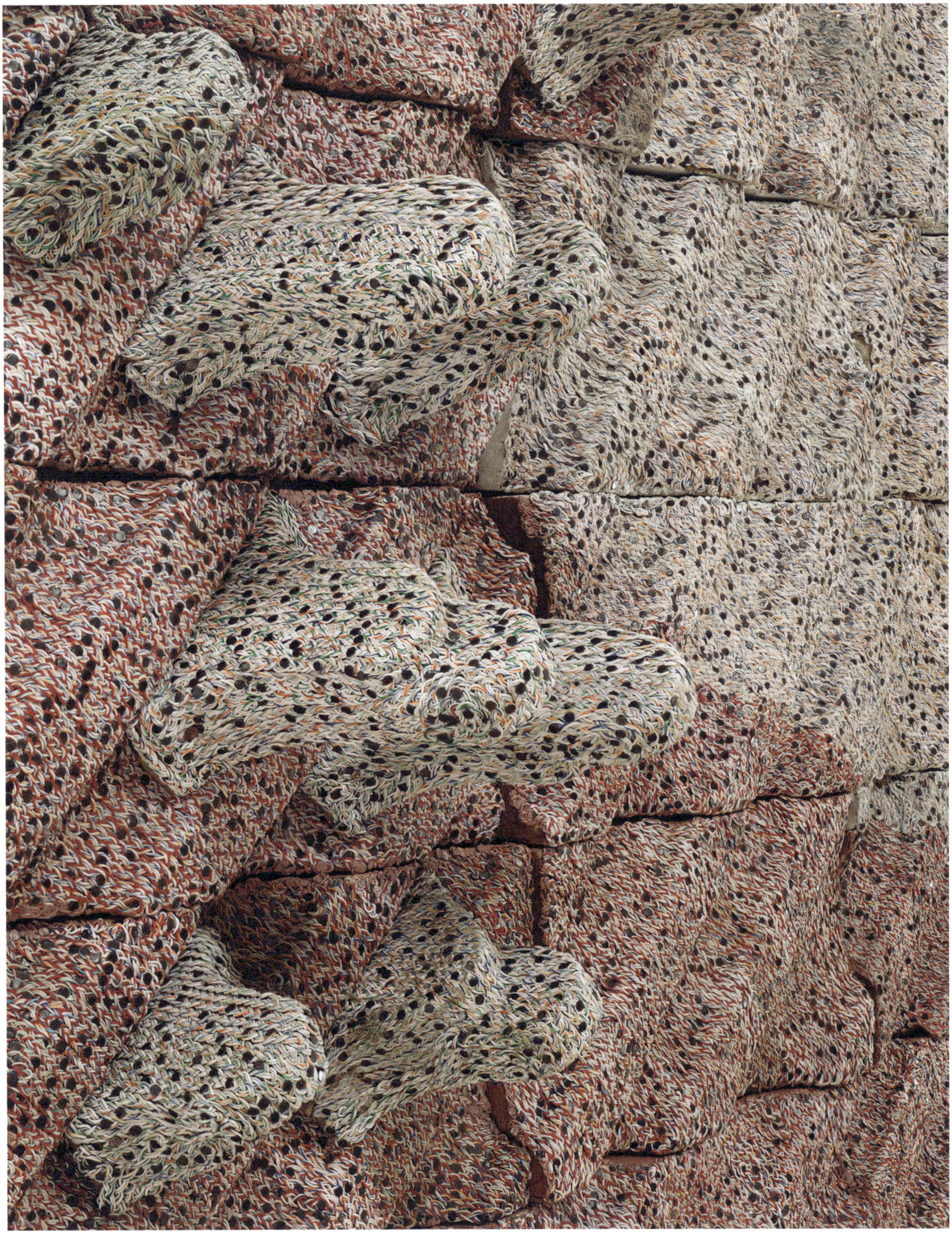

Veiled Whispers (detail)
2022, three-dimensional wall piece with woven electrical wires and other components on wood panels, 200.7 × 571.5 × 20.3 cm

like trainers or lawn furniture, into their component parts to reimagine cultural symbols and explore themes of identity and transcultural life. Still others, like Gupta and Anatsui, use recycled materials, found objects and repurposed commercial goods to call attention to the socio-political implications of discarded objects, globalisation and consumerism.

Sime's use of repurposed objects threads a line through these approaches, straddling abstraction and figuration and engaging with found materials that are both grounded in specific contexts and transformational in their sublime composition. As curator and art historian Ugochukwu-Smooth C. Nzewi states, 'Sime's practice is located at the intersection of the local and the global. The artist operates with a spacious creative license, addressing the experiences of his immediate environment while mirroring and transcending Ethiopia's rich artistic traditions, cultural heritage, and history to come into his own as an image and object maker. Sime insists that his work speaks not of Ethiopia or of Africa per se but of human experience.'[9]

Although Sime's artistic vision extends beyond geographical boundaries, his choice of materials and motifs reflects a deep connection to the history, culture and socio-political context of Ethiopia. At the same time, his integration of techniques borrowed from other contexts, and his use of deconstructed figural elements, enable his work to resonate with a broader global contemporary condition. Specifically, the braiding techniques present throughout Sime's work resonate across time and place — specific to Ethiopia and yet simultaneously international. Sime asserts that braiding patterns are not unique to an Ethiopian context, noting that braiding is a worldwide practice throughout human history, from images of ancient Egyptians, Greeks and Romans with braided hair to contemporary braiding styles used all over the world today.

Fostering a dialogue that extends beyond geographic and cultural boundaries, Sime's gridded surfaces are intentionally imbued with narrative content that speaks to our global experience. Works like *Tightrope: Noiseless 20* (2019) and *Tightrope: High Pitch and Low Pitch* (2021) incorporate different forms of circuitry and computer motherboards, seeming to reference our relationship with the built environment, evoking a fragmented urban landscape, the intricate structures of buildings and unknown aerial topographies. Similarly, the monumental tableau *Veiled Whispers* (2021) features elaborate braiding of wires and carved forms, recalling network systems and the interwoven nature of modern infrastructure, whether it be the electrical grid, telecommunications networks or the internet.

Notably, in his most recent works, Sime creates connections between our built and natural environments. In these works, the careful arrangement of wires and computer components mimics the delicate veins of leaves, ripples of water, the growth rings of trees, spirals of seashells or the fractal-like formations of organic material. In works like *Tightrope: It is Green 8* (2023), braided wire is layered and wrapped tightly around carved three-dimensional adornments of plants and flowers. In *Tightrope: We are all Green: Swollen Waves* (2020), the surface is divided and striated, with the top half in woven undulating wire and the bottom half in a multitude of green vine-like patterns, as if to map an undersea world of plant life.

The use of organic references here evokes a sense of interconnectedness, revealing the ways that mass-produced objects shape both natural and human-made realms. Just as elements in nature go through cycles of growth, decay and regeneration, the electronic components in Sime's art undergo a transformation from their original purpose to become part of a new artistic creation, echoing the natural cycles of birth, life, death and renewal. As he explains: 'Technology, no matter which way you look at it, is a product of nature because all the material that I use comes from the natural world. The material that I'm using is a product of nature, but the outcome of what is created from it is interfering with our natural behaviour or instinct and how and who we are as people.'[10]

Sime's art speaks to the interplay between the natural and the artificial, the organic and the technological. It prompts us to reflect on our relationship with the natural world, our reliance on technology, and the potential conflict and harmony that can exist between the two. This delicate balance between technological progress and environmental reckoning points to the labyrinthine world of globalised production, the environmental impact of raw material extraction and its inevitable evolution into e-waste.

Like Le Guin's carrier bag of fiction, the materials Sime transforms become vessels for complex stories that describe the world we live in from a multitude of perspectives. The discarded electronic components and wires that were once integral parts of technological systems, connecting devices, transmitting information and enabling communication, are transformed to reveal the inner workings of the objects that shape our global infrastructures, both literally and metaphorically. These new forms serve as a reminder that, beneath the surface of our visible world, there exists a complex network — an operating system that shapes our way of connecting to one another.

Just as Le Guin invites us to reconsider the narratives we prioritise, Sime compels us to re-evaluate our relationship with the objects that seem essential in our daily lives. He invites us to learn from their inner workings and the narratives they hold. In Sime's work, the carrier bag becomes a metaphorical bridge, connecting us to a network of ideas that challenge our prevailing notions about production, communication and technological advancement. Like a skilled alchemist, he uses his remarkable ability to transform the ordinary into the extraordinary, and in so doing invites us to re-engage with each other, build community and reconsider our mediated forms of communication in favour of human connection. In Sime's hands, repurposed materials preserve fragments of the collective human experience, revealing stories that lay dormant and inviting the viewer to contemplate the intricate threads that connect us all.

Tightrope: Echo!? (detail)
2021, reclaimed electrical wires and components on panel, 365.8 × 480.1 cm

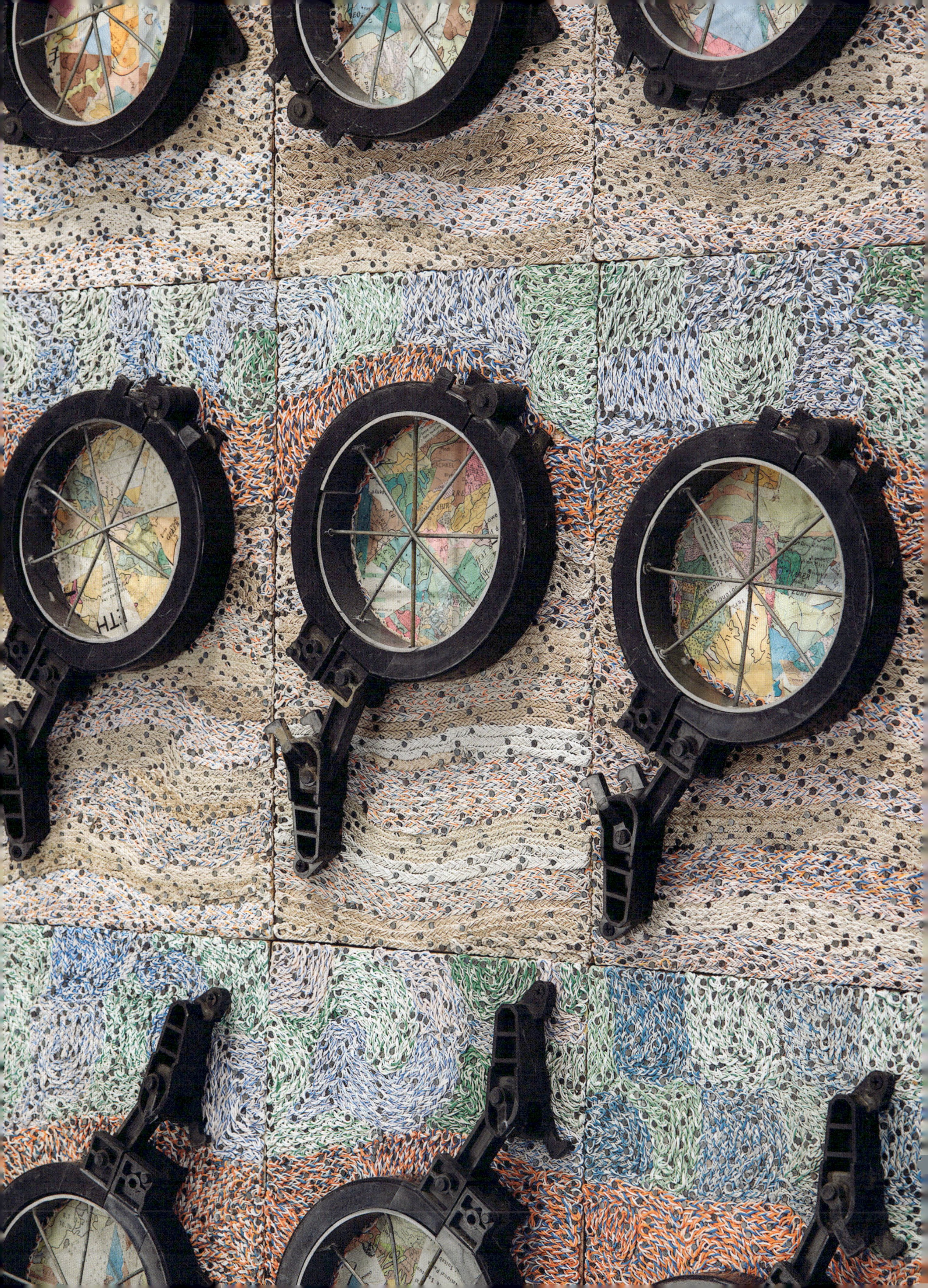

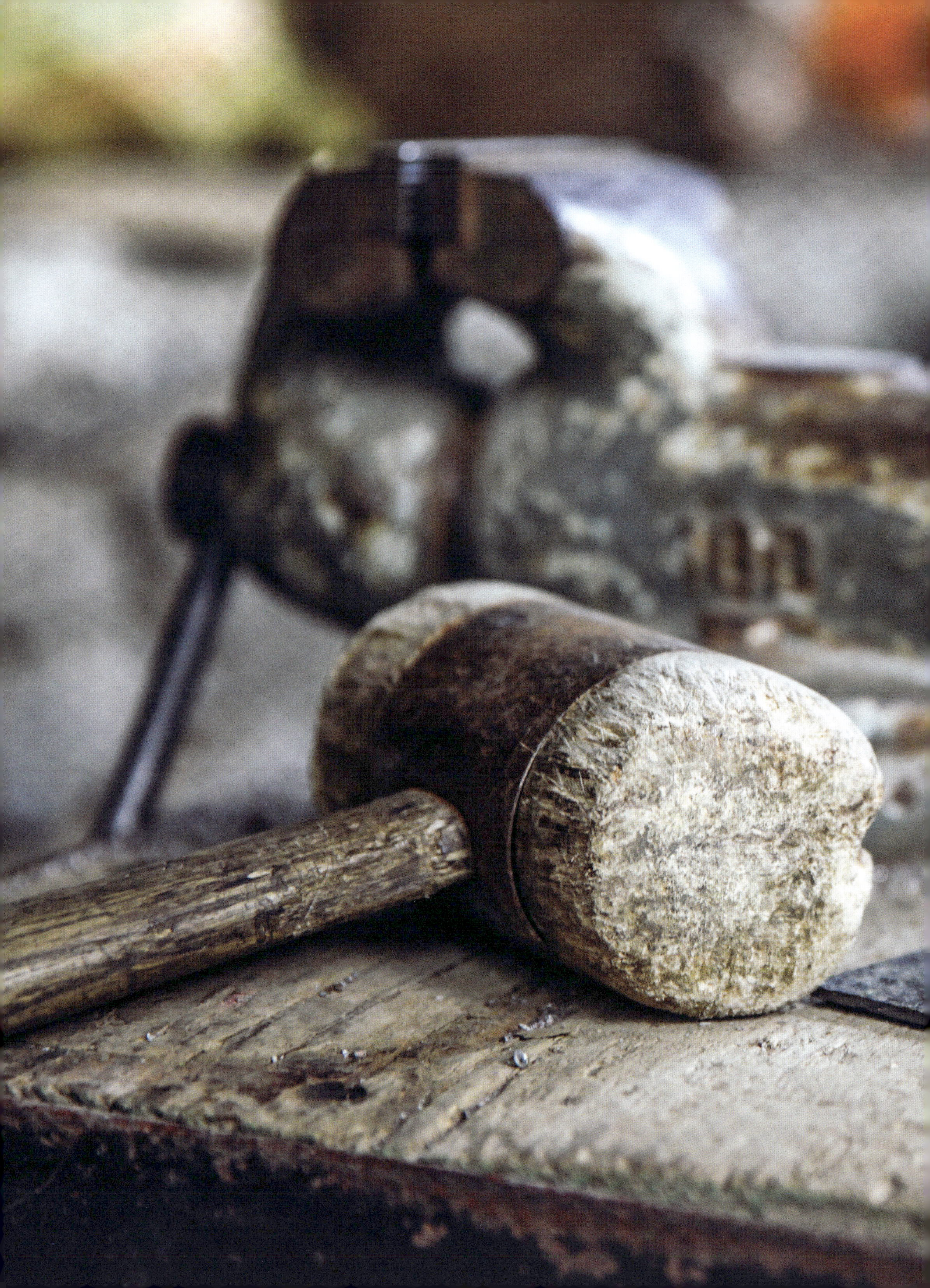

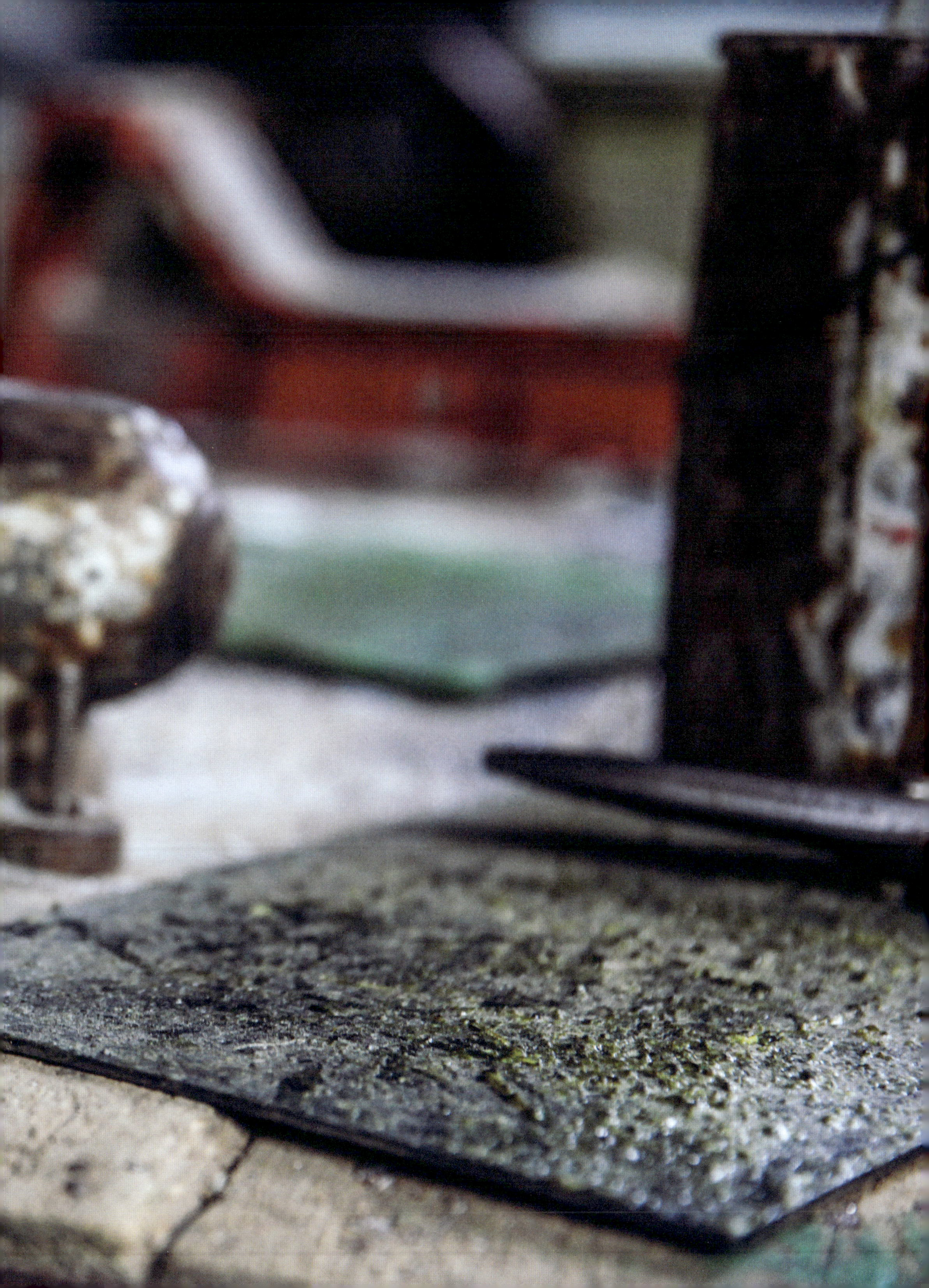

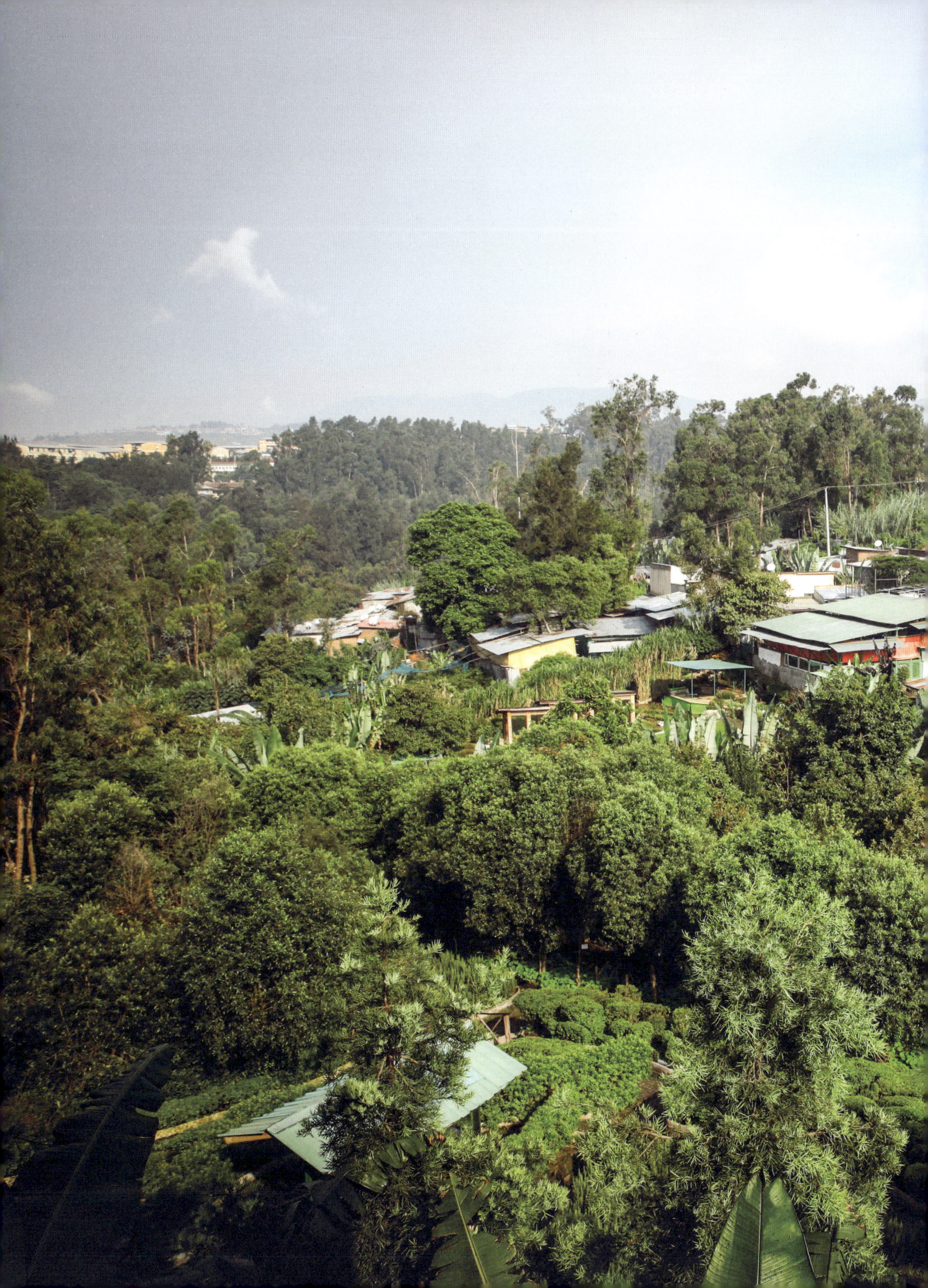

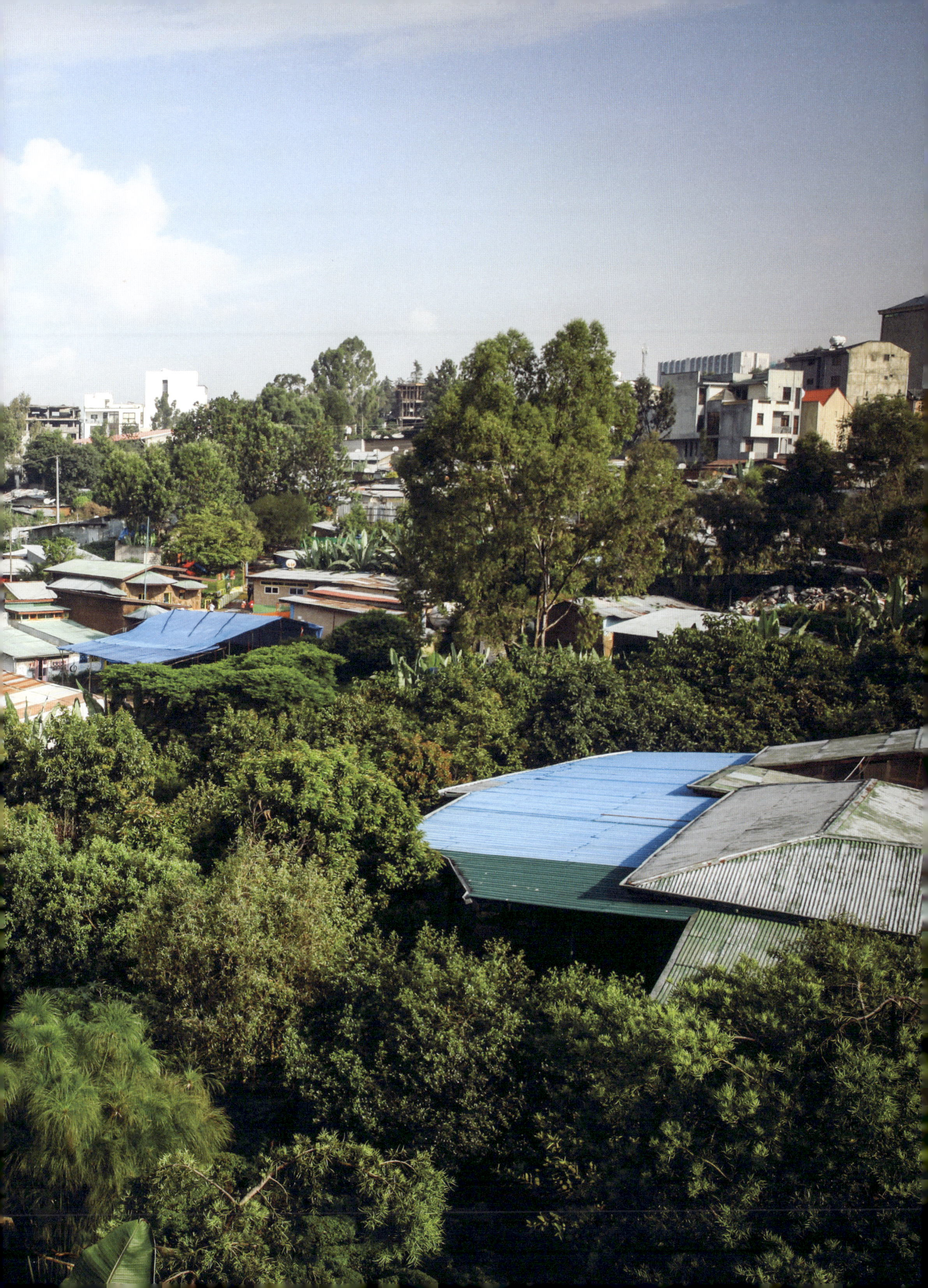

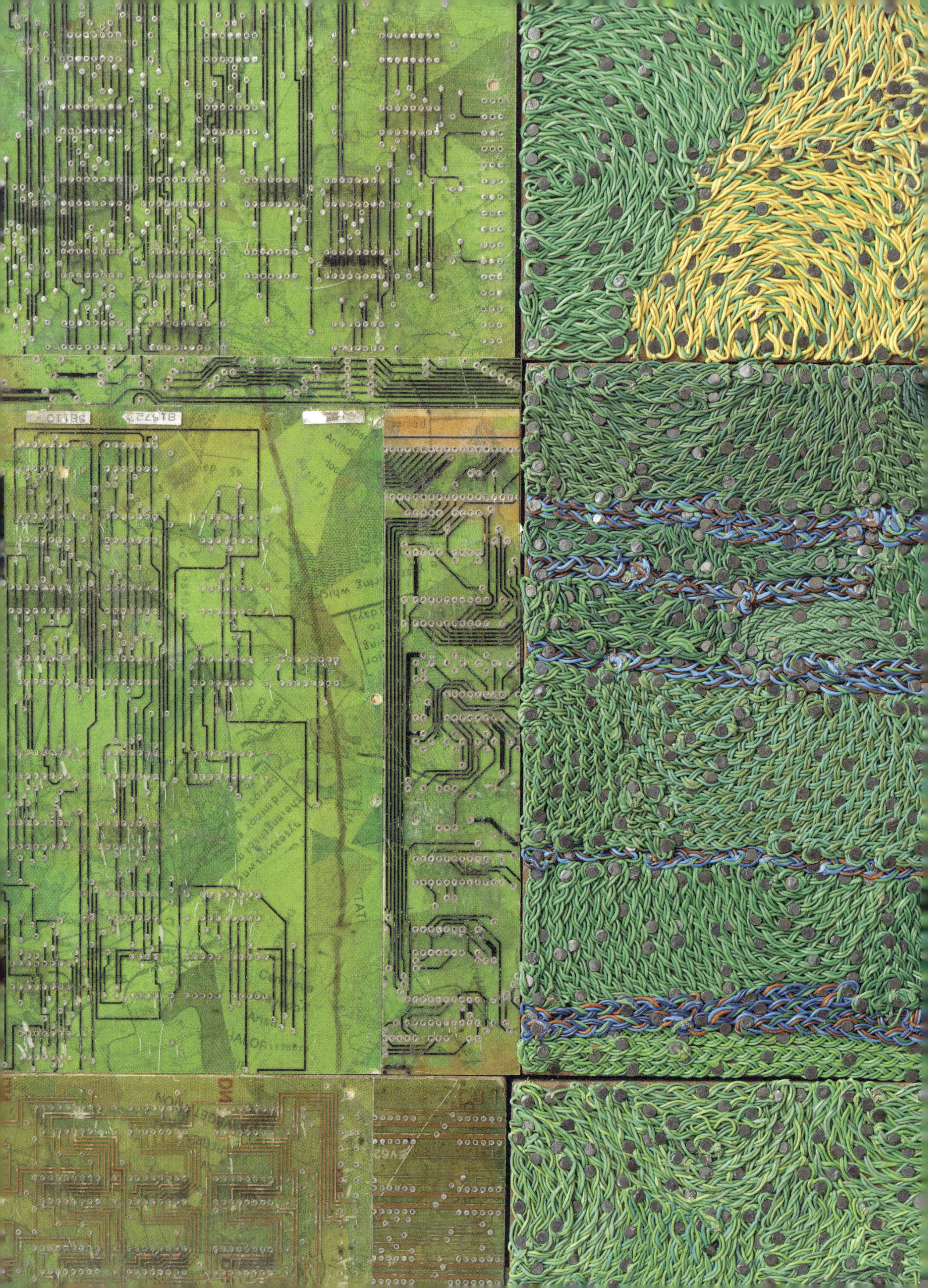

Nana Biamah-Ofosu

—

Zoma museum is an extension of the city... It is a love letter to a place—an unconditional act of devotion.

The collaborative practice of Elias Sime & Meskerem Assegued

BUILDING WITH LOVE

Resting above Addis Ababa in the valley of the Entoto Mountains, from which the sprawling urban landscape of the city can be observed, is Zoma Village Entoto—the latest collaboration between artist Elias Sime and curator and cultural anthropologist Meskerem Assegued.

Nearing completion, this will be the third iteration of Zoma in Addis Ababa.[1] Like its predecessors, located within the city and in the Dire Dawa region of Ethiopia, Zoma Village Entoto is a manifestation of a close and grounded connection to the site, from which buildings emerge not merely as a form of shelter but as an expression of love, craft and dedication to historic building cultures and techniques.[2]

To understand Zoma Museum as a project, it is important to ground the collaboration between Sime and Assegued. Sime is an Ethiopian artist whose practice narrates the human condition and our connection to the natural and technological world. His large-scale canvases, sculptural reliefs and (more recently) in situ installations braid, thread and assemble carefully selected materials into rich, layered, abstract compositions filled with rhythm, lyricism and narrative. Using electronic components—computer keyboards, circuit boards, wires and mobile phone parts—Sime creates compositional landscapes that suggest topography and landform. These large works require you to look closely and calmly, with intention, to register their depth. The reward for such focus and stillness is to understand through his practice the story of a global civilisation—Sime clearly emphasises that 'It's not about Ethiopia. It's not about Africa,'[3] a limitation often placed on African artists. His materials are sourced throughout Africa, and other parts of the world, including the Menyalesh Tera[4] section of the Merkato market in Addis Ababa, one of the continent's largest open-air markets. Sime's assemblages tell stories through visual means; however, they are also a commentary on our relationship to technology and the environment. In Sime's work, this is interrelated with his approach to time, an aspect of the human condition which can be narrated through our engagement with technology—'I am not one of those people who says technology is not good, but I am one of those who says, "Let's talk about it. Let's stop and think about it."'[5]

Tightrope: Behind the Processor No.1 (detail)
2023, reclaimed electrical wires and components on panel, 276 × 160 × 2 cm

In thinking about technology, Sime is exploring time, evolution, information, communication and, by essence, the condition of human history. His work reflects on the tenuous nature of our seemingly and increasingly interconnected world. It explores the duality and often binary nature of such interconnectedness, suggesting the conflict between tradition and modernity, physical and virtual connection and the natural and the man-made.

Assegued translates Sime. Their relationship is one of kinship — based on a shared language both literally and metaphorically. Sime typically communicates in Amharic, which Assegued translates into English. Inherent in this act of translation is trust; it is an act of negotiation — finding rhythm in the natural pauses of one's speech, catching the intonations that express more than mere sound. The act of translation goes beyond linguistics, semantics and syntax — it is inflected circumstance, context and condition. Speaking metaphorically, Assegued's translation of Sime is found in how she positions his practice through writing and curation. Assegued, who was born and raised in Addis Ababa, studied psychology before switching disciplines to cultural anthropology, which, for her, encapsulated a deeper understanding of human history, conditioning and narrative.[6] It is this cultural understanding that she brings to her interpretation of Sime's work.

She categorises his artistic evolution into two distinct periods: 1990 to 2000 and from 2001 to the present. Sime's work between 1990 and 2000 was, as Assegued describes, an extension of his art school training under the Stalinist Derg era in Ethiopia's political history. These works, often portrait-based, carried certain communist ideals concerned with melancholic depictions of the working class. The material language of his earlier works — reassembled and stitched fabric, threads, buttons, plastic, animal skins and horns — speaks to the 'idea of continually mending life, an important philosophical aspect of humanity.'[7] Assegued describes the week-long live exhibition, *Addis Abeba Zare* as a transformative moment in Sime's work.[8] Through this performance piece, his work extended beyond the figurative and towards art as a living artefact, and by extension a building culture. Assegued wrote about this work as a turning point in Sime's artistic career, when he was 'breaking the labels and boundaries imposed on him' and becoming neither a collage artist nor a sculptor, but an artist.[9] The beginnings of Zoma and the depth of the collaboration between Assegued and Sime is articulated in this pivotal work, connecting an art practice with the larger conditions of human existence, particularly how we build.

Mekanisa, a typical urban neighbourhood of Addis Ababa, is the place where Zoma Museum begins. Inside the compound, past its walled and gated entrance, you are greeted by an eco-climate and atmosphere distinct from the urban life outside. Within the tight compound, consisting of a mat of hand-carved paving slabs decorated with images of wildlife such as lizards and turtles and a rich garden filled with indigenous plants bursting with colour, sit four individual buildings — a small, double-storey gatehouse, two simple rectilinear structures carved from stone and a monumental circular building made from sculpted mud.

Initially conceived as a home for Sime himself, these buildings have become a gallery and artist residence. Sime and Assegued first acquired the house (at the time, an old, languishing structure) in 2002, when the concept of Zoma as a centre for contemporary art was first formed. Strict government regulations meant that the existing massing could not be altered. Sime credits these restrictions for the nature of the place they created. Described as a 'Gesamtkunstwerk'[10] — a total work of art — this is a project that engages with material and ecology, as well as construction as a codified practice, dealing with local building regulations, techniques and craft.

Entering the compound, you encounter the monolithic yet human-scale elevation of the paired rectilinear structures. The monolithic appearance is due to the fact that they are constructed from

 Kitchen and bedroom, 'little Zoma'

Button mosaic, bathroom ceiling, 'little Zoma'

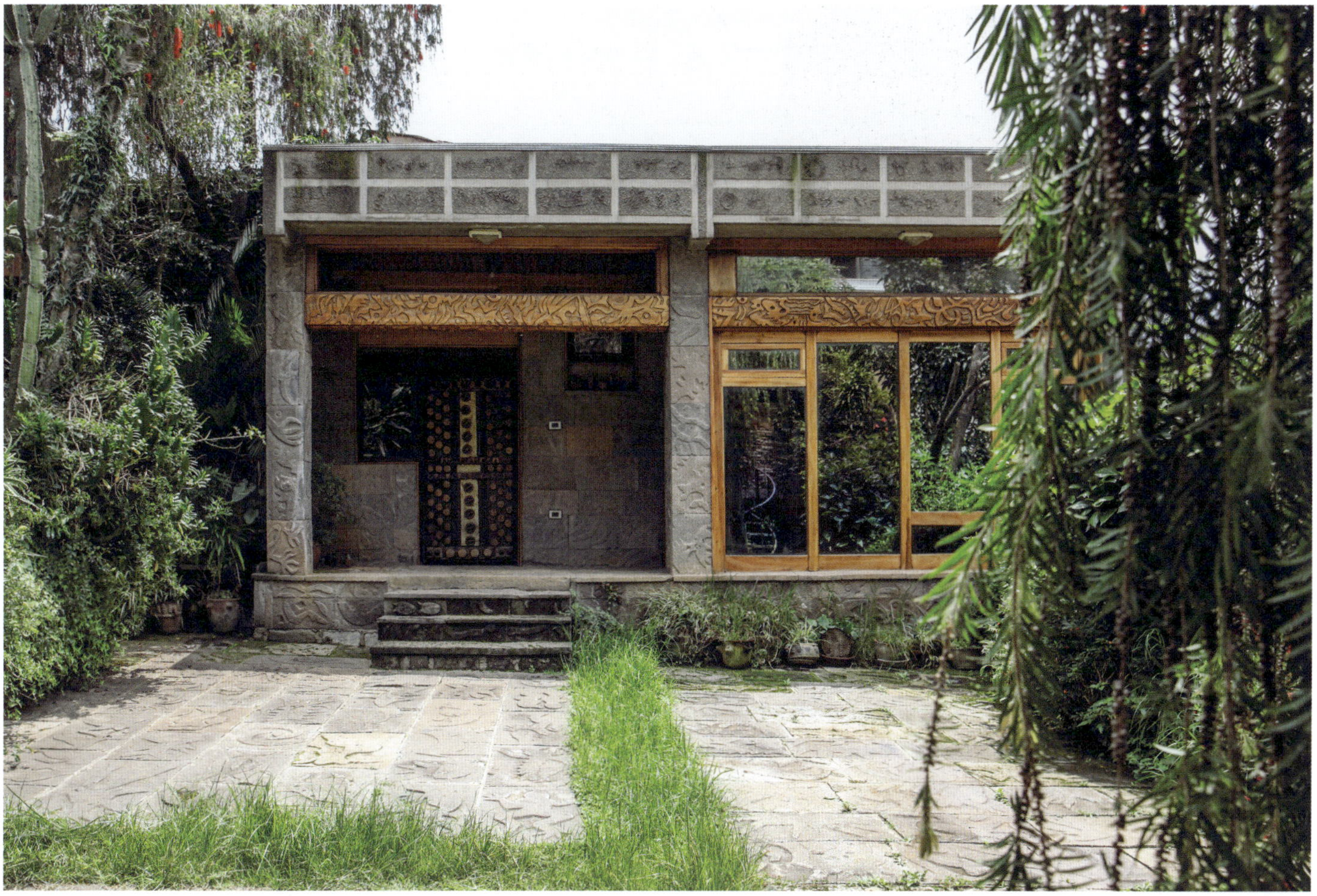

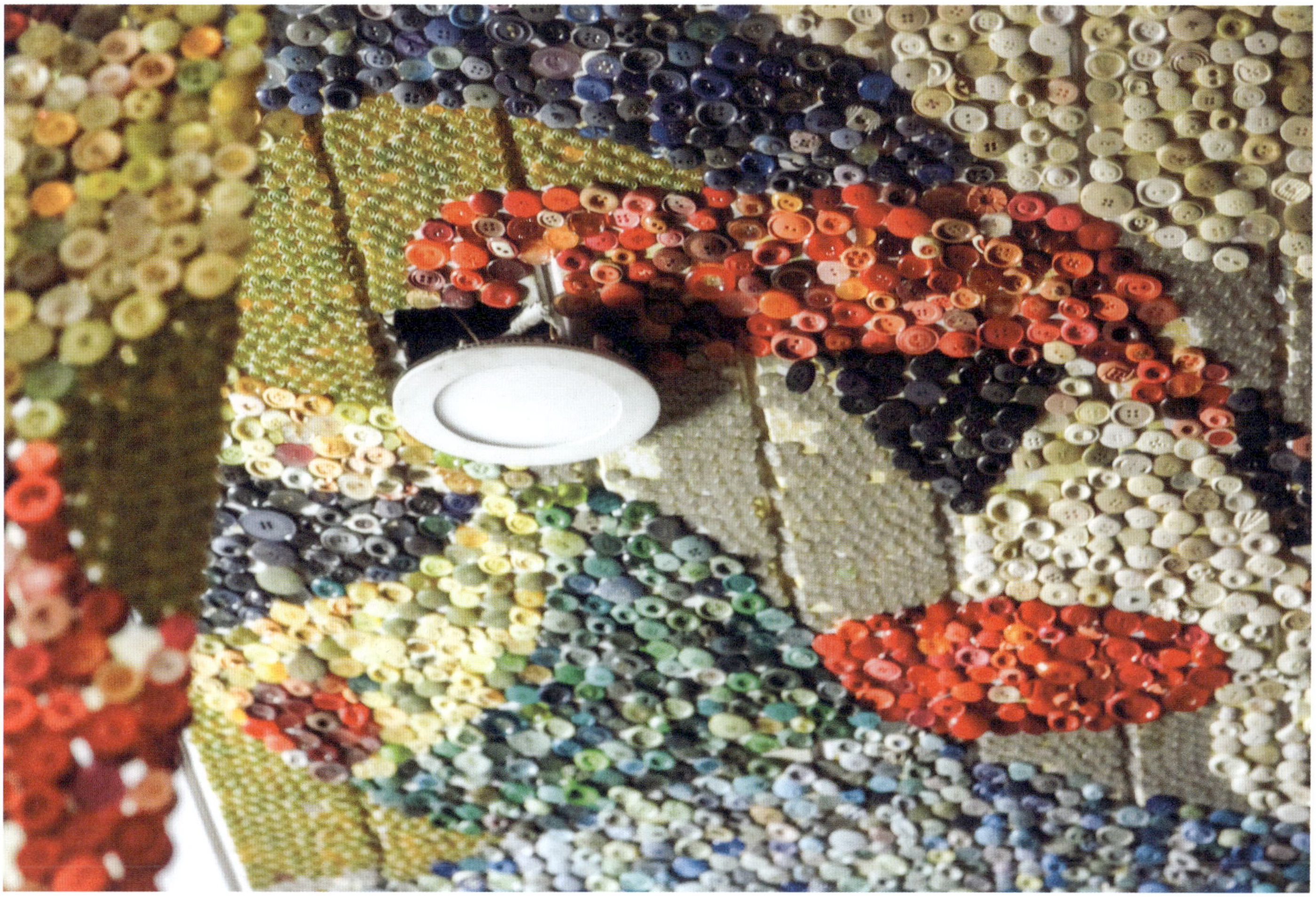

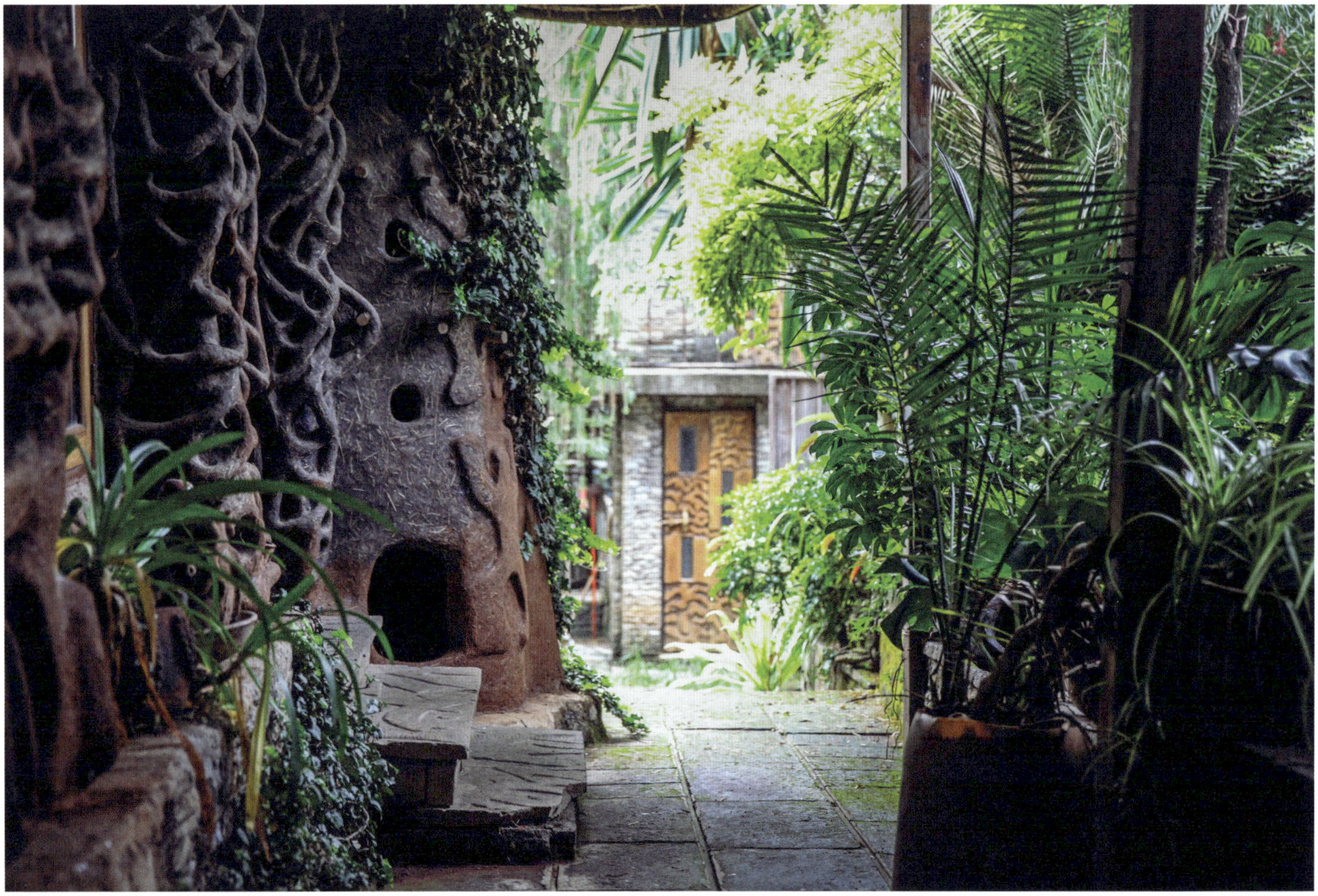

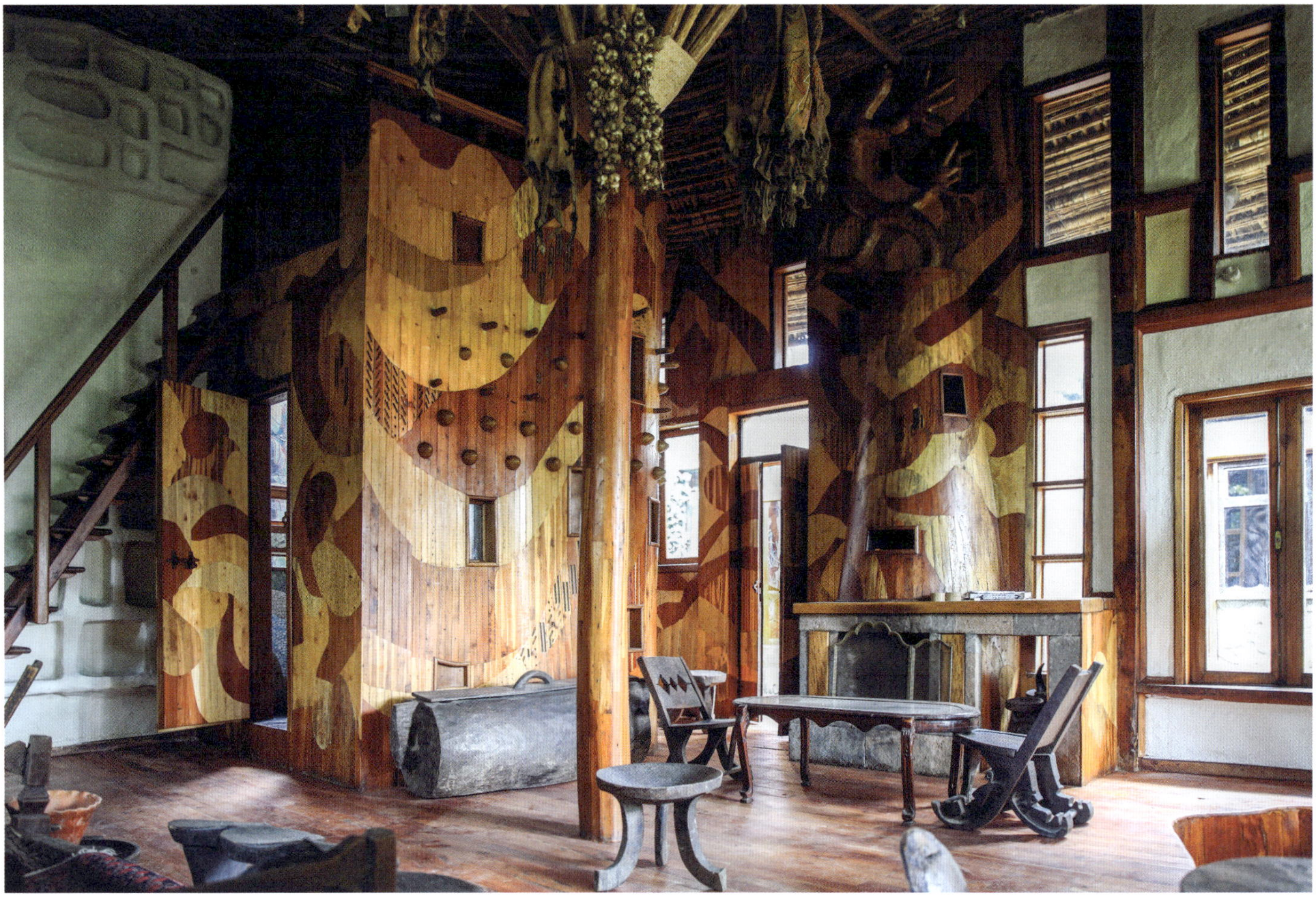

large stone blocks cut on all sides and laid with precision. This impression is further emphasised by the choice and treatment of the stone — like the ground, it is also hand-carved with stories from ancient folklore describing sea creatures, microscopic beings and land animals. This offers a sense of continuity, as though the buildings themselves are rising from the ground up. This feeling of solidity and connection to the ground is amplified by the buildings' raised plinth, which lifts them two steps from the ground, providing a demarcation between the public and private realm. Learning from traditional Ethiopian construction, this monumental use of stone can be found in everyday buildings such as the simple two-storey farmhouses in the Amhara region, themselves inspired by the building culture of pre-Aksumite civilisation in Ethiopia.[11]

This monumentality of the stone is gently tuned using timber joinery; hand-carved timber panels form entablatures which frame generous openings. The use of timber and stone continues within the interior; however, a plastered wall finish creates a more domestic character. The simple, restrained interior of the main room gives way to an almost cosmic experience in the bathroom — a bright mosaic made from buttons found in the markets of Addis Ababa covers the ceiling; looking up feels like looking into an ancient cosmos. The twin rectilinear buildings were initially designed as gallery spaces — their simplicity allowed for various forms and media of works to be shown here: video screenings, Sime's large, embroidered canvases and works by celebrated artists like David Hammons, as well as emerging artists such as Ernesto Novelo.[12] Yet the scale and proportion of these rooms also allows them to be used as domestic spaces, providing accommodation for visiting artists. This ease of transformation reinforces a key principle in Sime and Assegued's practice — rather than setting out to create so-called masterpieces, their work presents art 'not just as something that is collected and kept by the elite, but also owned and touched and engaged in by every stratum of the community.'[13] Here, making a good room is an art form in its own right.

Like a traditional Ethiopian homestead, the central gathering space of the compound is a circular standalone building. Constructed in earth, its elaborate, handwoven mud walls grow out of the ground like the intertwined branches of an ancient tree. The exterior walls, which are about 25 centimetres thick, reinterpret a traditional wattle and daub construction method known as chikka. This technique consists of a timber frame interlocked with strings, upon which a mix of fermented mud and straw is fixed. While the mix is wet, it is soft and malleable, allowing it to be engraved, carved and crafted with chameleons, lizards, spiders and their webs, roots of plants and mortar and pestle. The earth and straw walls are left to dry, giving it its rich dark brown tone. Within a month, the mud hardens, becoming as dense as stone. Finally, a mixture of flour, lime and cactus juice is applied, making the wall construction waterproof.[14] These walls sit on a plinth made from the existing stem walls of the original buildings on site; using them to support the new structures, it could be argued that this was a restoration project rather than a new construction, thus allowing mud to be used as the main building material.

A veranda provides a transitional space between inside and outside as well as an external seating space under the overhang of the voluptuous straw roof structure. At night, the compound can be transformed by candlelight emanating from the small niches in the walls, casting warm glows and flickering shadows created by the mythical forms embedded in the mud. In the interior, the conical roof is supported by a single column made from a eucalyptus trunk, its splayed branches fanning out to become supporting underside beams for the ceiling. The mud walls are washed in white render in contrast to the rich, two-toned juniper wood panelling decorated with organic and mythical shapes. Openings are strategically placed along

Garden and building, 'little Zoma'

Interior, 'little Zoma'

the circumference of the space, framing particular views back into the compound. A small sleeping area in the eaves of the roof, accessed via a timber ladder, doubles up as a stage, a place from which recitals, poems and performances can be seen from a vantage point by those gathered below in the main space. Like the tukuls that are common to the region's architectural heritage, this building is a convivial space, designed for gathering, sharing stories and the act of dreaming — it is a space defined by a 'swirl of ancient techniques and ecstatic imagination.'[15]

The wisdom of old seen in this first iteration of Zoma Museum, often referred to locally as 'little Zoma', is evident in the next incarnation of Zoma. Opened in 2019, the complex includes a gallery, school, library, restaurant, an amphitheatre and botanical and herbal gardens — all of which are accessible to the public. If 'little Zoma' is a homestead, then Zoma Museum is the village where the singular is intrinsically linked to the whole.

The project began in 2013 when Sime and Assegued started assembling land close to the Akaki River, financed through personal funding from both Assegued and Sime and the sales of Sime's work. It is an exercise in building from the ground up — it starts with the earth, contemplating the terrain of the landscape. The two-acre plot was considerably polluted due to its downstream location, which meant it received contaminated water from the upper part of the neighbourhood. Consequently, a series of channels carved into the network of exterior spaces create a significant wastewater management system which collects, cleans and reuses this water. The remediation of the land was the next stage of the construction process — decades of poor farming practices had left the ground topsoil in poor condition and contaminated with waste. The waste removed from site was burned and its ashes turned into fertiliser for the new growth to come. With the land revived, the terracing of the landscape, laid with dry stone walls and cobblestone walkways, could begin. The process begins with intuition, by walking the land. For Assegued, this embodied and experiential way of designing is important — 'by walking, your body will tell you whether this is a comfortable slope.'[16] Finally, a series of rooms create a network of sheltered spaces intertwined with the landscape.

For Sime and Assegued, place and programme are linked. Zoma Museum is a place of indigenous knowledge — learning from the land, culture and building heritage of a place. The project recalls, recollects and reinterprets tradition, history and memory, creating a bridge between indigenous systems and contemporary art and architecture. The site is roughly divided into two. Perched on the hill and facing the urban fabric of Mekanisa is Zoma School, while the gallery and public spaces are located downhill, connected by meandering paths and walkways lined with edible gardens. The school, which offers classes from nursery to grade six, is an intrinsic part of the complex. It follows a historic form of education known as 'Ye kes timirt bet' which, long before standardised western learning, provided literacy education to young children in this region. For Assegued, who oversees the running of the school, it was important that this place offered an educational space that could foreground alternative forms of learning — where children are exposed to nature, where general sciences are taught through planting or looking after the cows who are also residents here, where art and physical exercise are intertwined with play and gardening, and where Amharic (a semitic language descended from Ge'ez) is taught with the same significance as the English language.

Further down the sloping terrain, a series of buildings emerge on a clearing. The main gallery space is flanked by a series of smaller structures that accommodate exhibition spaces, a library and a café. The gallery space is designed to be flexible and allow a wide range of media to be shown here. The museum does not hold a permanent collection but rather it is a place of continuous experimentation, giving space to celebrated international artists as well as those emerging.

 School buildings, Zoma Museum

Student feeding the goats, Zoma Museum

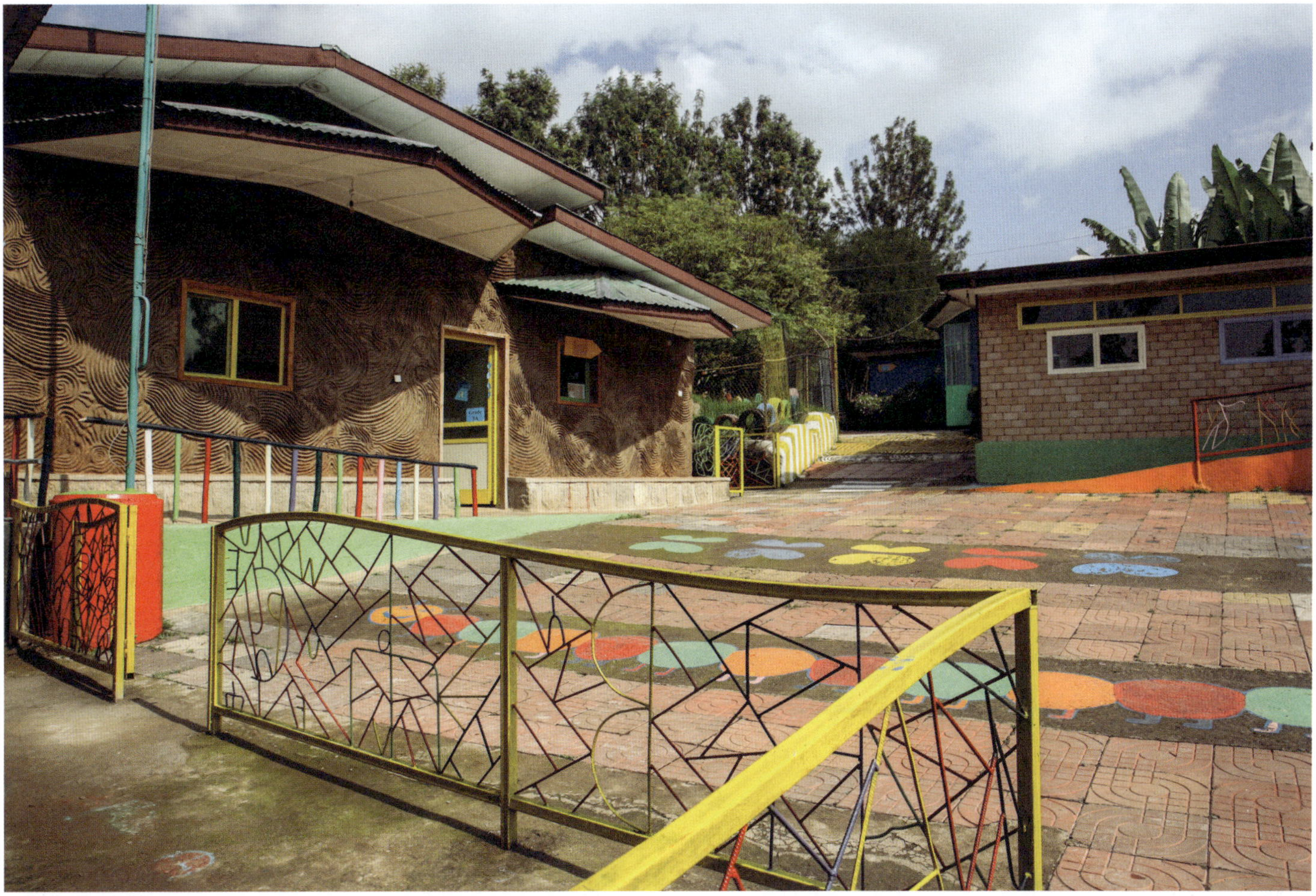

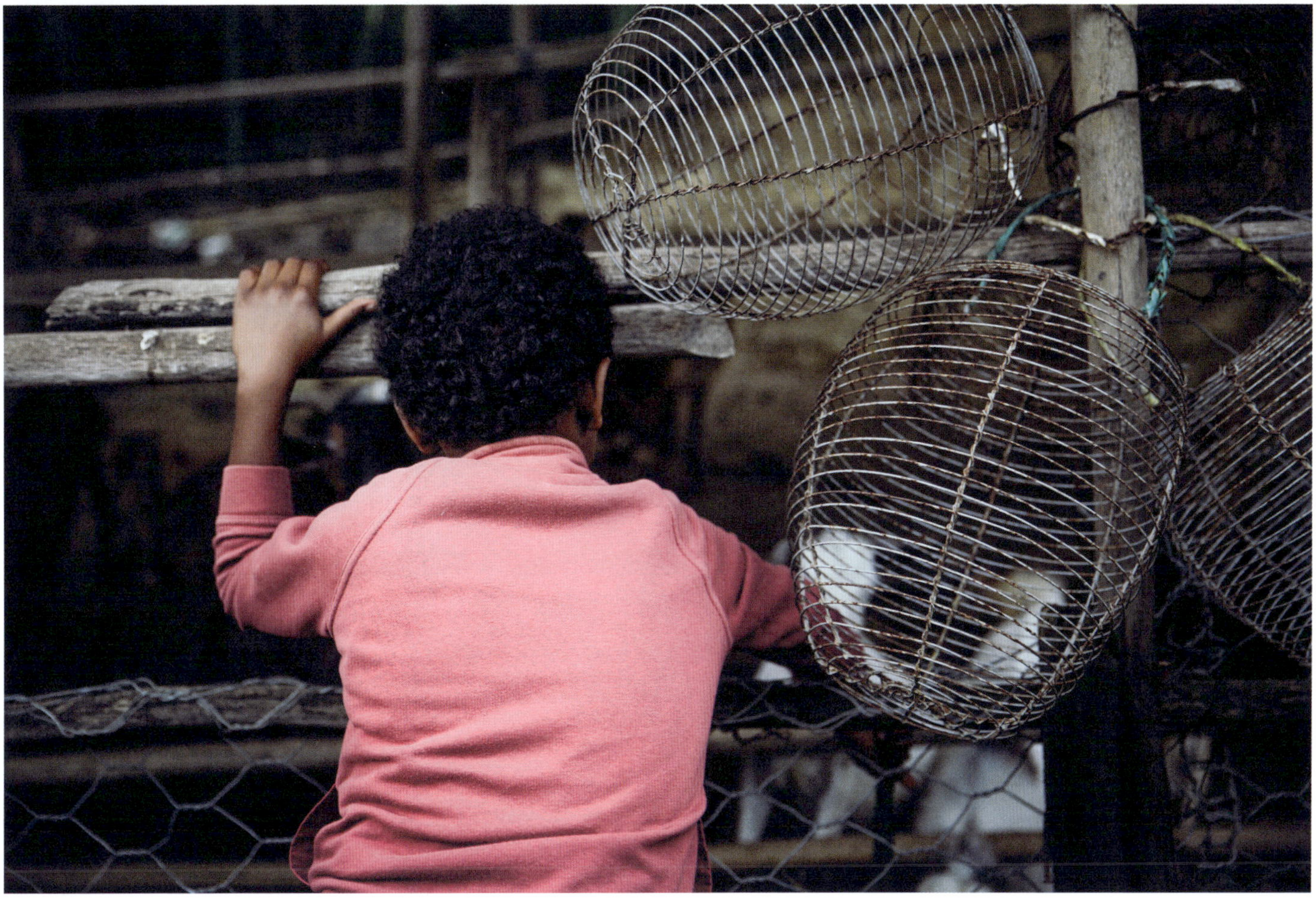

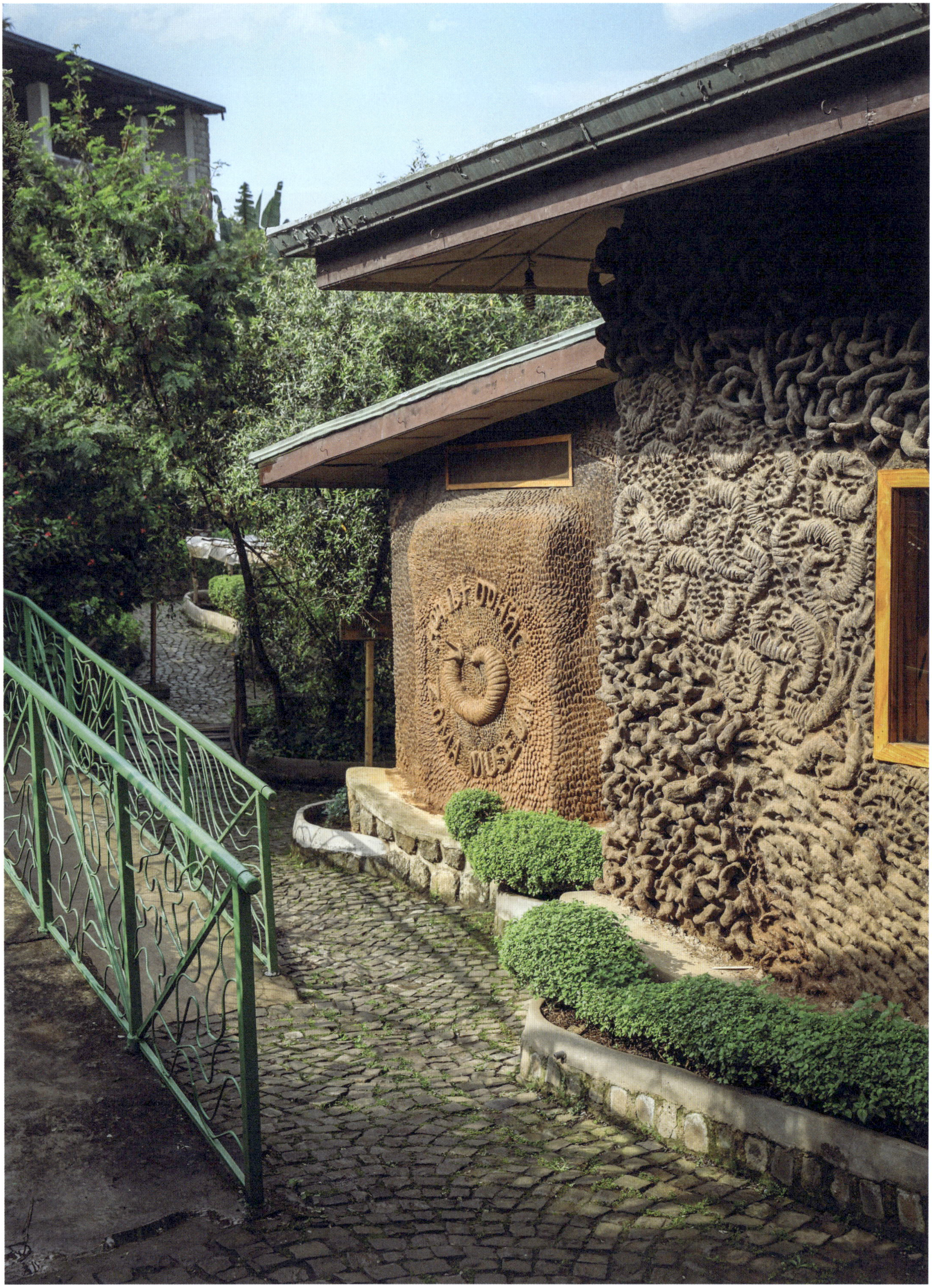

Like 'little Zoma', Zoma Museum emphasises the merits of learning from traditional methods of construction and reinterpreting for contemporary architectural practice. The traditional wattle and daub construction is reprised here and the buildings bear imprints of their maker's hands. The mud becomes a canvas for vivid imaginations and the retelling of significant events in Ethiopian culture — one wall incorporates Ge'ez, one of the oldest written languages in the world. Its inclusion here is a symbol of precolonial African civilisations — a reminder that the history of a place should be told by its own people. The engraved mud also explores the relationship between human civilisation and the natural world with depictions, such as the four stages of the life cycle of the butterfly, like the cave art of earlier civilisations. Internally, the warmth of the juniper timber used for doors, furniture, wall finishes and decoration provides a warm atmosphere. Every building is a chapter of a larger story and, like every good story, it is held together by an overarching structure. Here, the ground is the story's narrative — physically and metaphorically, it is the structure that holds this village of buildings together.

Leaving Addis Ababa for the Entoto Mountains, one encounters Assegued and Sime's latest project — a vast, sprawling arts centre nestled in the cool, quiet valley perched above the city. In this triptych of projects — which operate from the scale of the homestead up to that of the village — Zoma Village Entoto represents the scale of the settlement. It is a vision for a new kind of urbanism, contextualised by its natural surroundings. Here the binary conditions of urban and rural, man-made and natural, modern and traditional dissolve and make space for a contemporary form of placemaking. The use of concrete, to achieve the required spans and structural integrity, is a necessary departure from the earth construction used in previous iterations of Zoma. However, like the other incarnations of Zoma, the material is used knowingly, with grace and in deference to the landscape. A series of walkways meander through the steep slope of the site. Retaining dry stone walls are decorated with intricate mosaics created and constructed by Sime and his team of construction workers. Planters filled with indigenous flowers line the walkways while terrazzo mosaics depicting native animals and birds are embedded into the ground. A series of buildings are strategically placed to take advantage of the vast, picturesque views offered by this landscape. Approaching the site from the top of the slope, the first building is an external room. Under a waffle slab roof, ingeniously created using the ubiquitous plastic water containers as formwork and supported by a forest of columns, sits an arboretum of sorts. Like a clearing in a forest, it provides space and shelter for human inhabitation within the landscape. From this vantage point, looking up towards the hills, one registers other buildings which will host galleries, workshops and domestic spaces for visiting artists, curators and scholars. The form of the main building, an open-plan space sheltered by a roof supported by a strategically defined grid of columns, follows that of the existing landscape, opening towards expansive views and sometimes closing to create intimate corners and nooks which frame particular moments within the landscape. Here, under the dark, grey and thunderous skies of Addis Ababa in June, one is witnessing, as has been said about Sime and Assegued's practice, 'a philosopher's invocation'[17] where dreams are carved from the ground and the imagination expanded through the recollection and translation of indigenous knowledge systems.

To build in a contemporary manner is a holistic and gradual process. It is the practice of looking at tradition and culture with intent. It is an act of translation, where the artist, builder or maker becomes a mediator between historical knowledge and modern practice. Similar to his artworks, Sime and Assegued's building practice is an act of transformation. Like the thousands of electronic components Sime assembles on wooden blocks, their design and construction work is a slow and grounded process. It is about working with what is found, looking with intent to find the essence of a material, a site or a space, and then, with a combination of modesty and grandeur,[18] giving them a contemporary life. For Assegued and Sime, it is a practice of building with love — Zoma Museum is a place created, built and finished with love.[19] It is simultaneously about the past and the present, about ancient rituals and traditions and modernity. Zoma Museum is an extension of the city, rooted specifically in its history, culture and context. It is a love letter to a place — an unconditional act of devotion.[20]

Zoma Village Entoto, Entoto Mountains

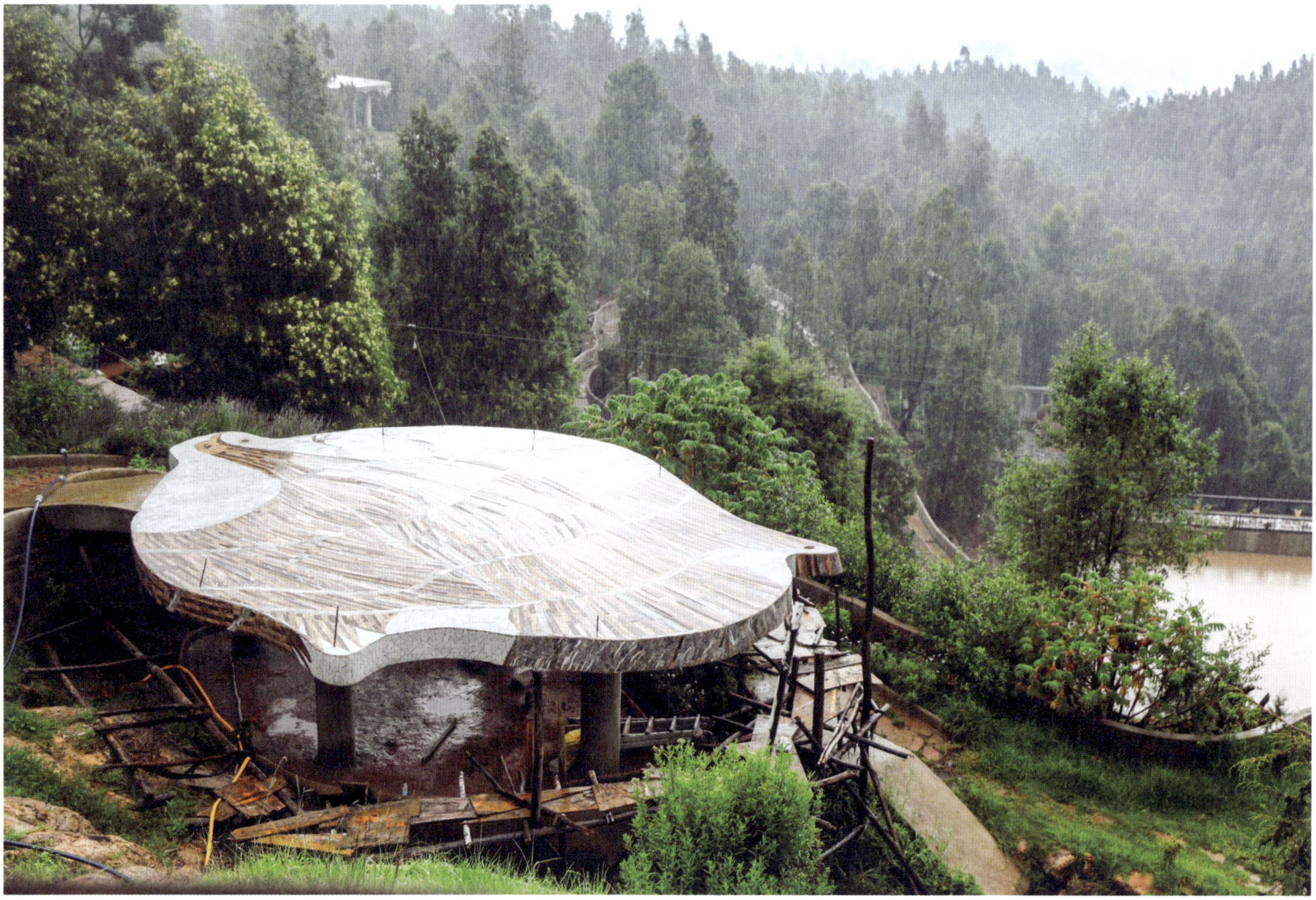

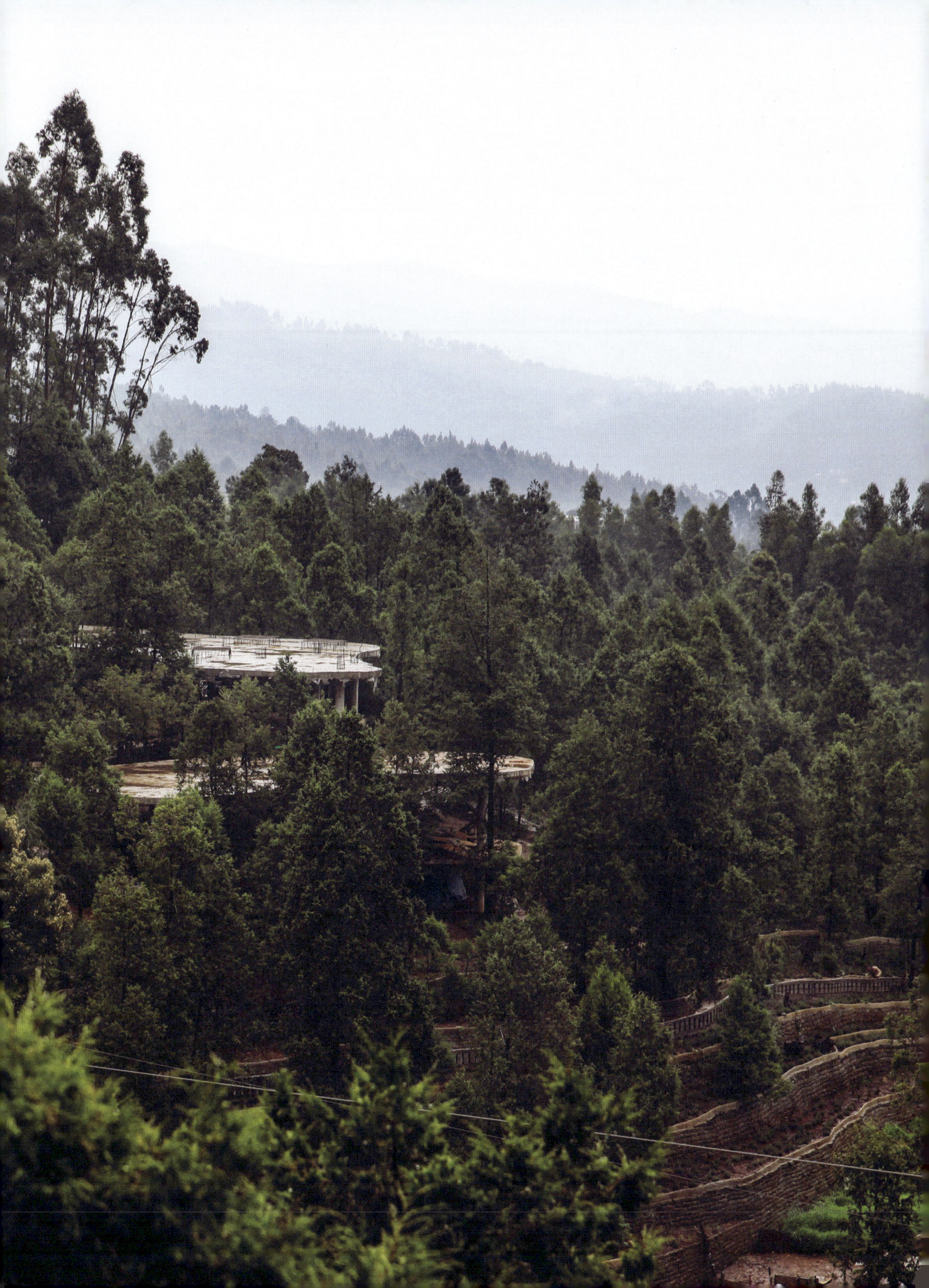

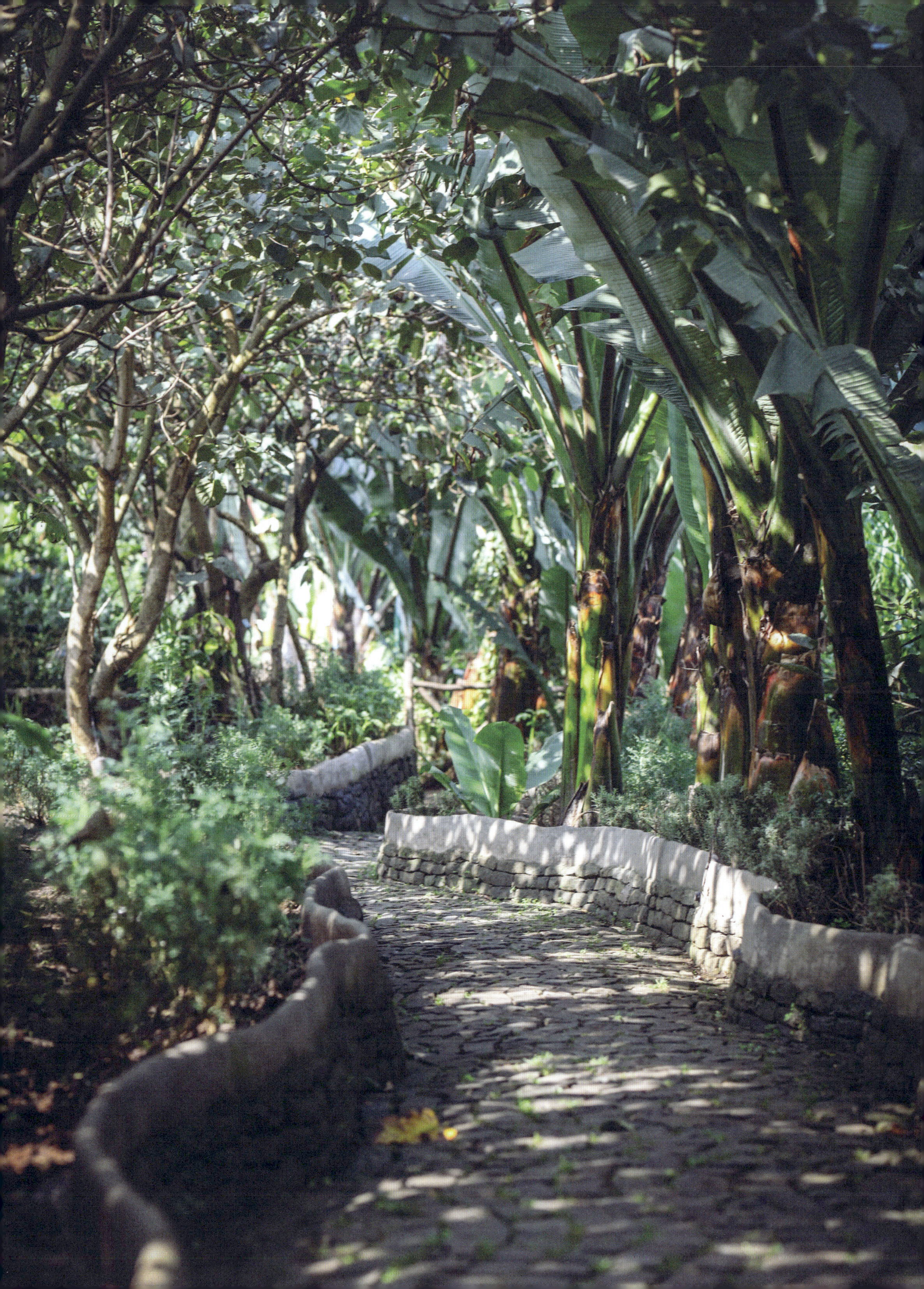

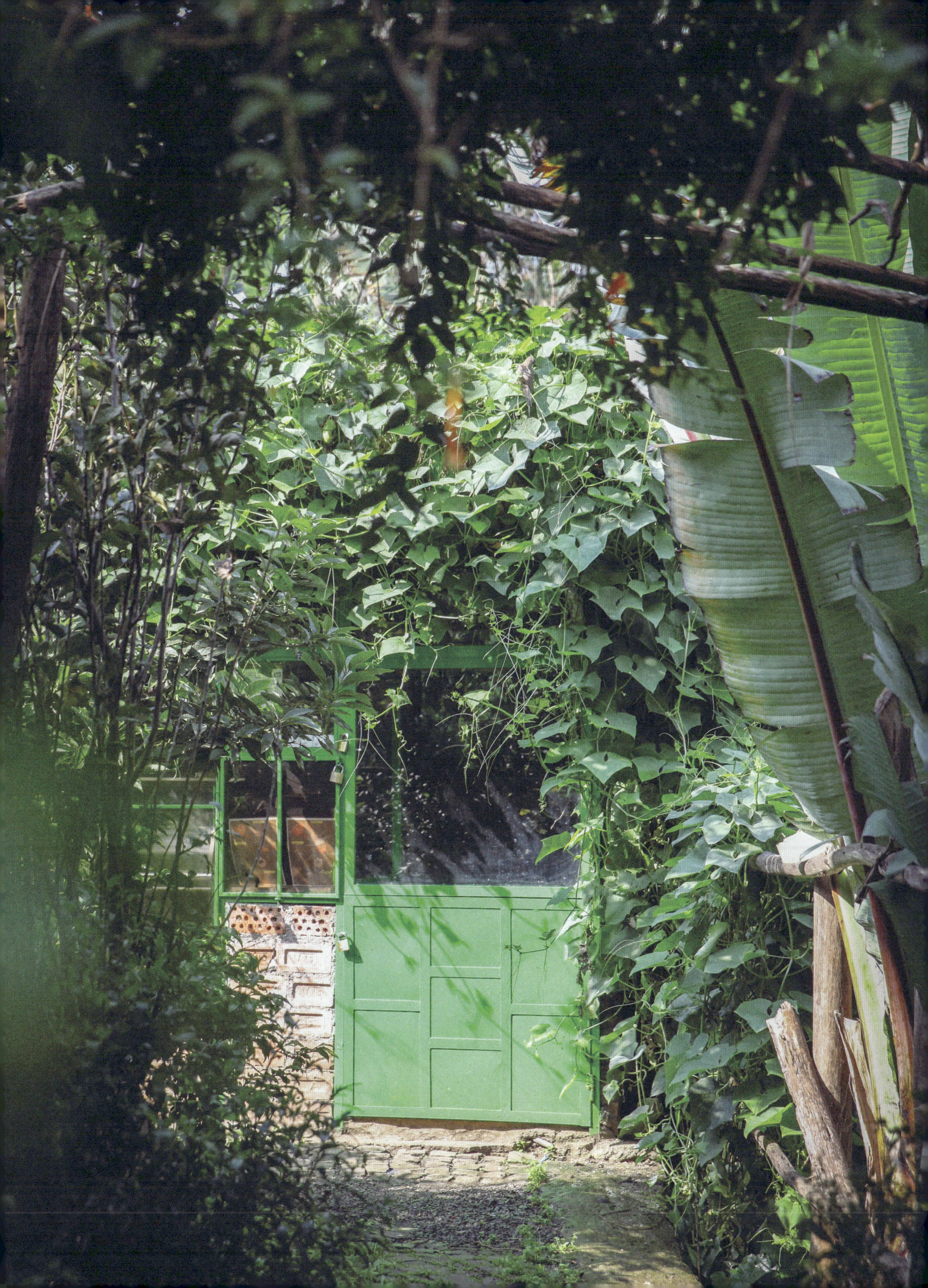

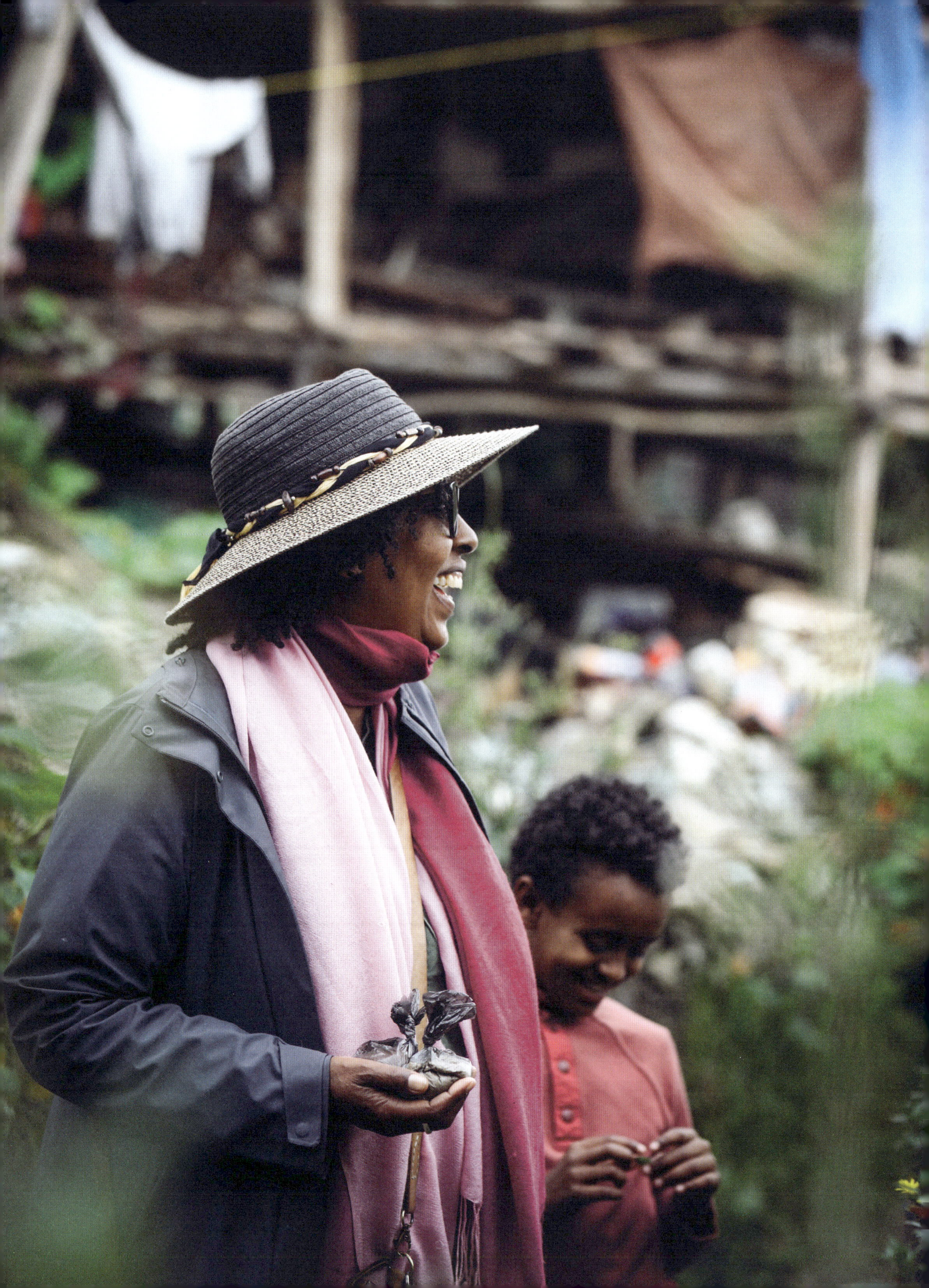

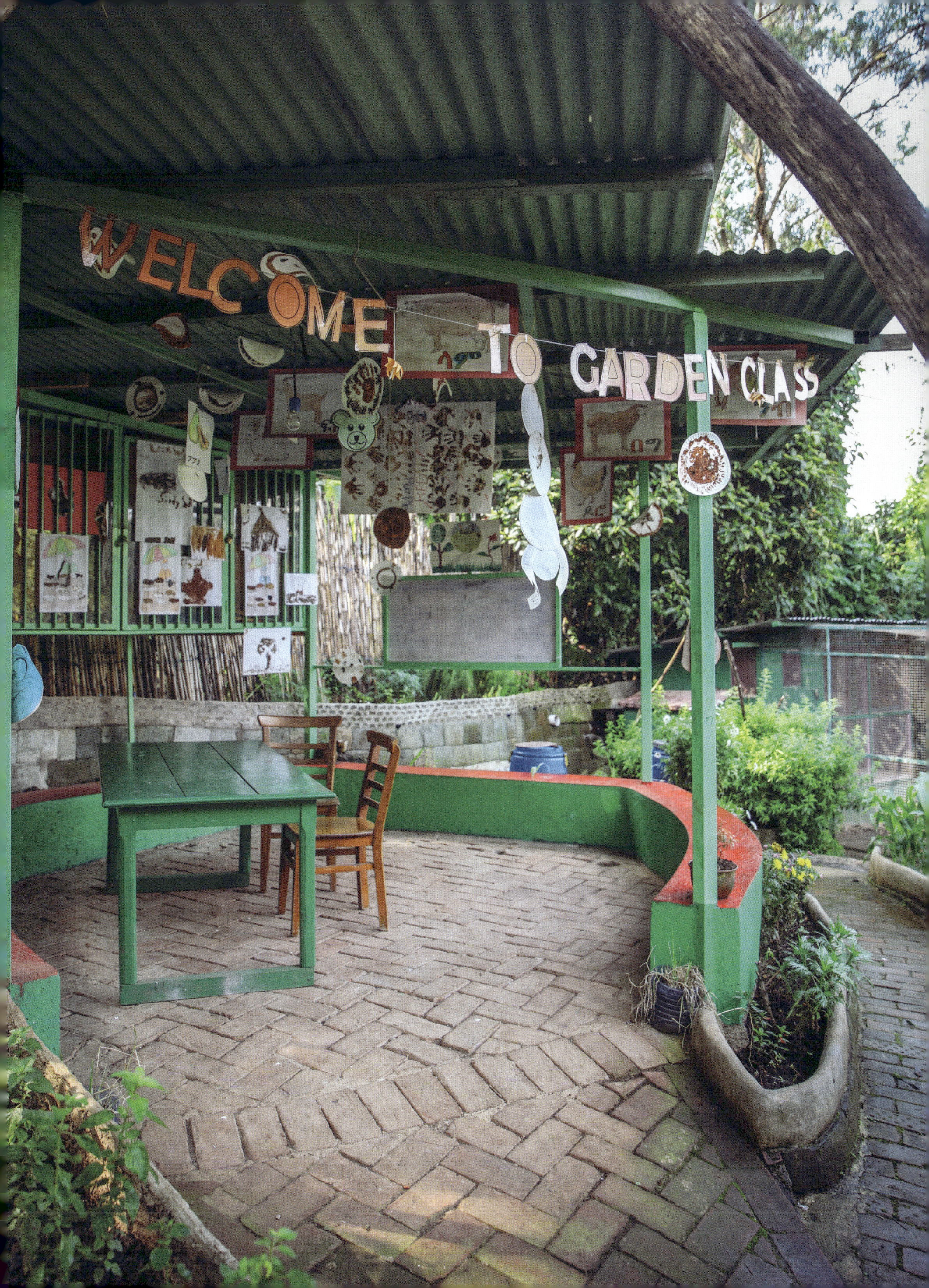
WELCOME TO GARDEN CLASS

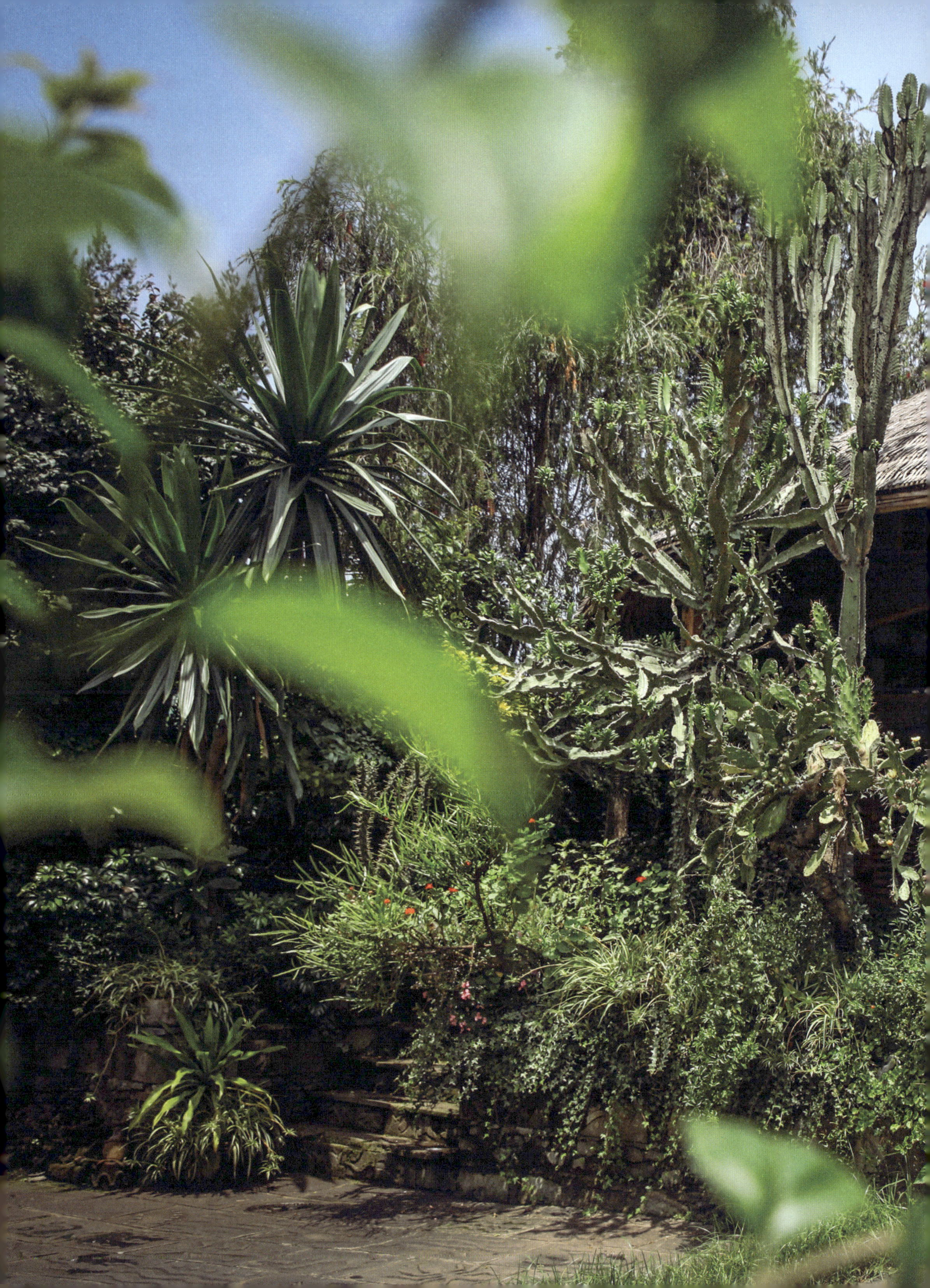

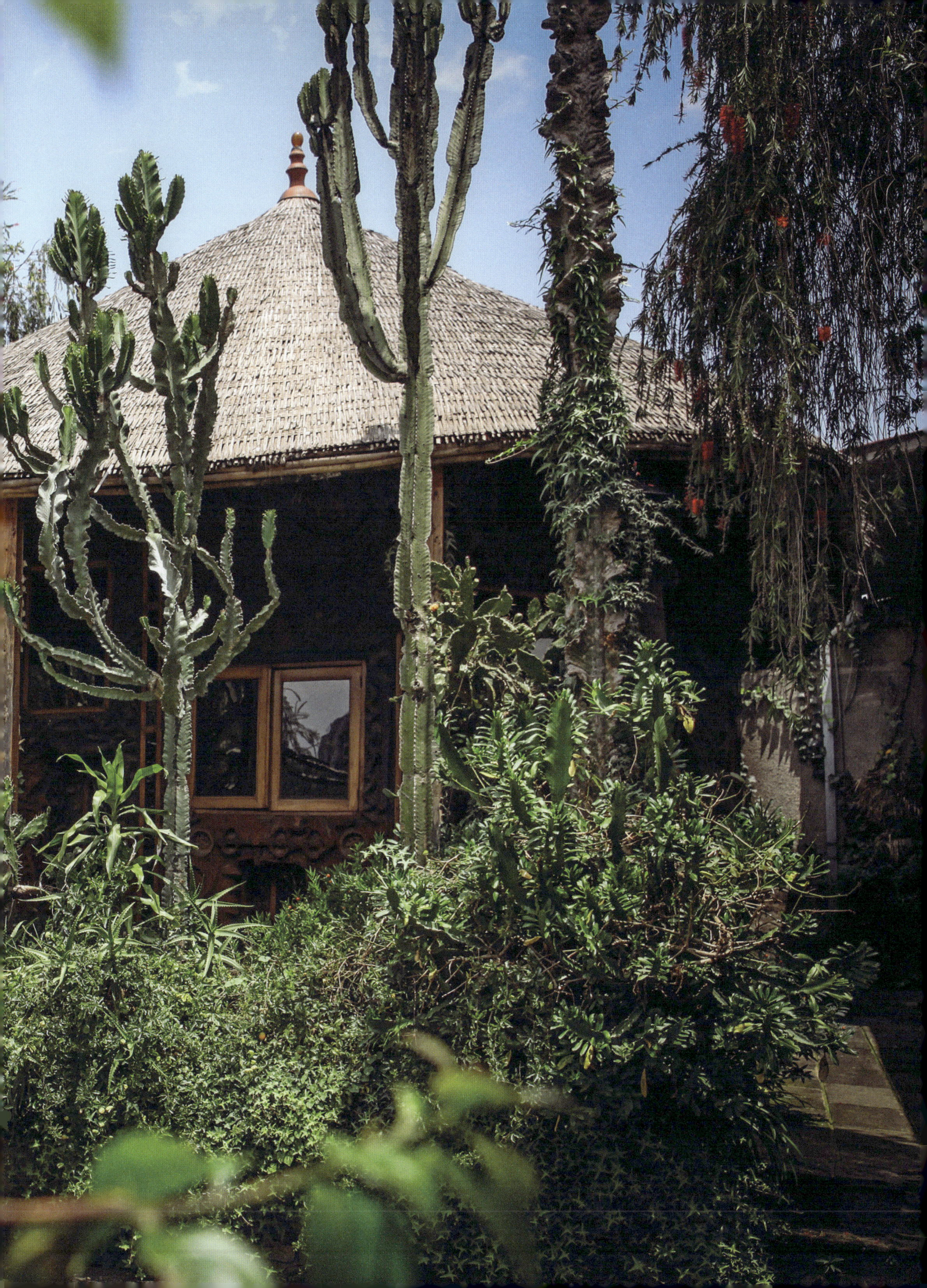

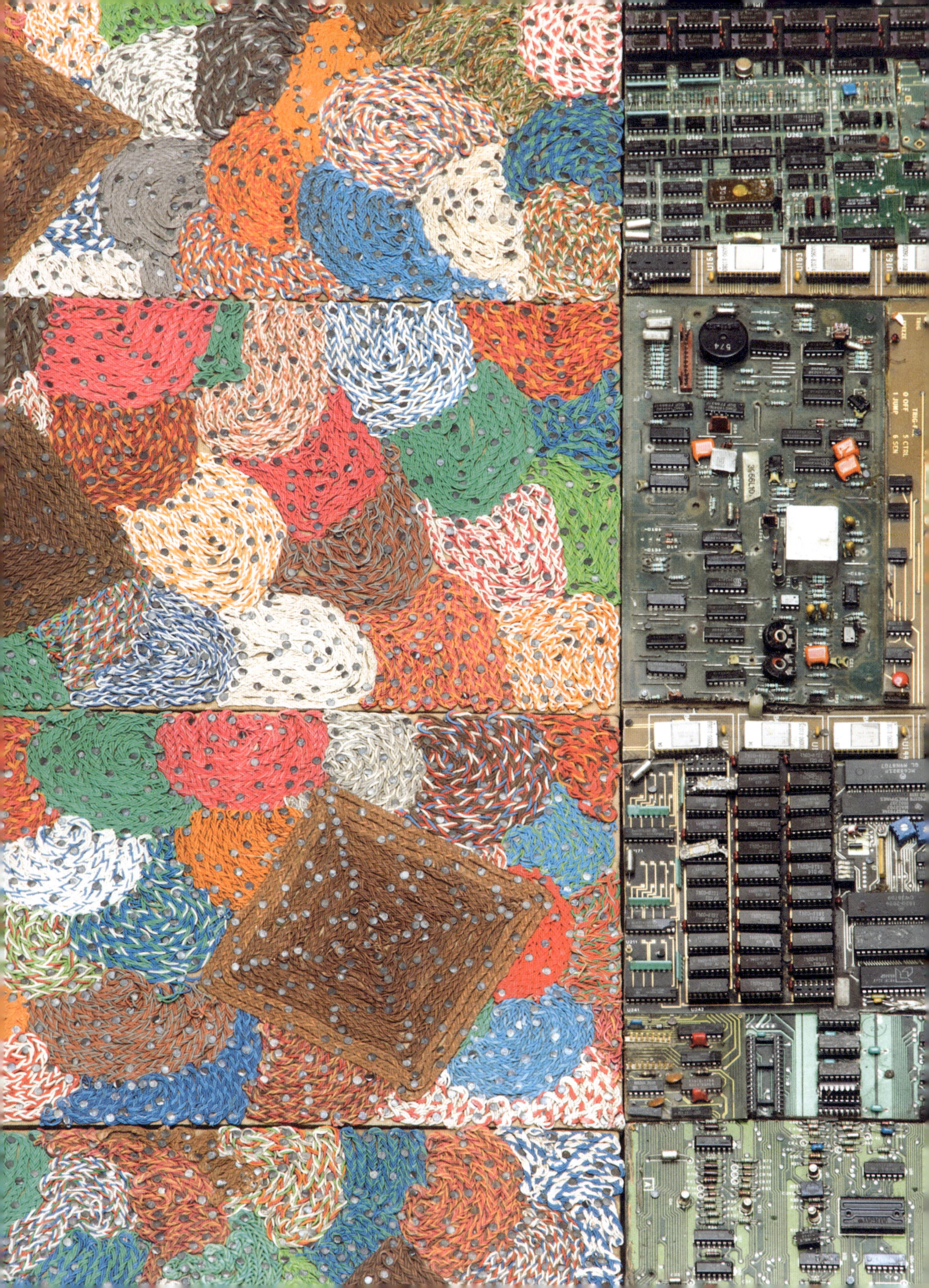

SELECTED EXHIBITED WORKS

Tightrope: Behind the Flowers
2017, reclaimed electronic components and wire on panel, 162.6 × 320 cm

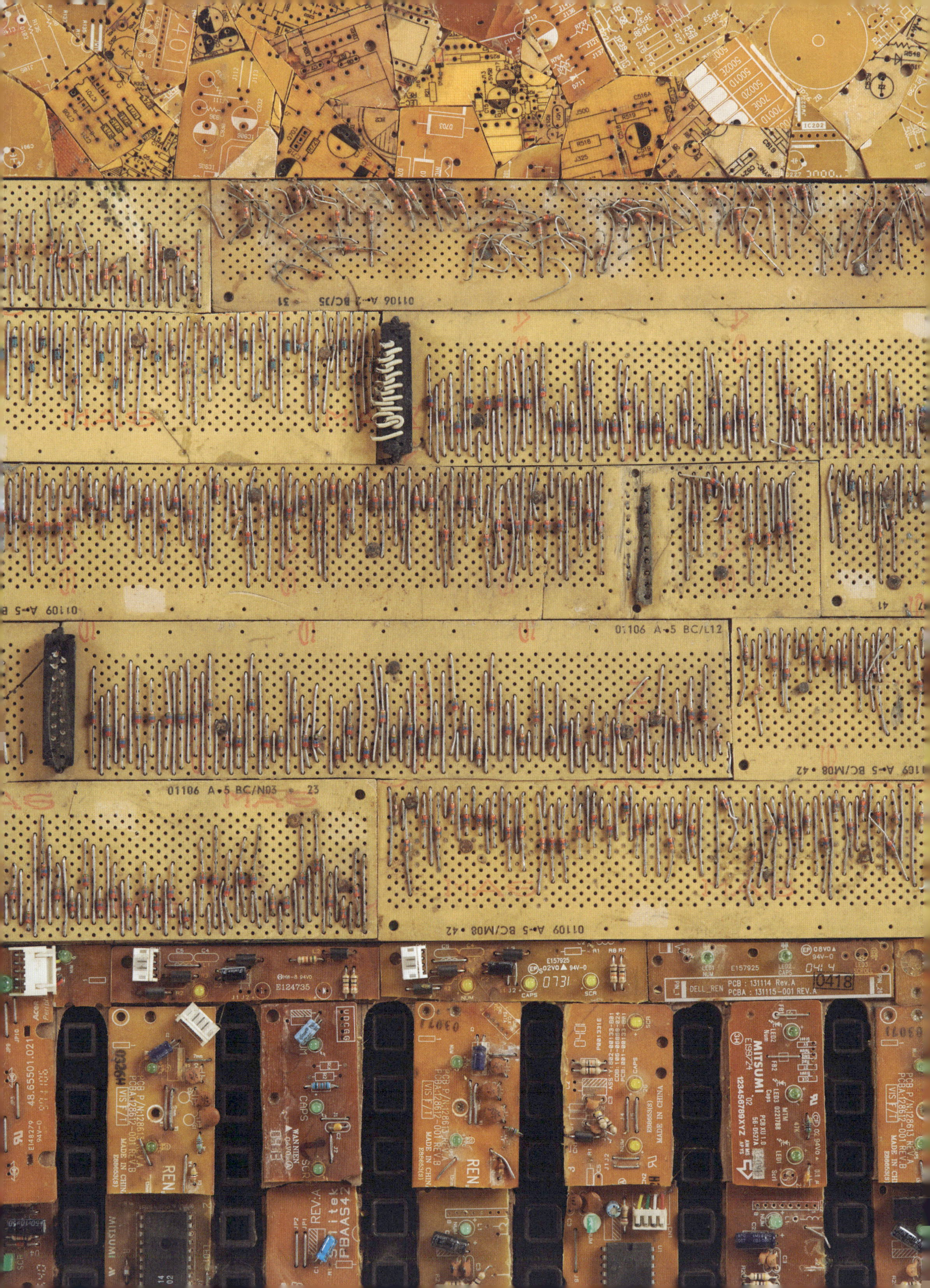
01106 A-5 BC/L12
01106 A-5 BC/N03 23
DELL_REN
PCB : 131114 Rev.A
PCBA : 131115-001 REV.A
0418
E157925
MITSUMI

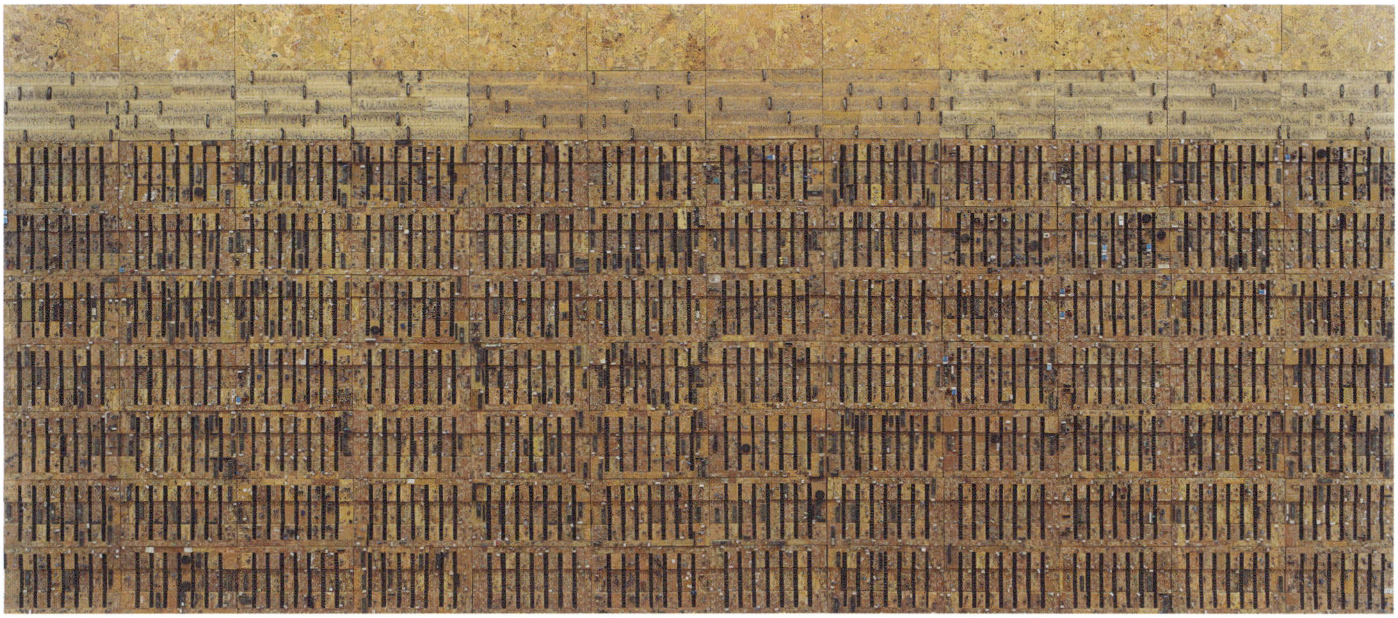

Tightrope: High Pitch and Low Pitch
2021, reclaimed electrical components on panel,
208.3 × 481.3 cm

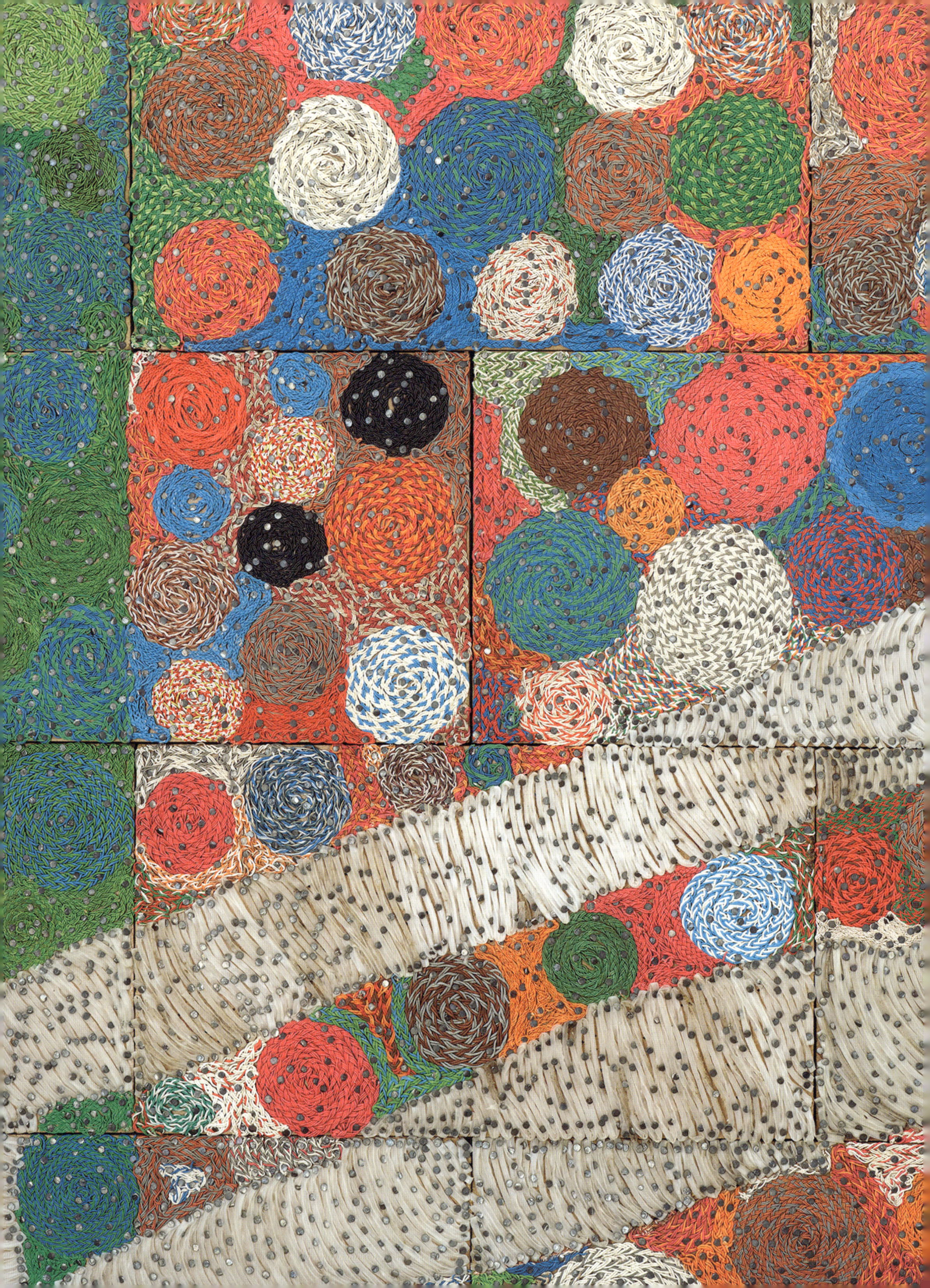

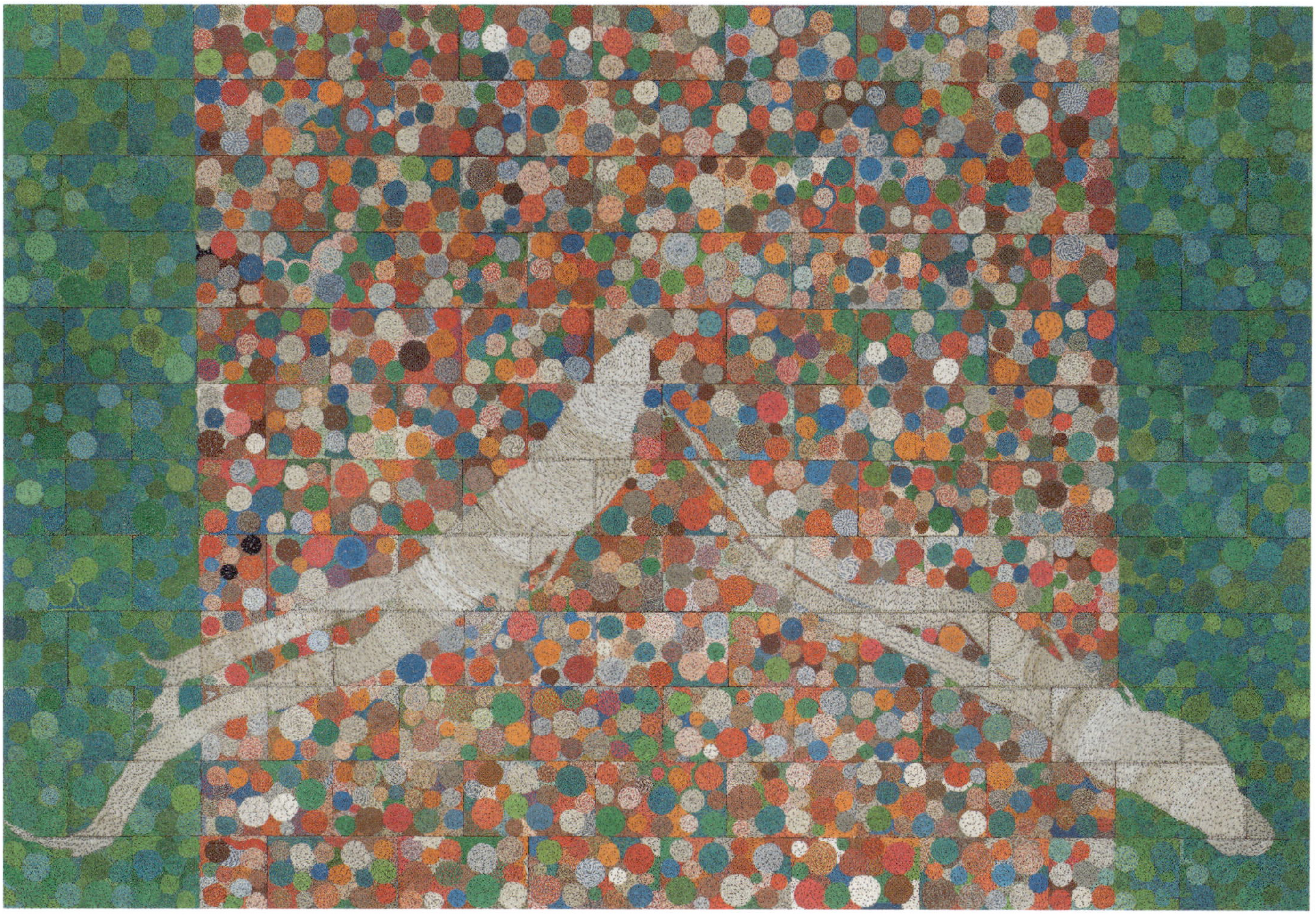

Tightrope: Evolution (1)
2017, reclaimed electrical wires on panel,
279.4 × 422.3 cm

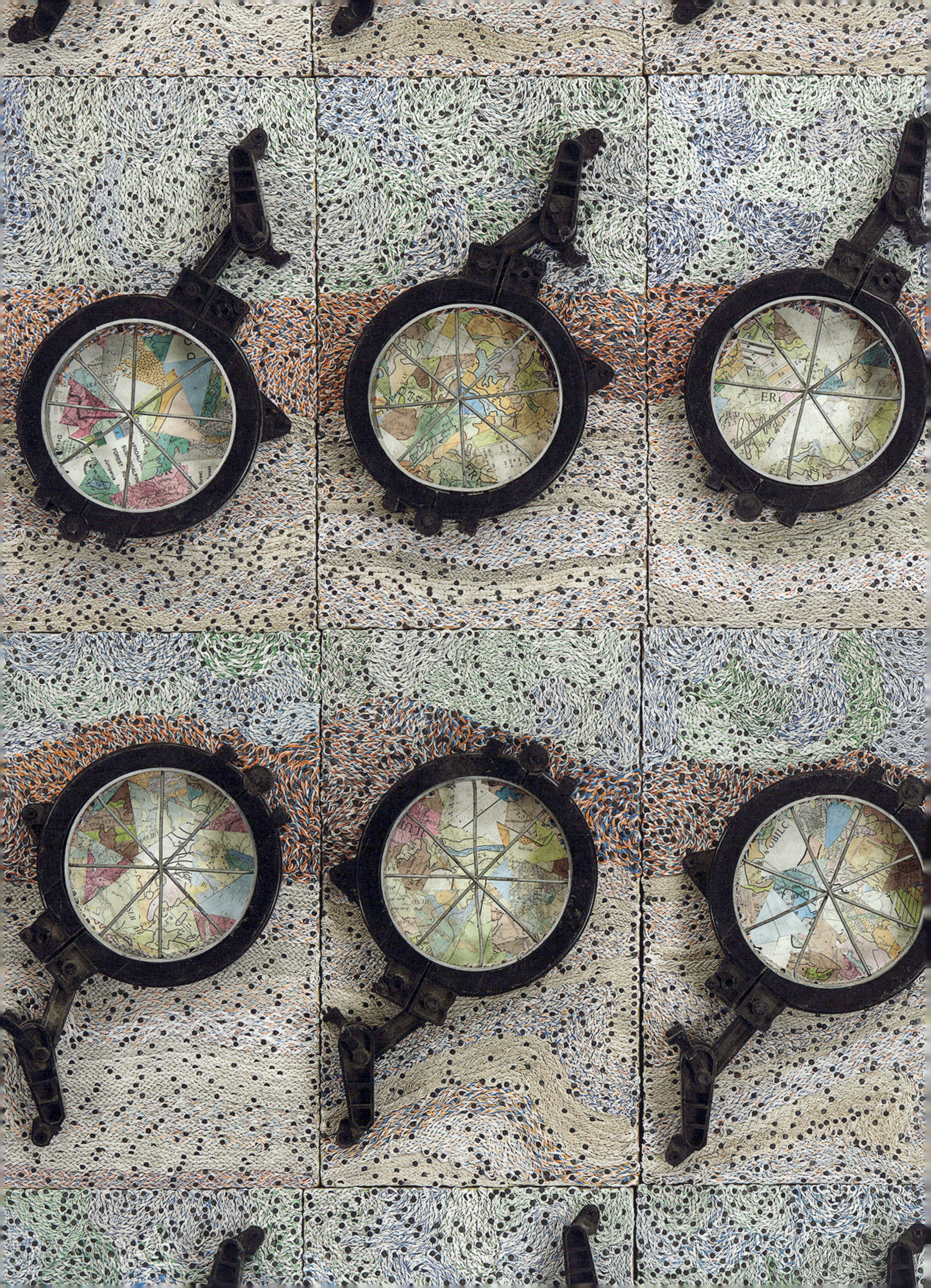

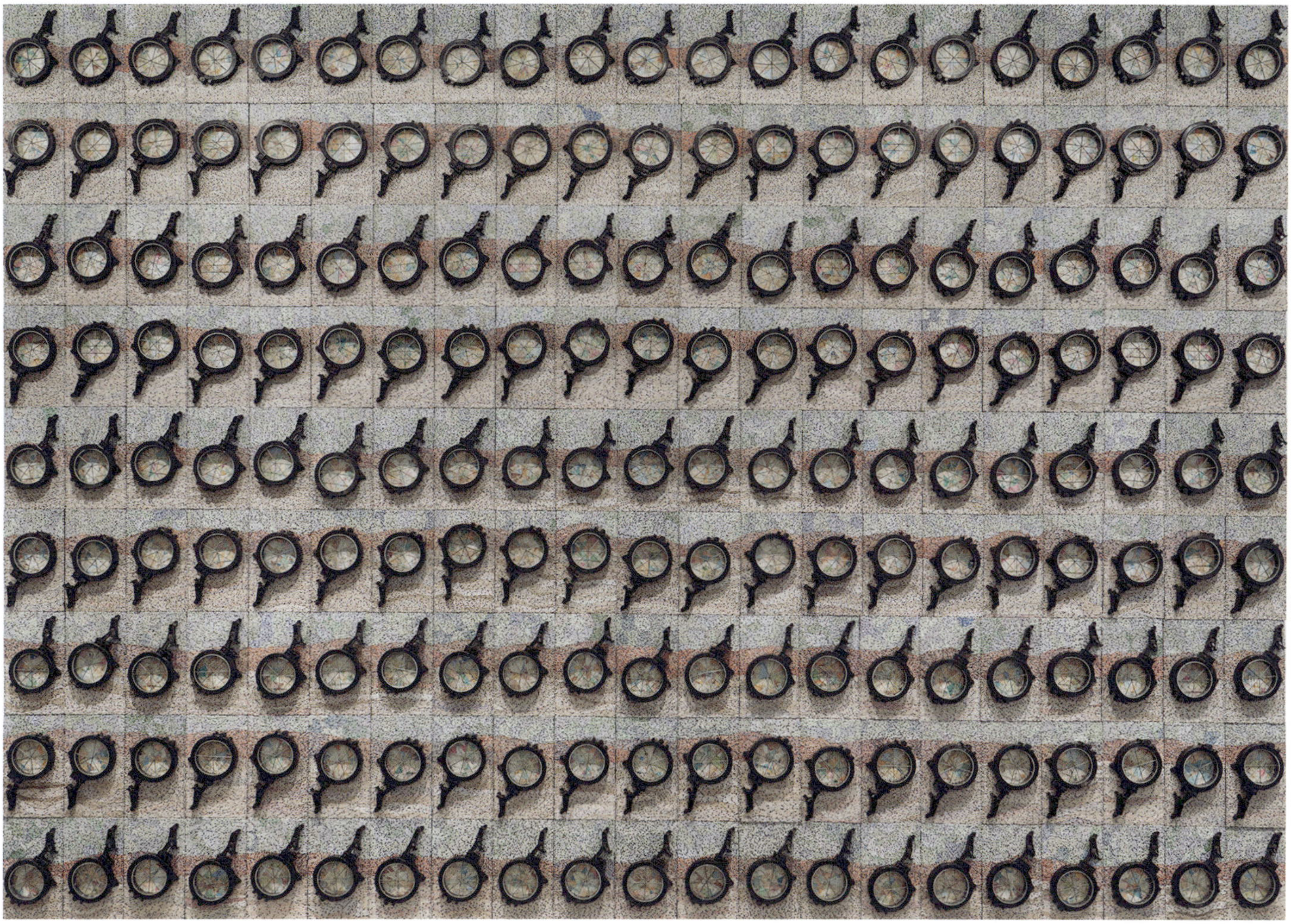

Tightrope: Echo!?
2021, reclaimed electrical wires and components
on panel, 365.8 × 480.1 cm

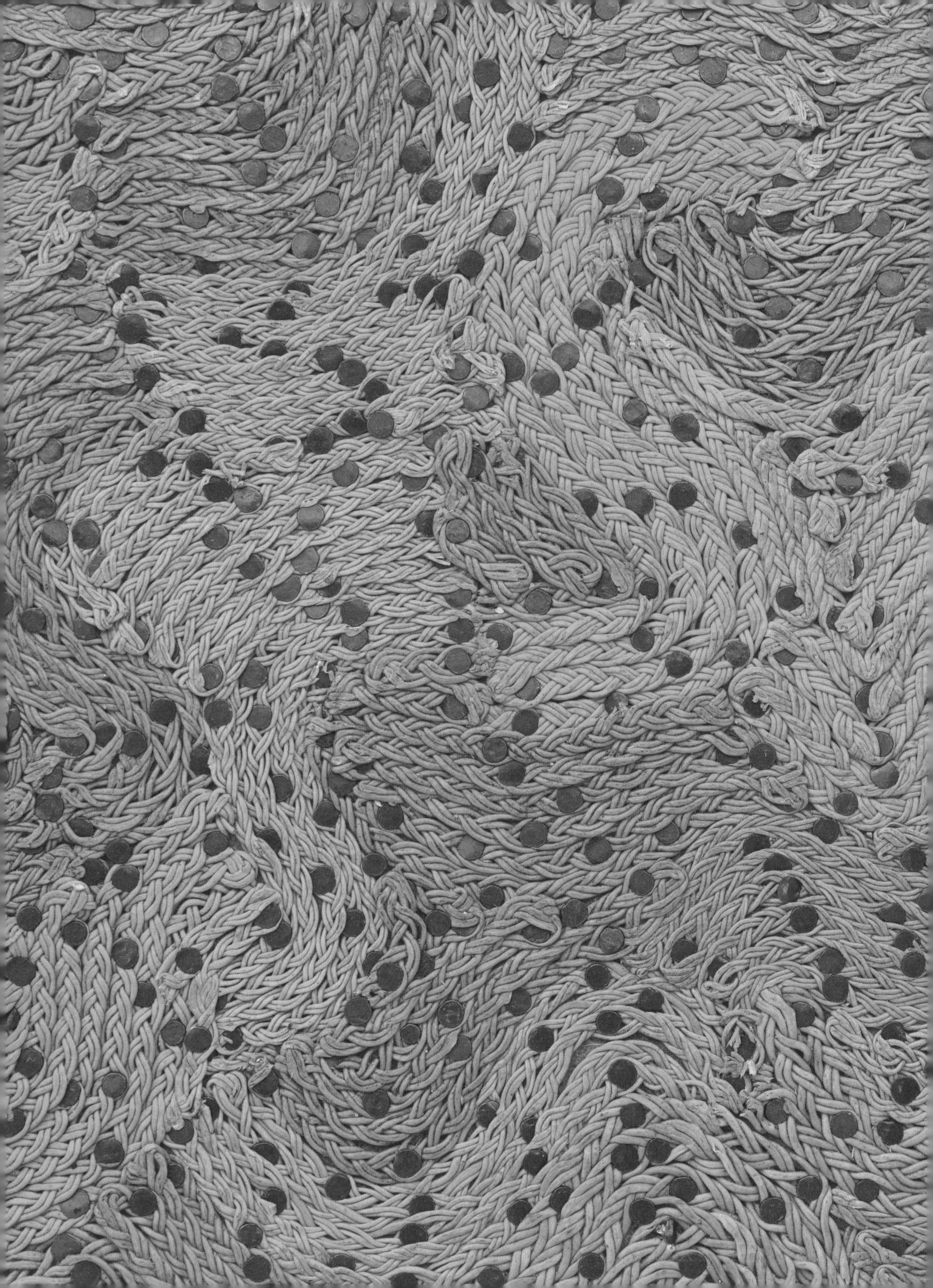

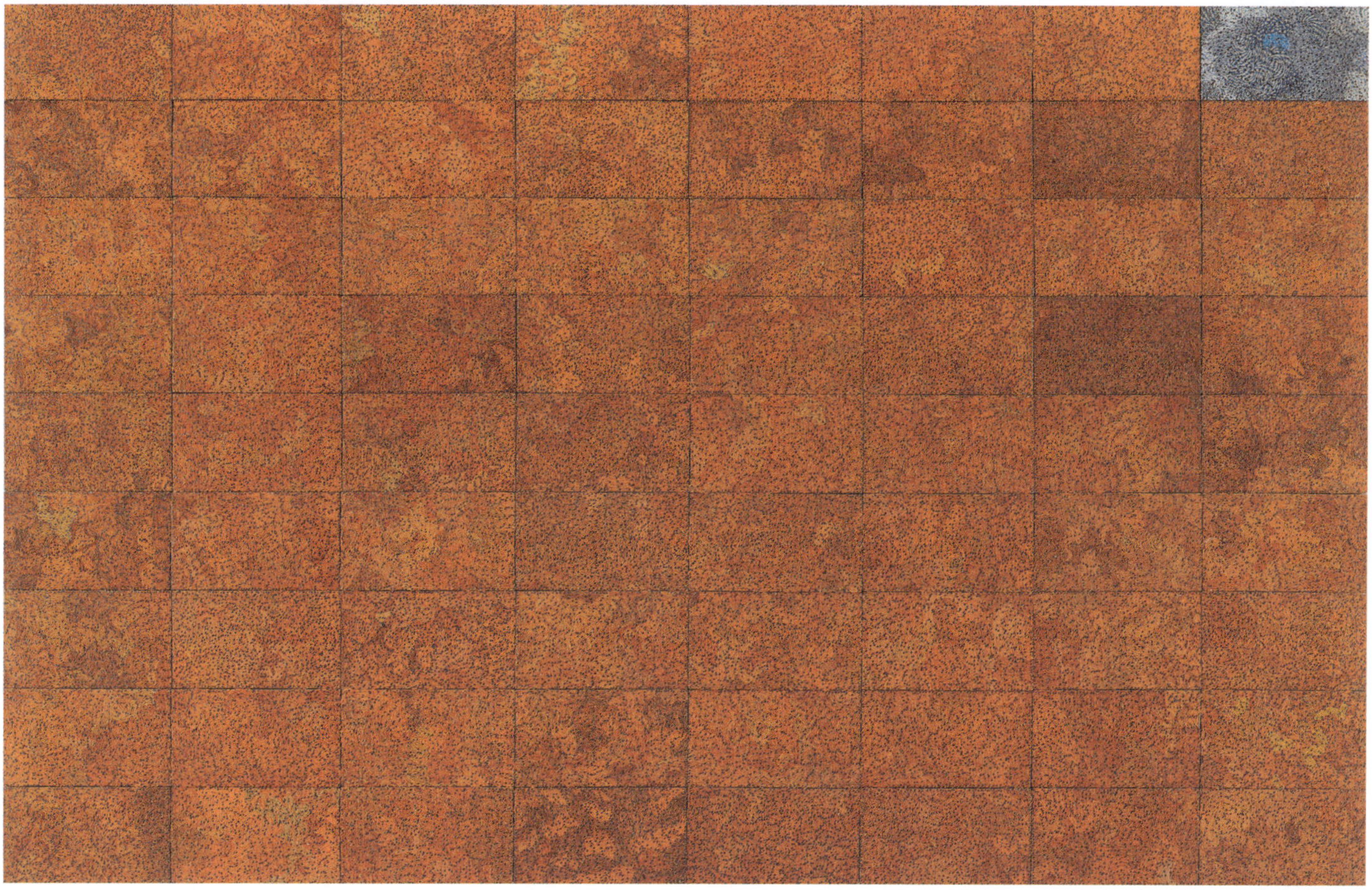

Tightrope: (20) While Observing...
2018, reclaimed electrical wires on panel,
208.6 × 321.3 cm

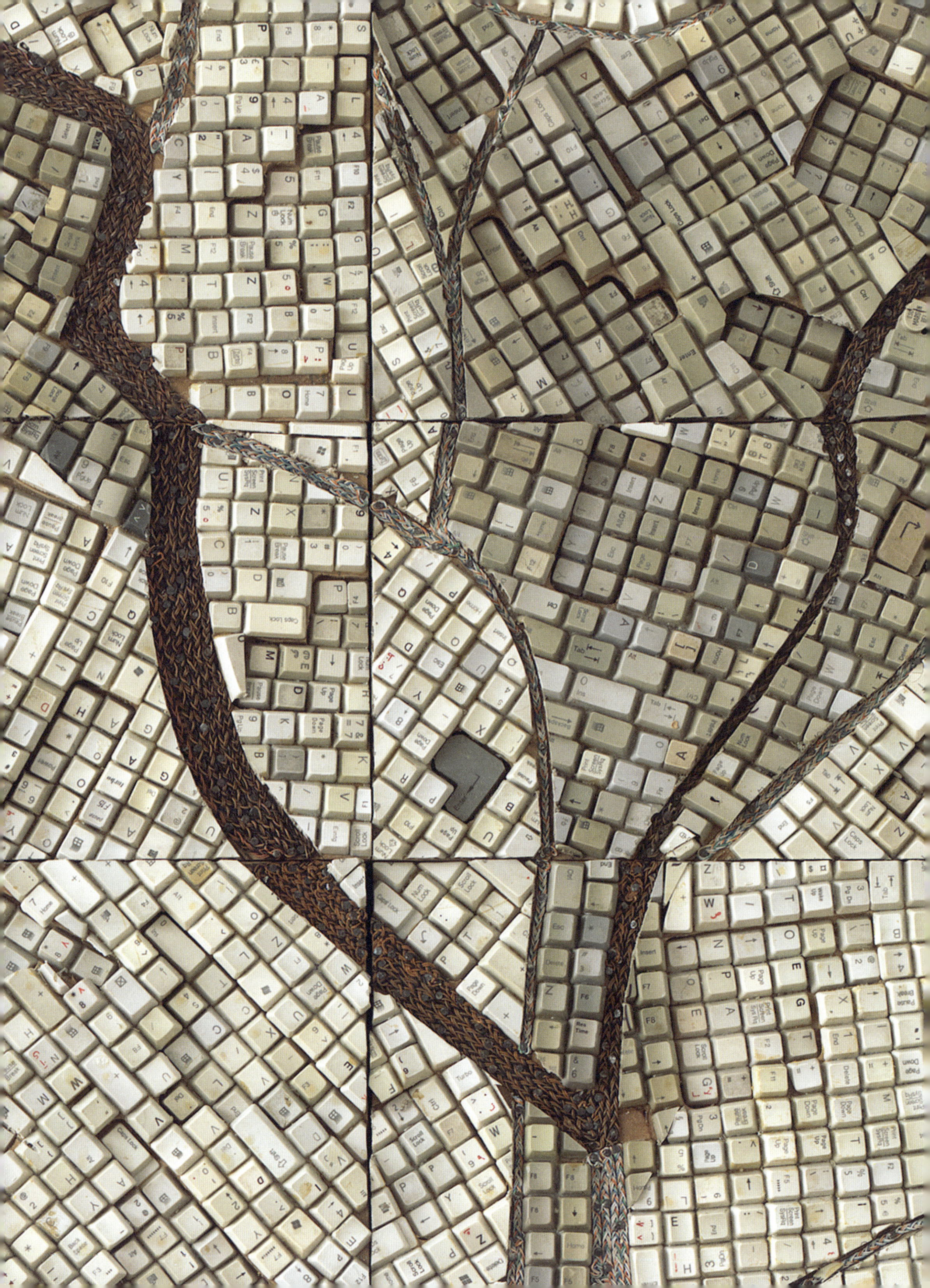

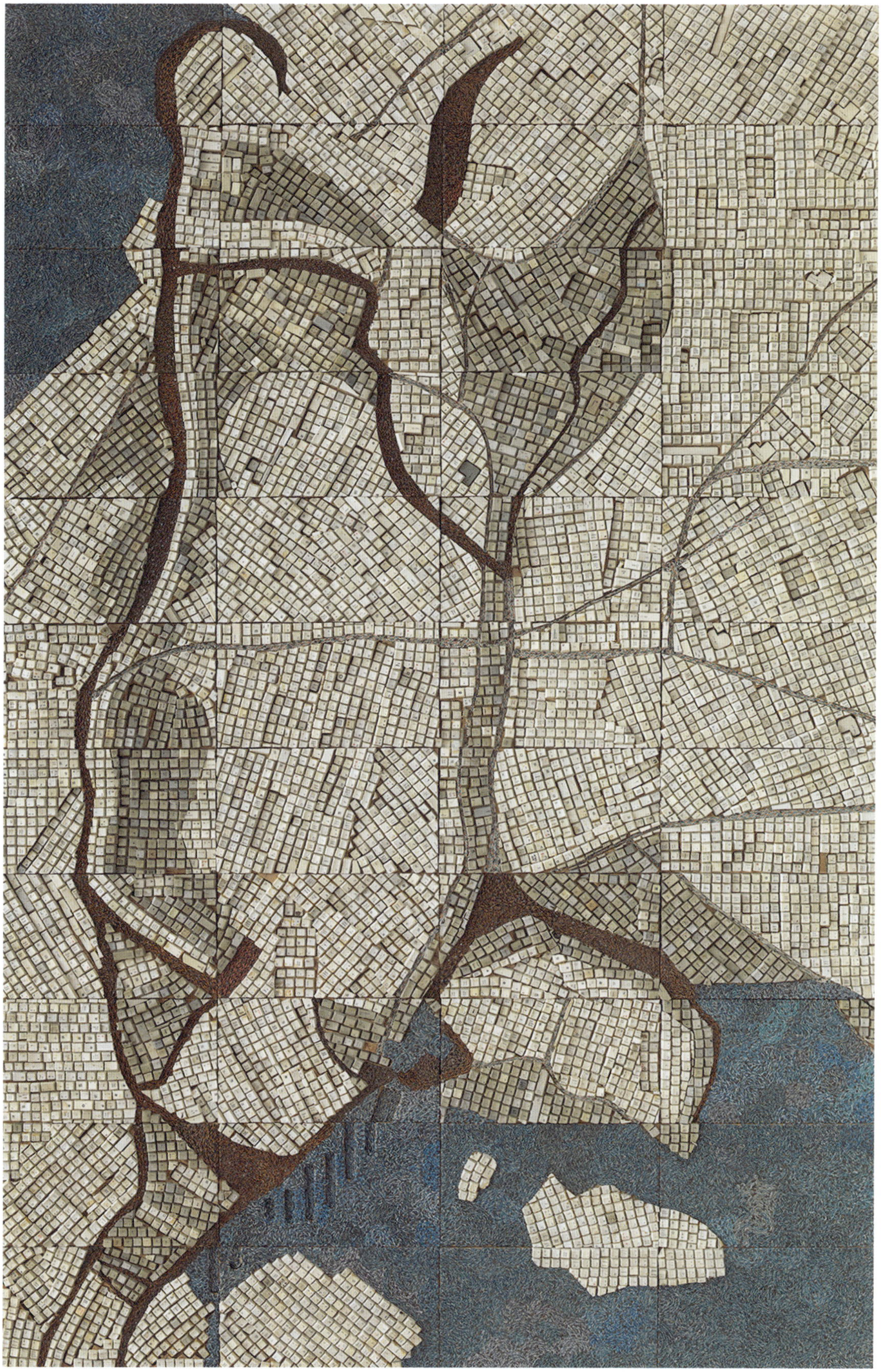

Tightrope: Noiseless 18
2019, reclaimed electrical wires and components on panel, 254.6 × 160.7 cm

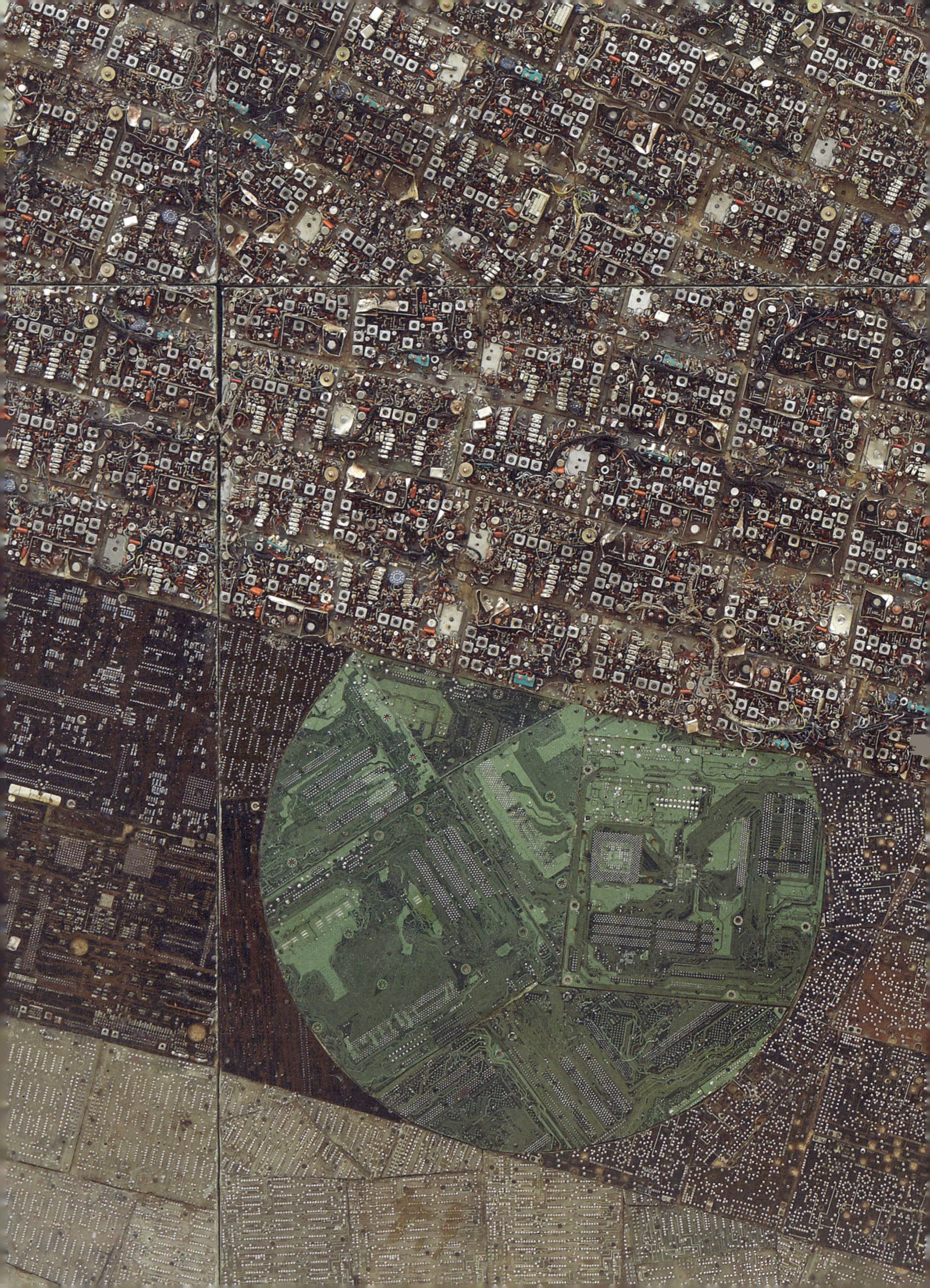

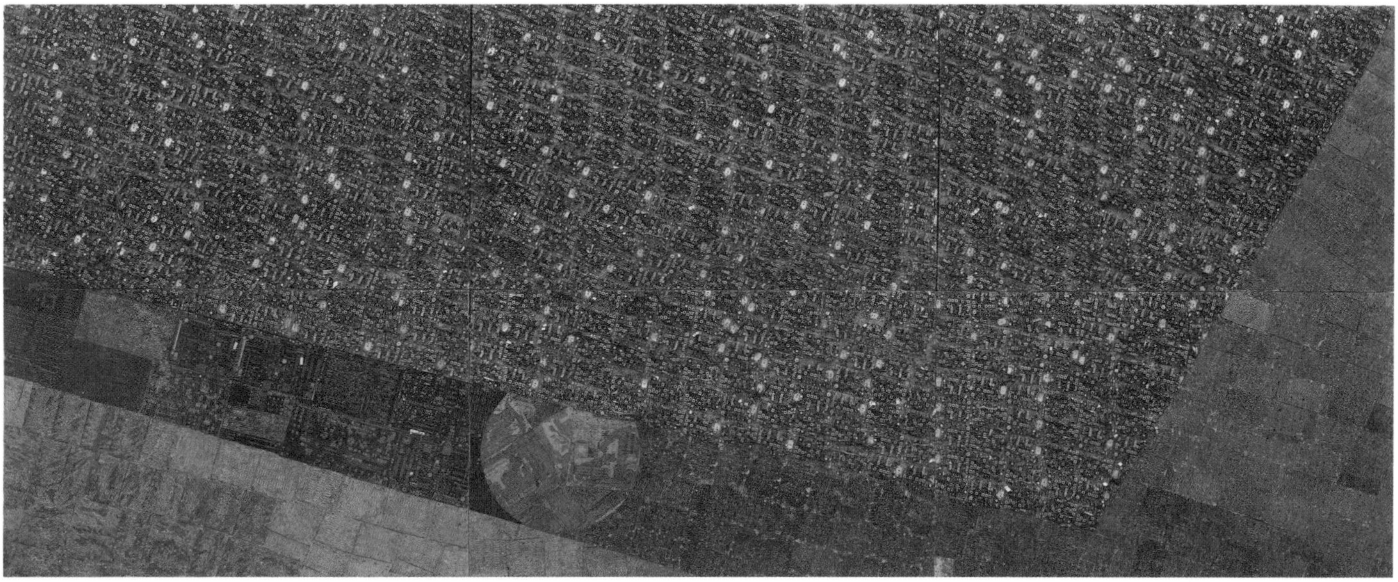

Tightrope: 99
2009–2014, reclaimed electrical components
on panel, 200 × 481.3 cm

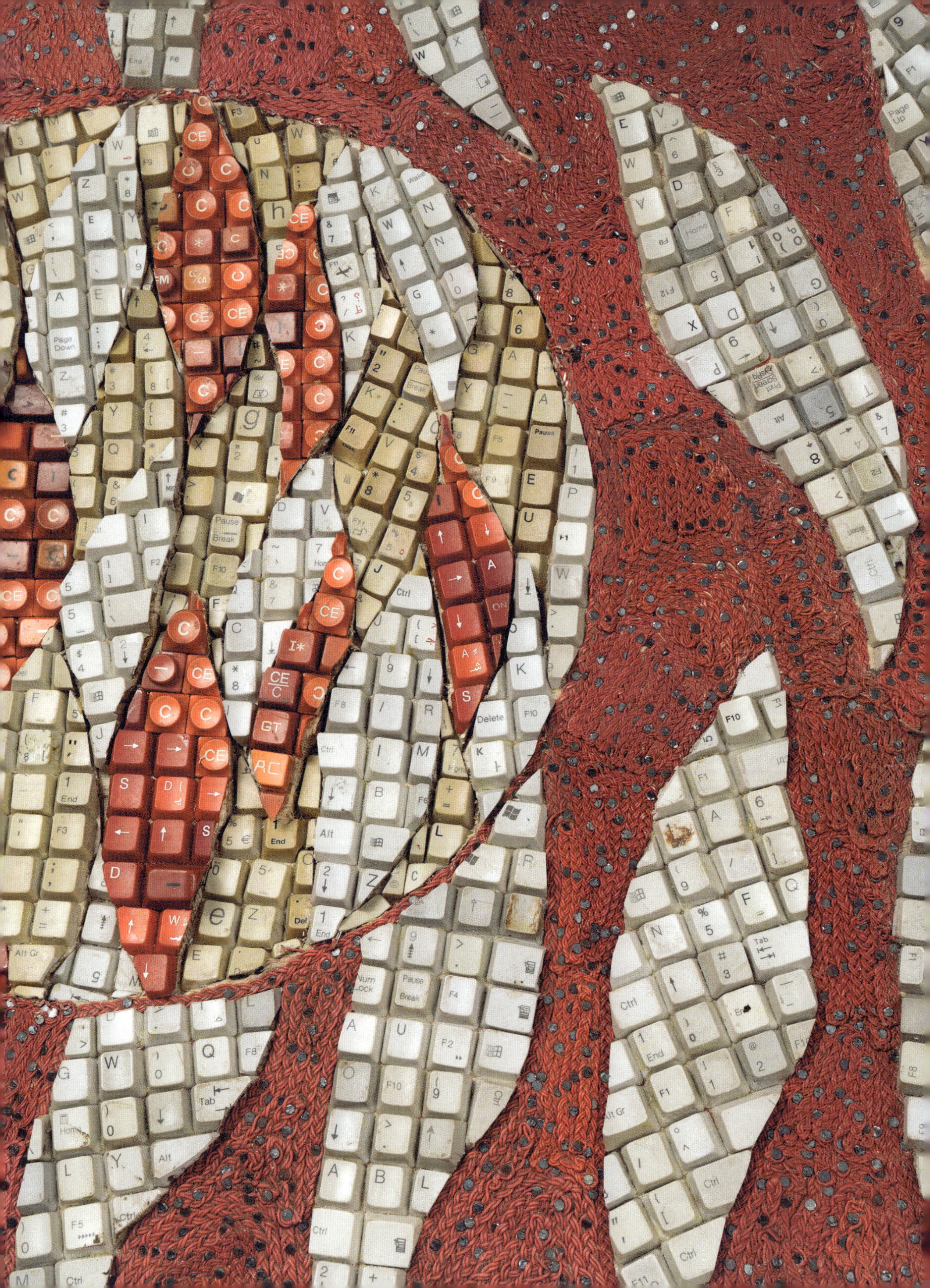

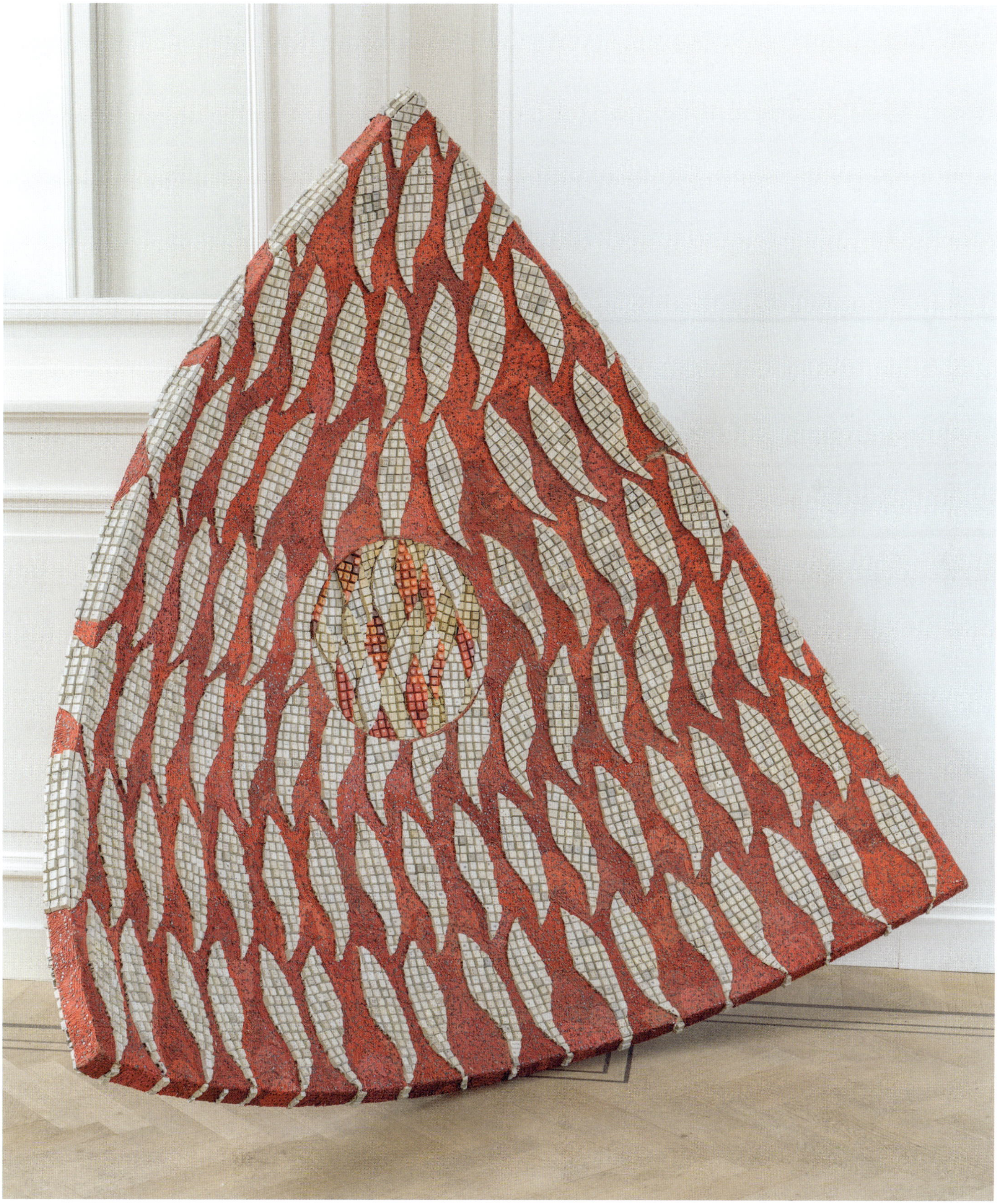

Tightrope: Concave Triangle No.2
2020, reclaimed electrical wires and computer keys
on wood, 185 × 185 × 60 cm

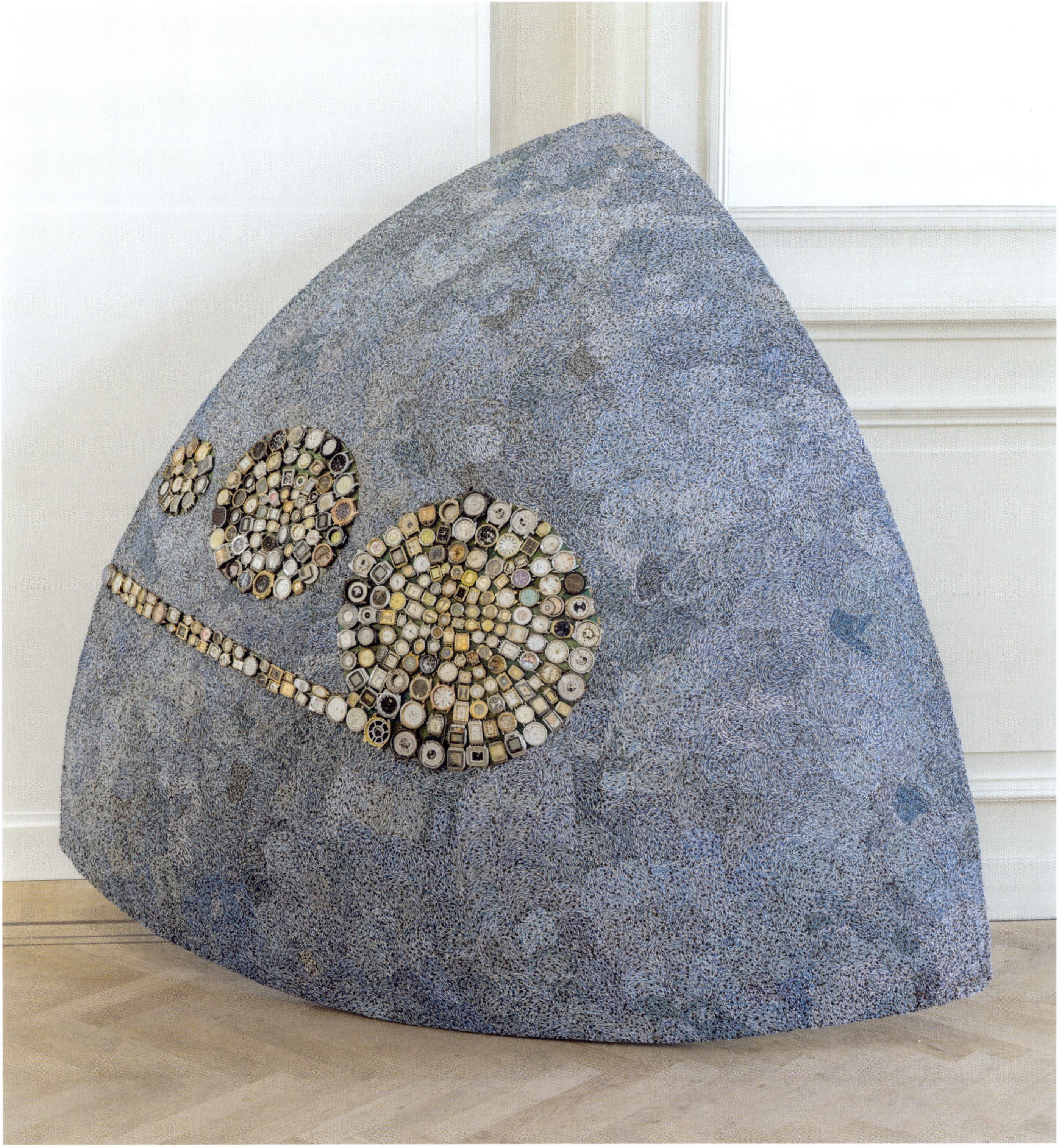

Tightrope: Concave Triangle No.3
2020, reclaimed electrical wires and watch faces on wood, 185 × 185 × 60 cm

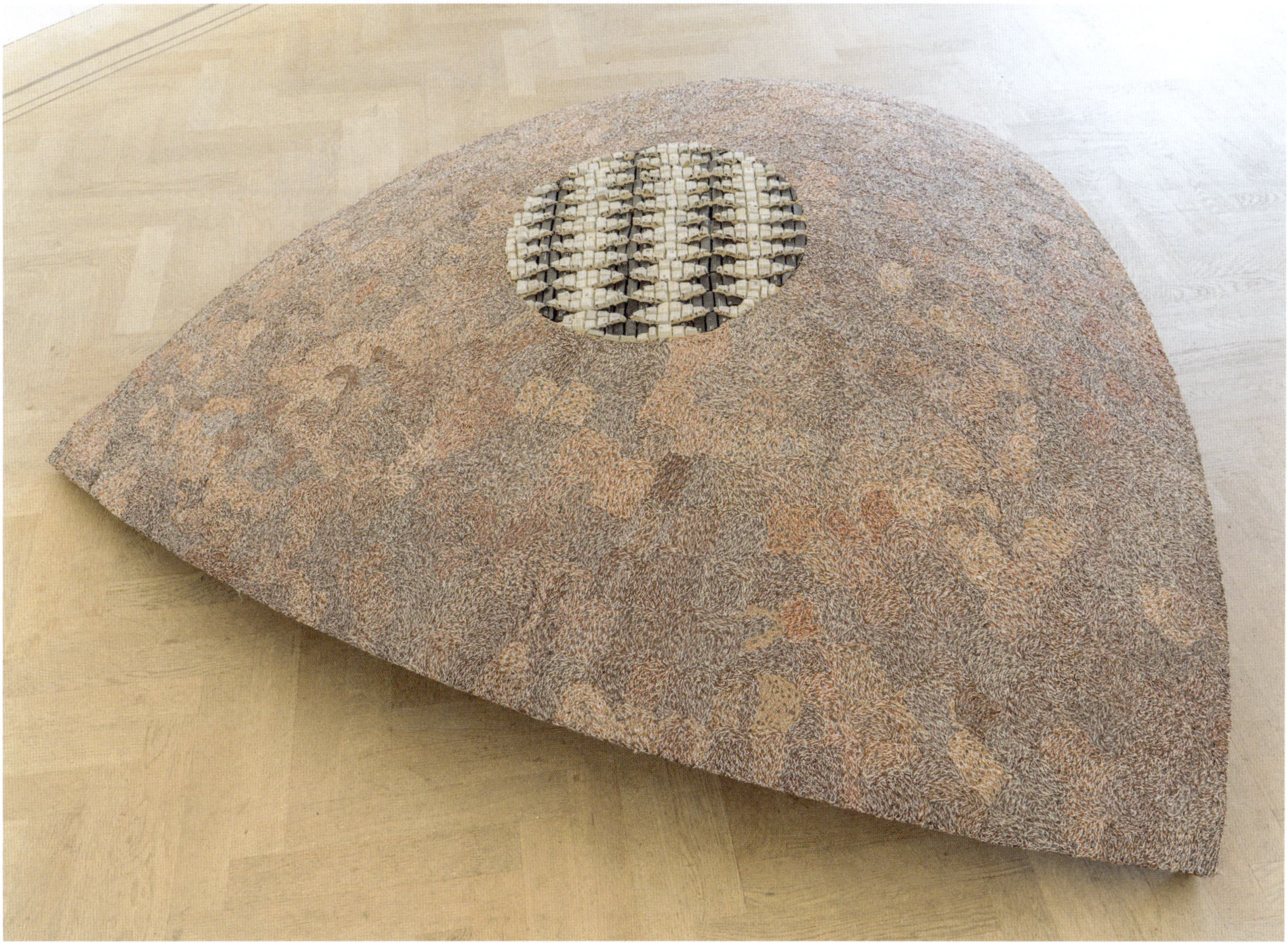

Tightrope: Concave Triangle No.4
2020, reclaimed electrical wires and computer keys
on wood, 185 × 185 × 60 cm

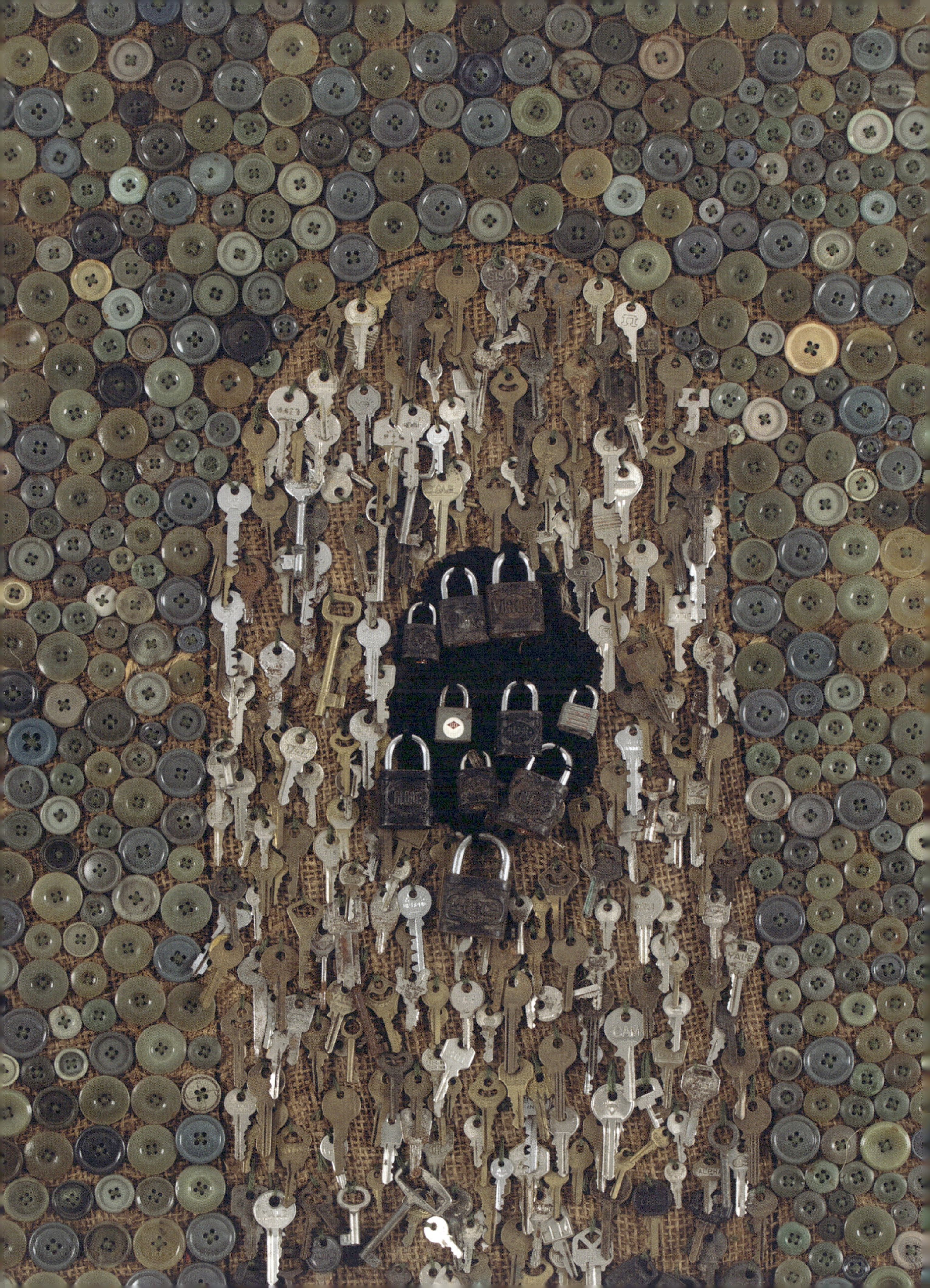

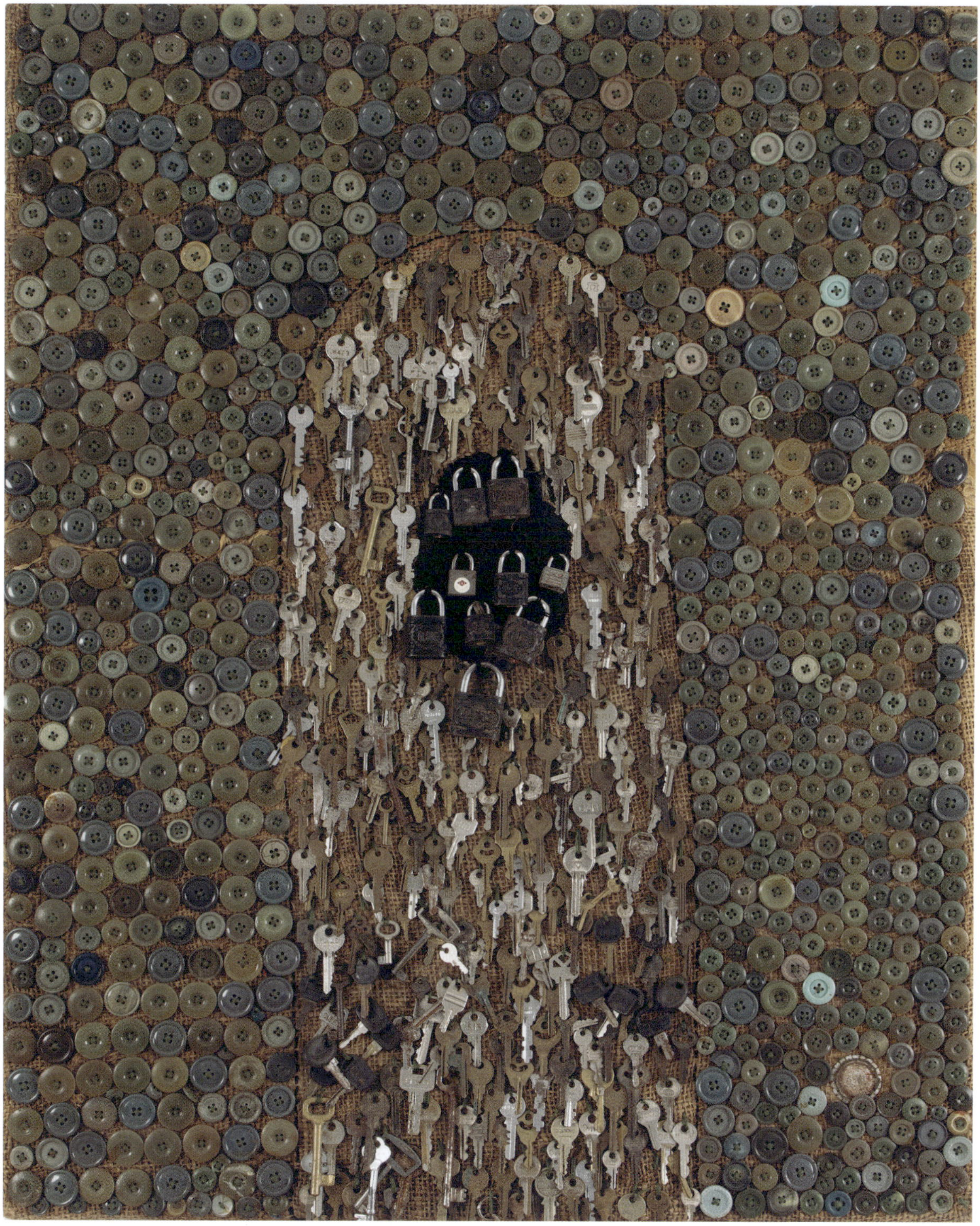

Mewezageb
date unknown, metal, cloth and buttons,
96 × 75 cm

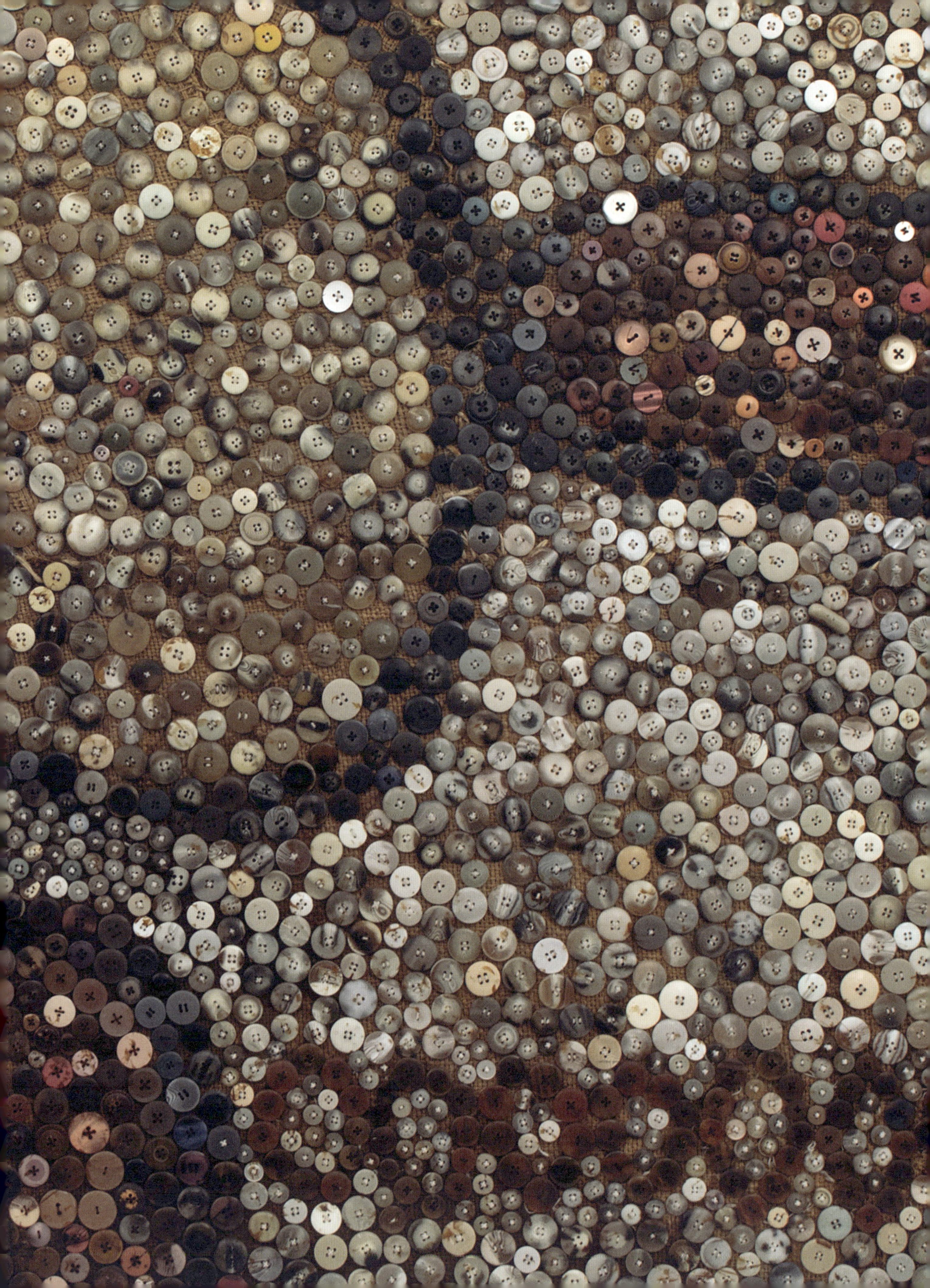

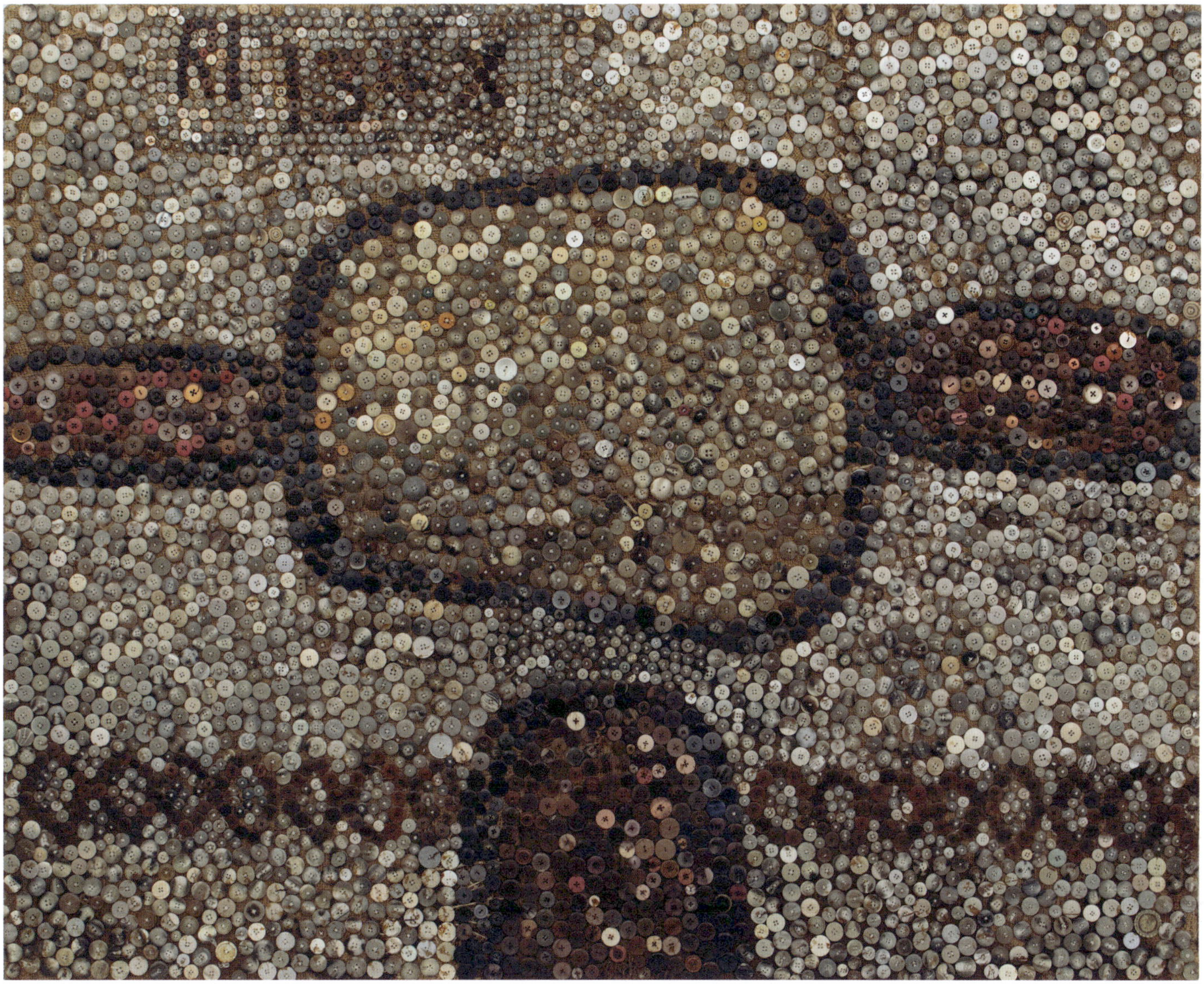

Melayo
2003–2004, buttons on hessian,
130 × 163 cm

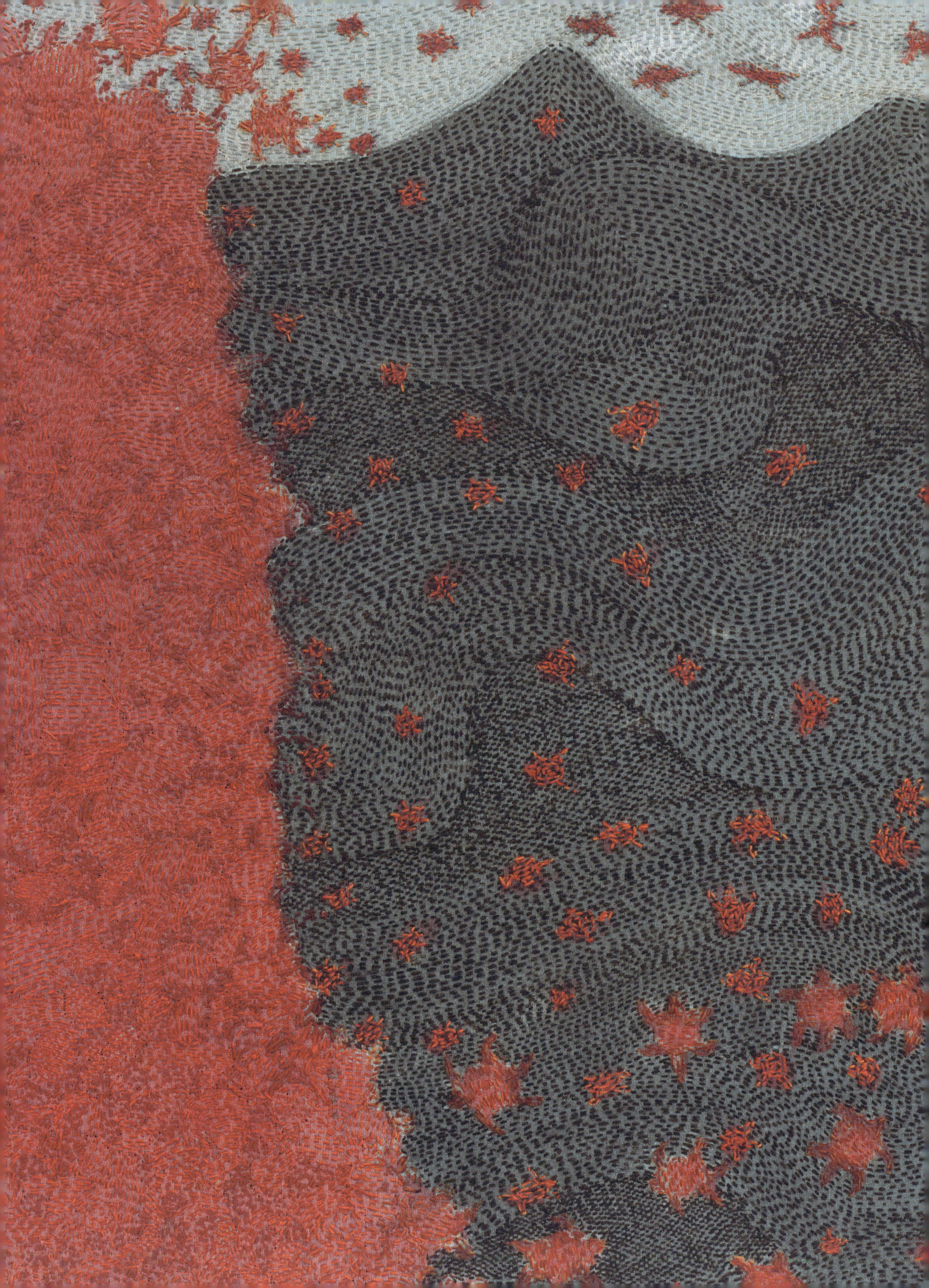

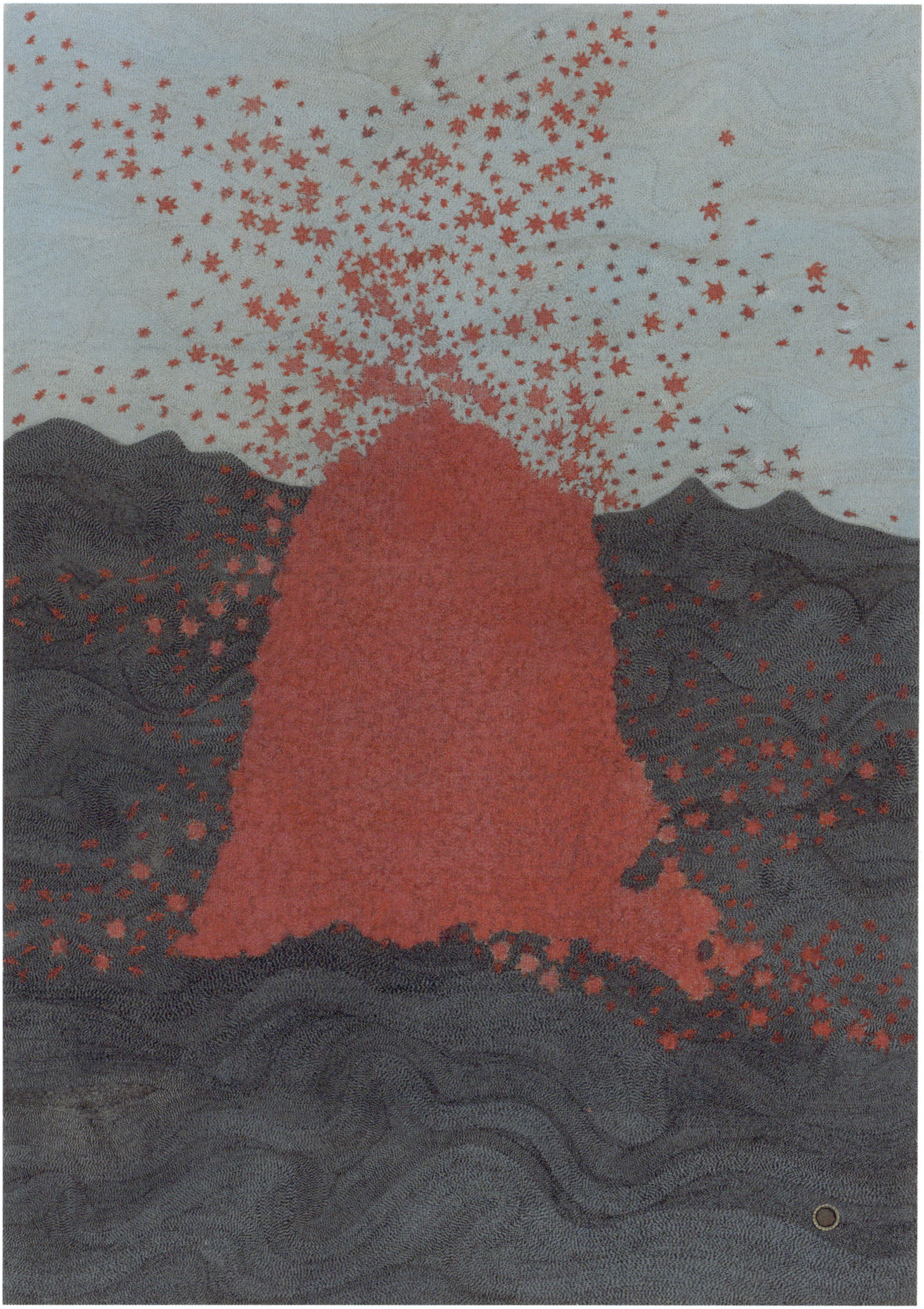

What is Love? (1)
2007, yarn and stitch on canvas,
188 × 132 cm

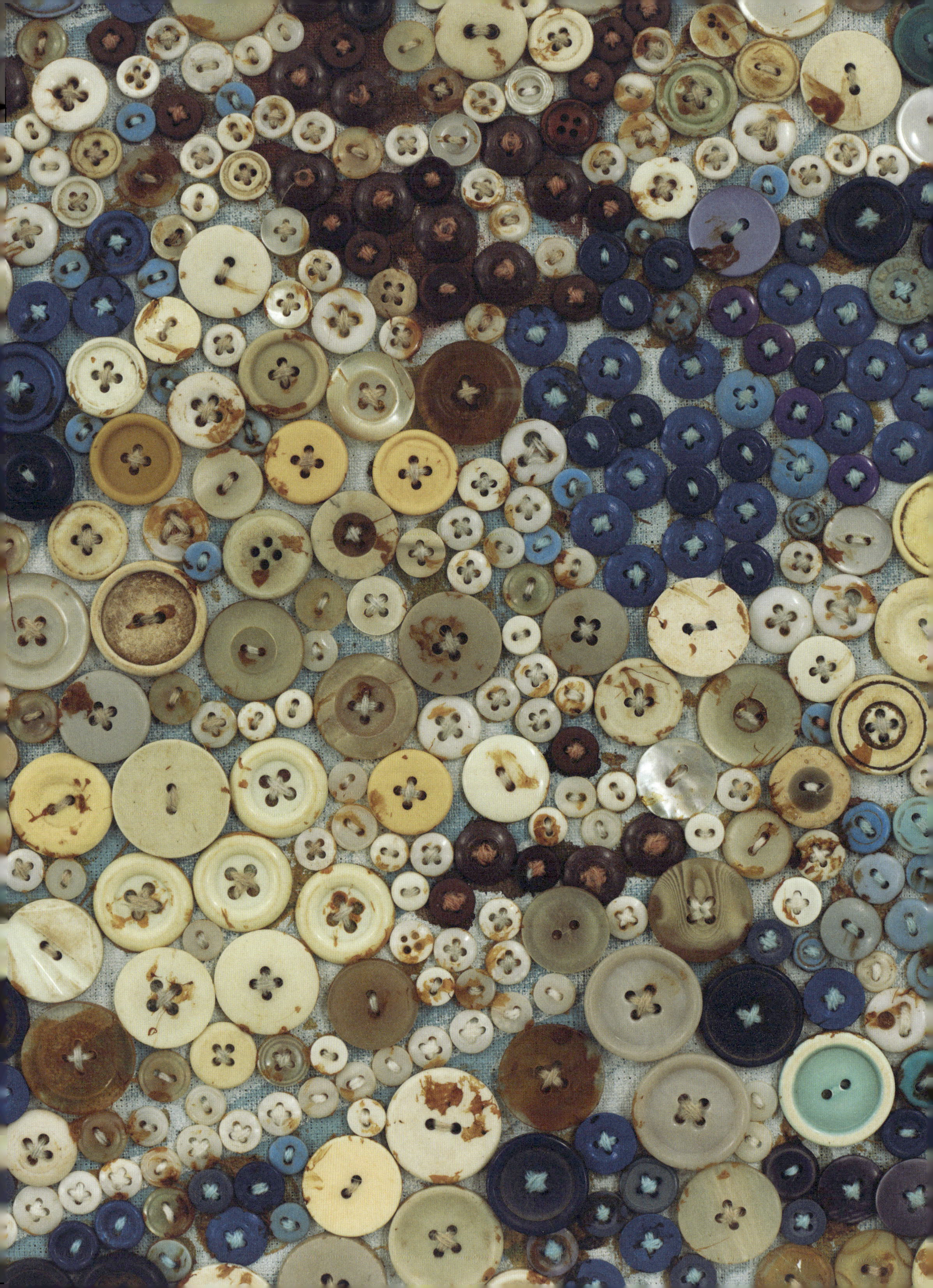

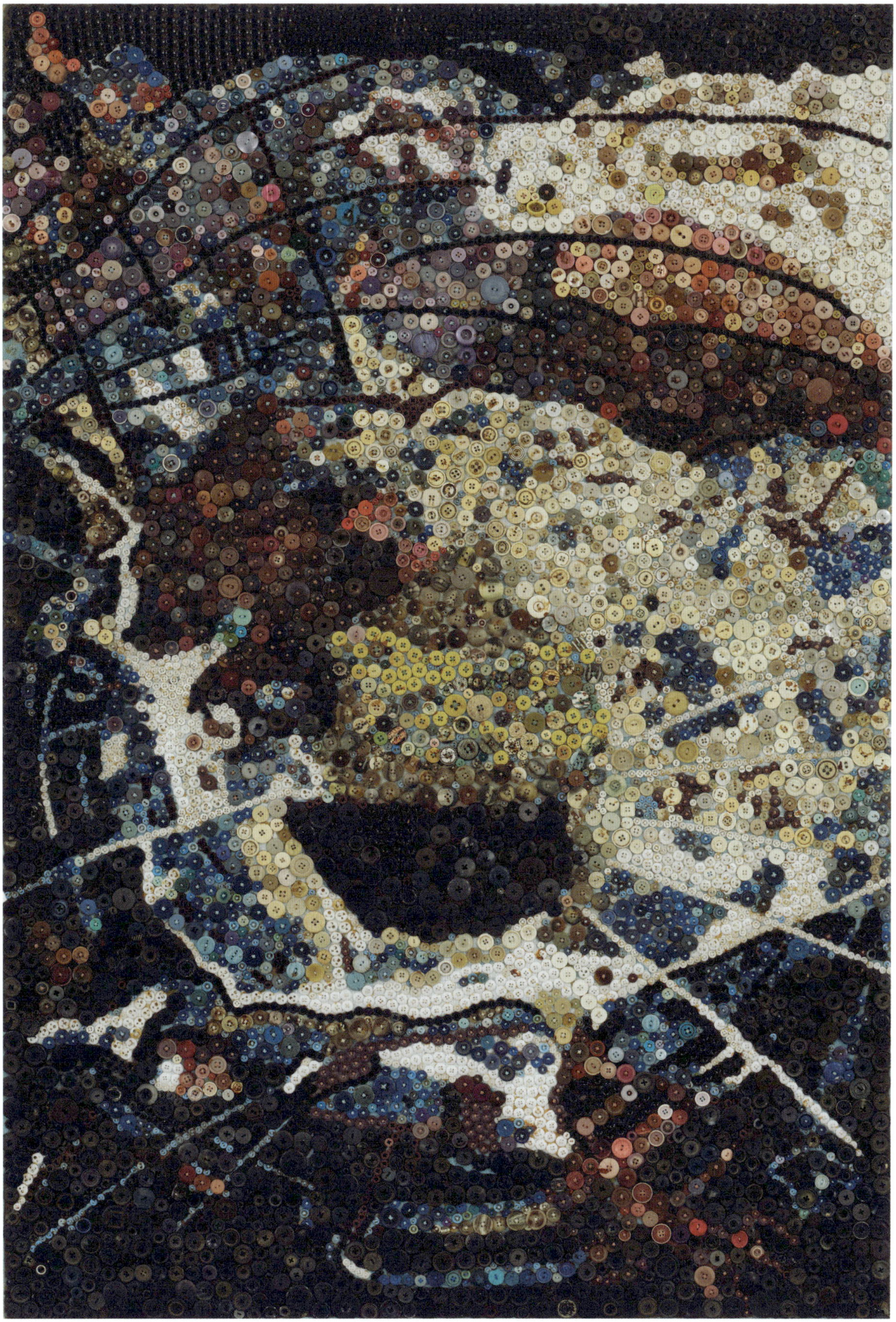

Yemegnot Alem
2001, yarn, stitch and buttons on canvas,
190 × 164 cm

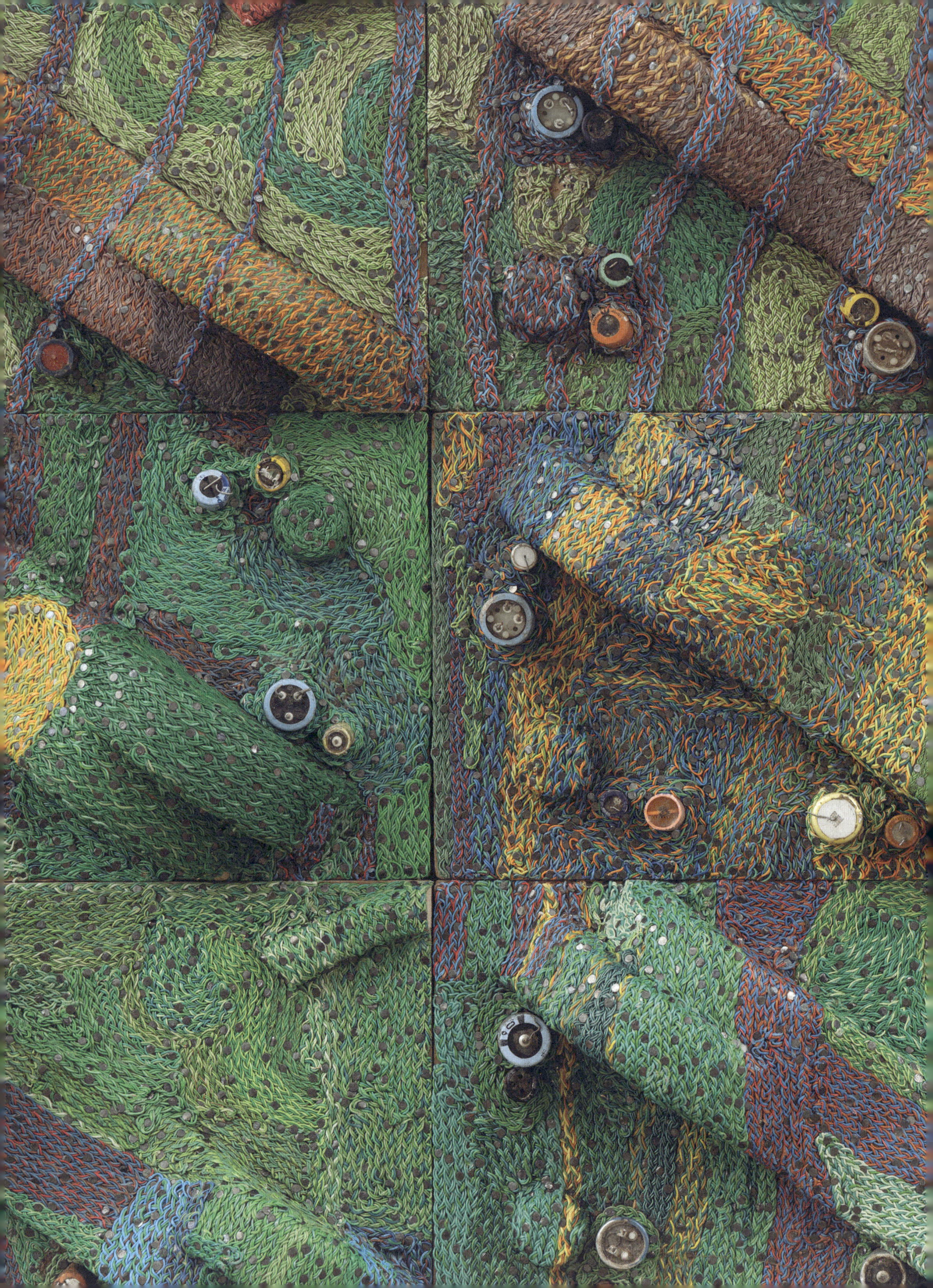

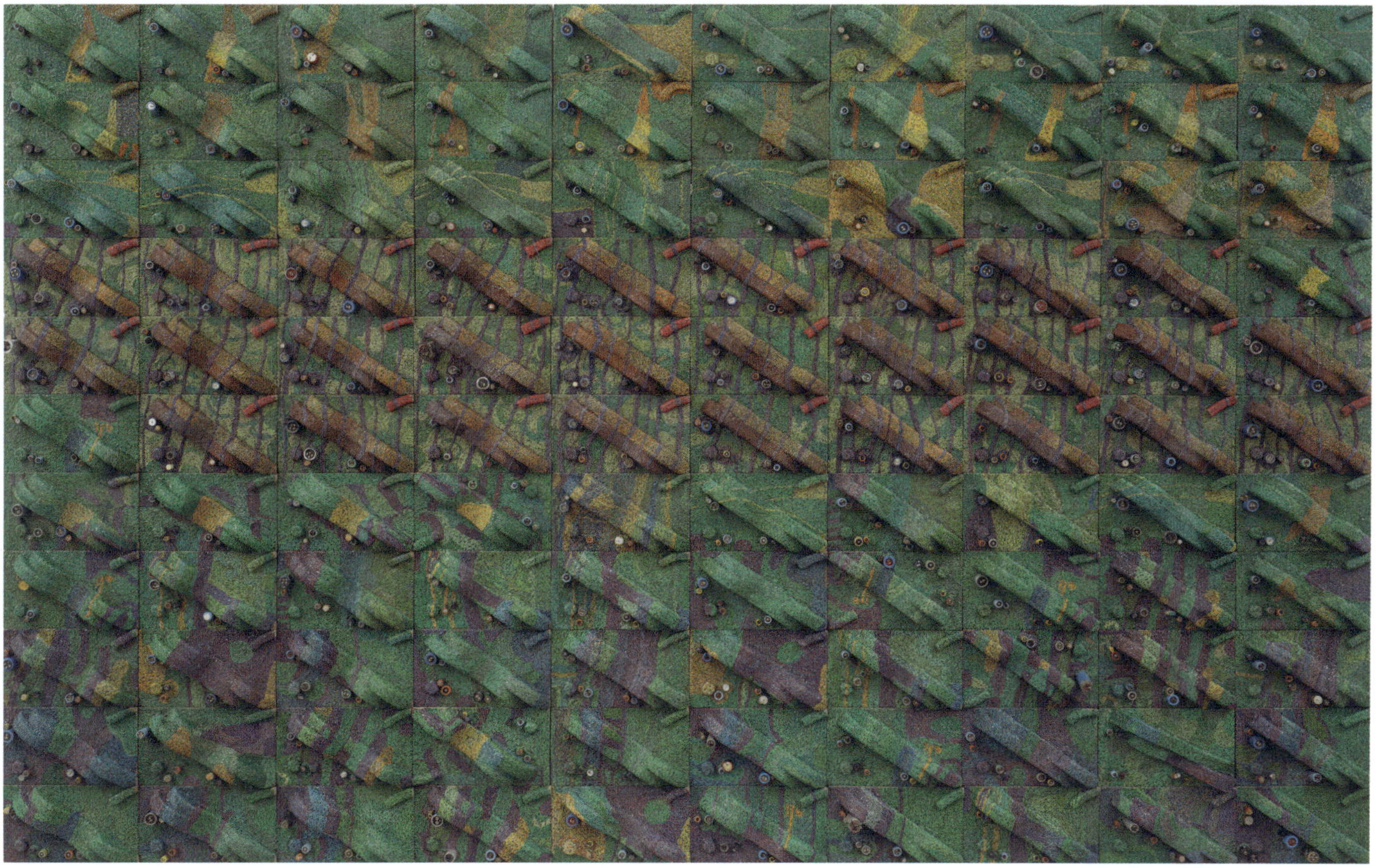

Tightrope: Behind the Processor No.6
2022, three-dimensional wall piece with woven electrical wires and other components on wood panels, 253 × 400 × 12 cm

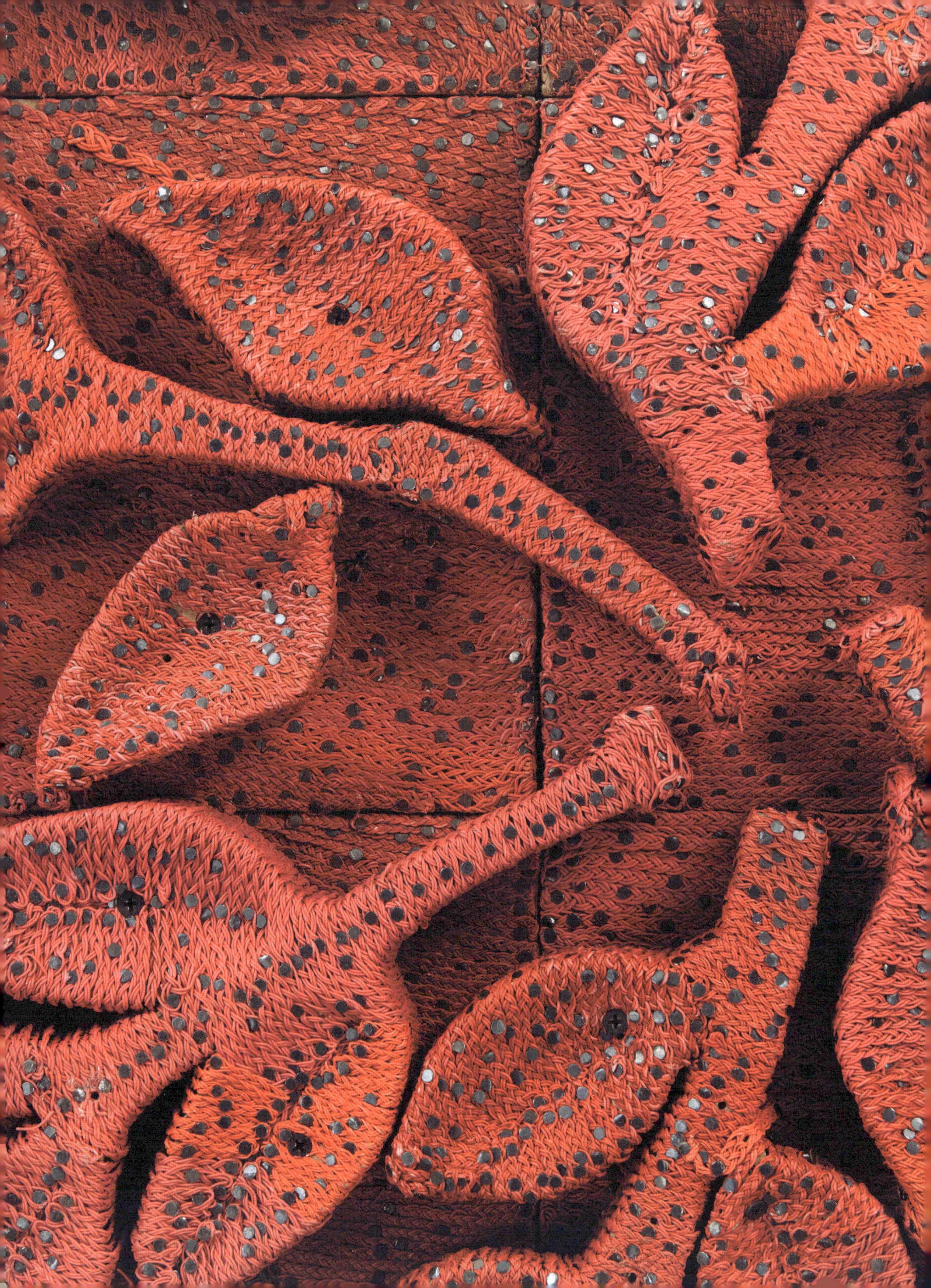

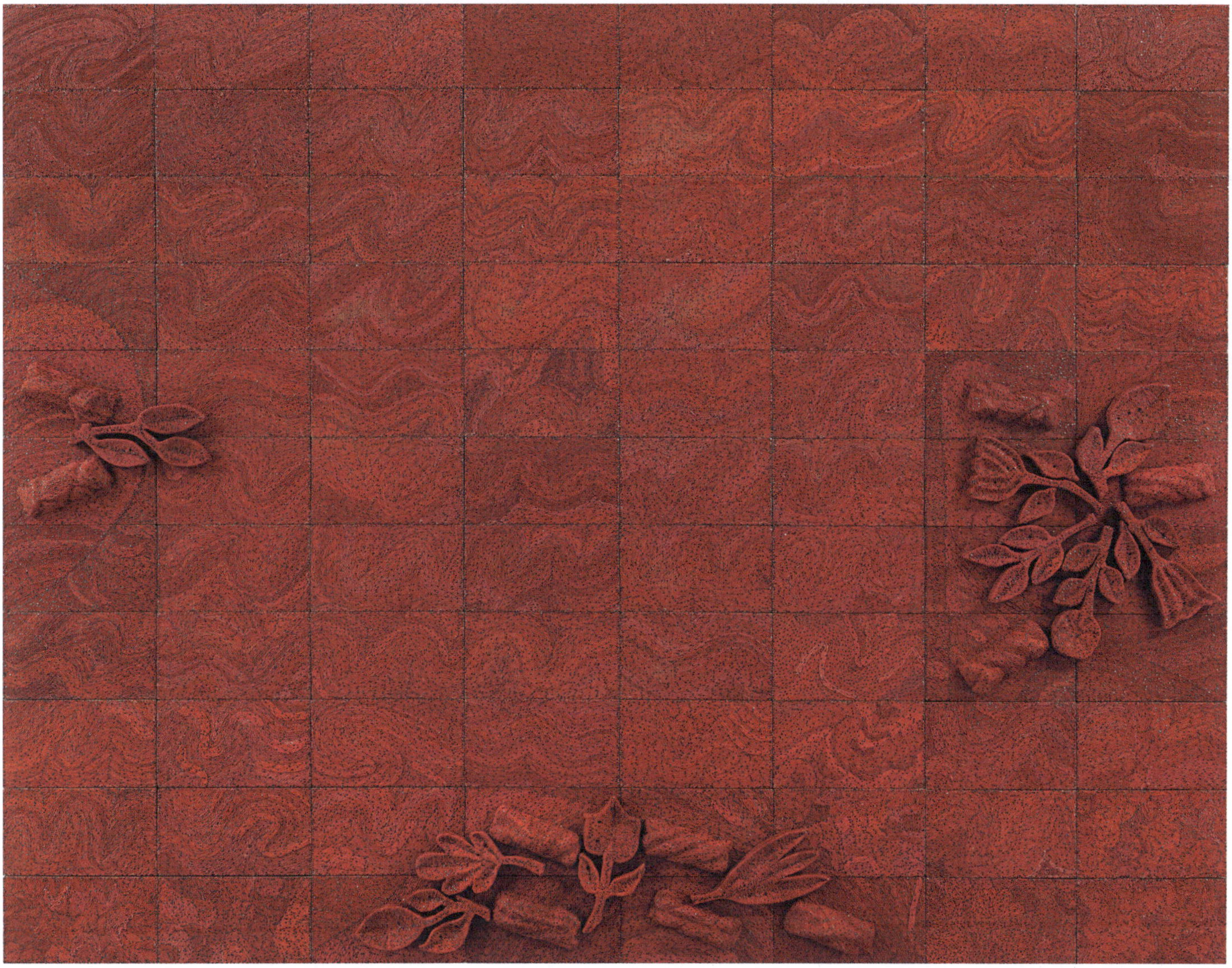

Tightrope: It is Green 8
2023, three-dimensional wall piece with woven electrical wires on panel, 318.8 × 251.5 × 8.9 cm

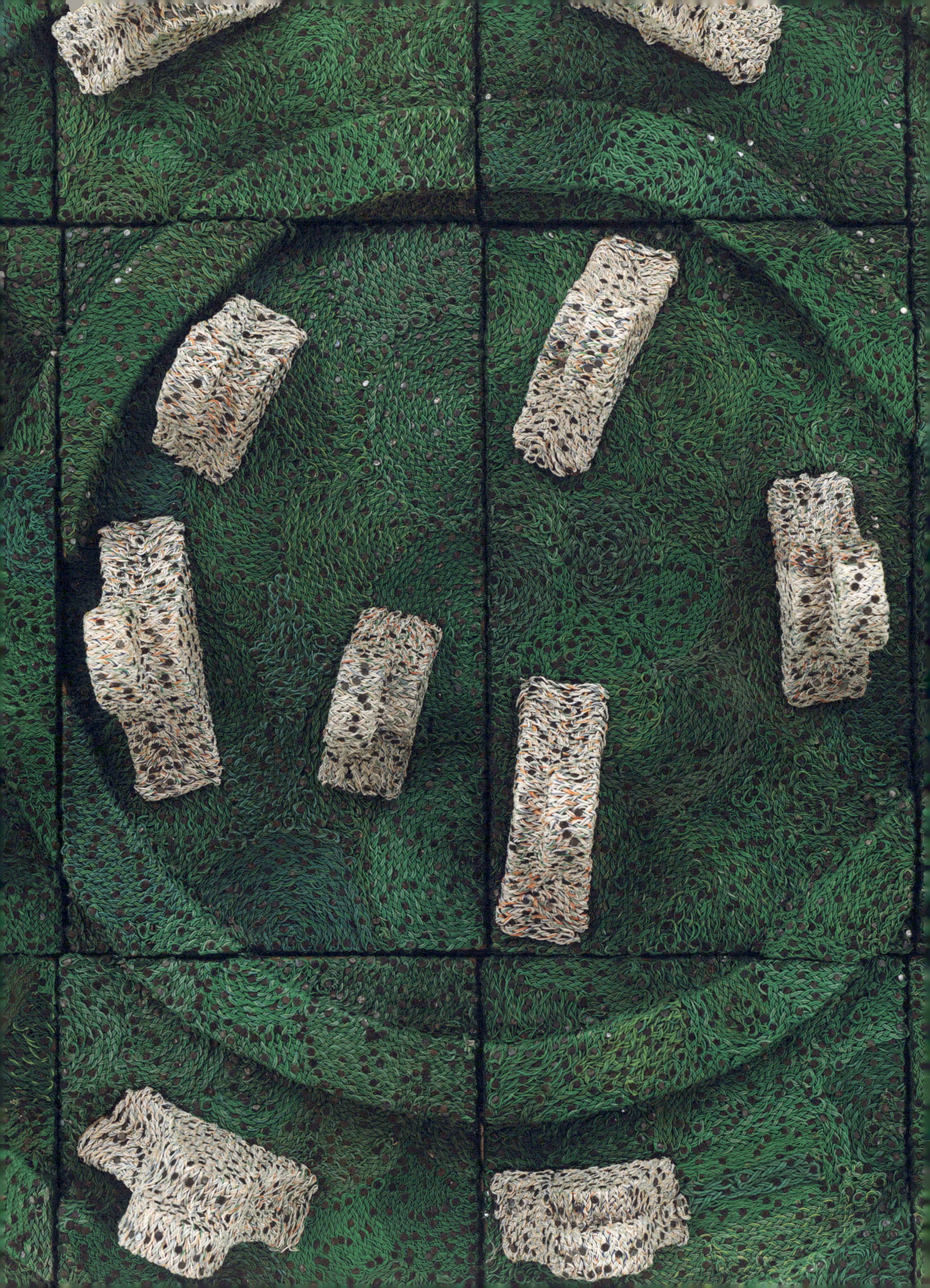

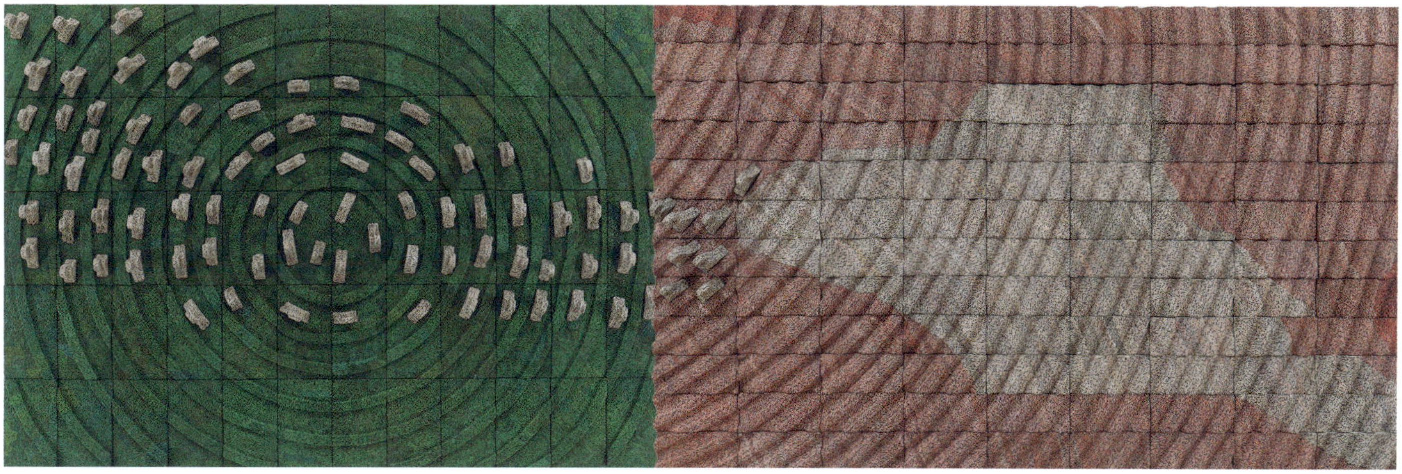

Veiled Whispers
2022, three-dimensional wall piece with woven electrical wires and other components on wood panels, 200.7 × 571.5 × 20.3 cm

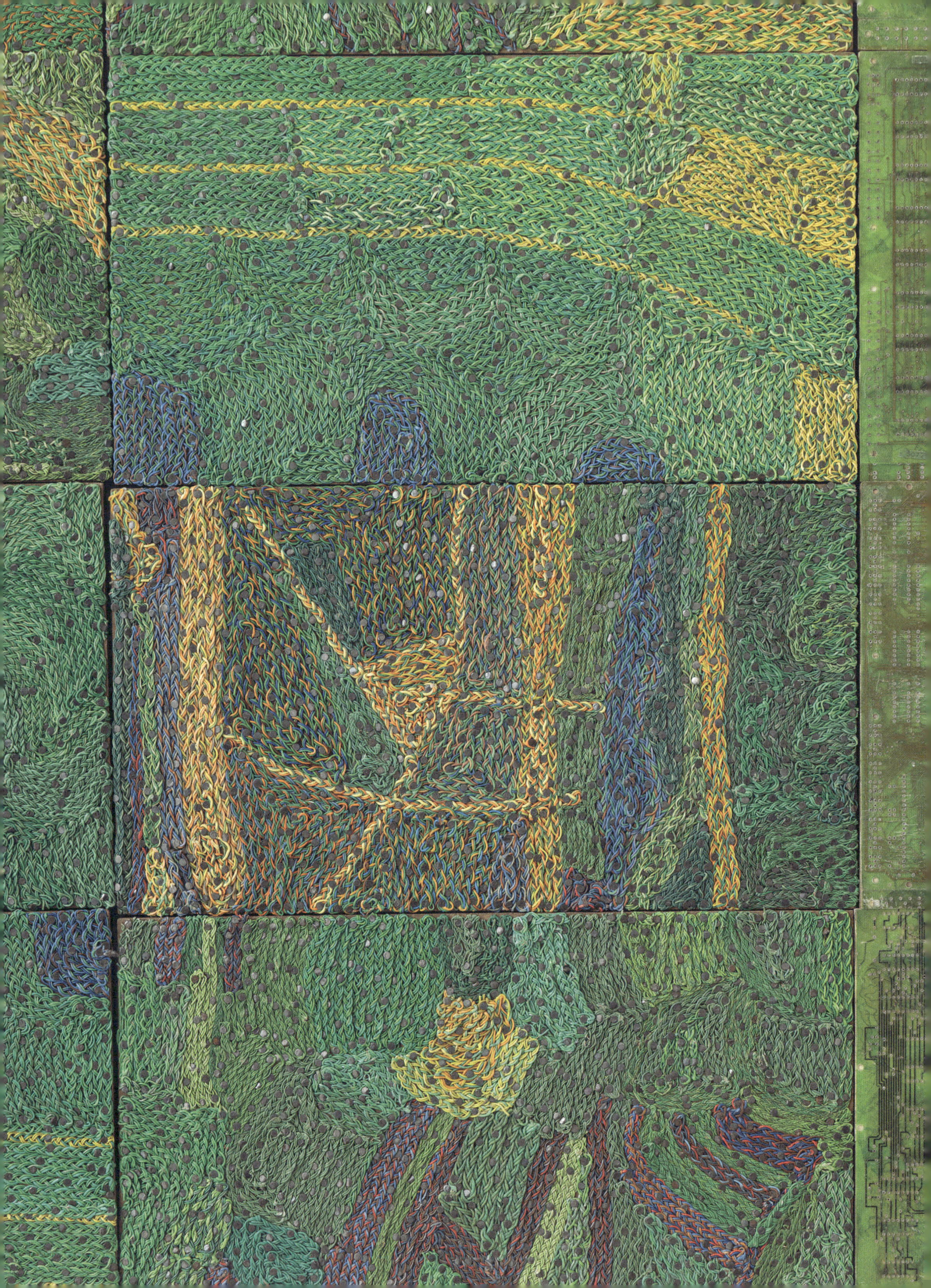

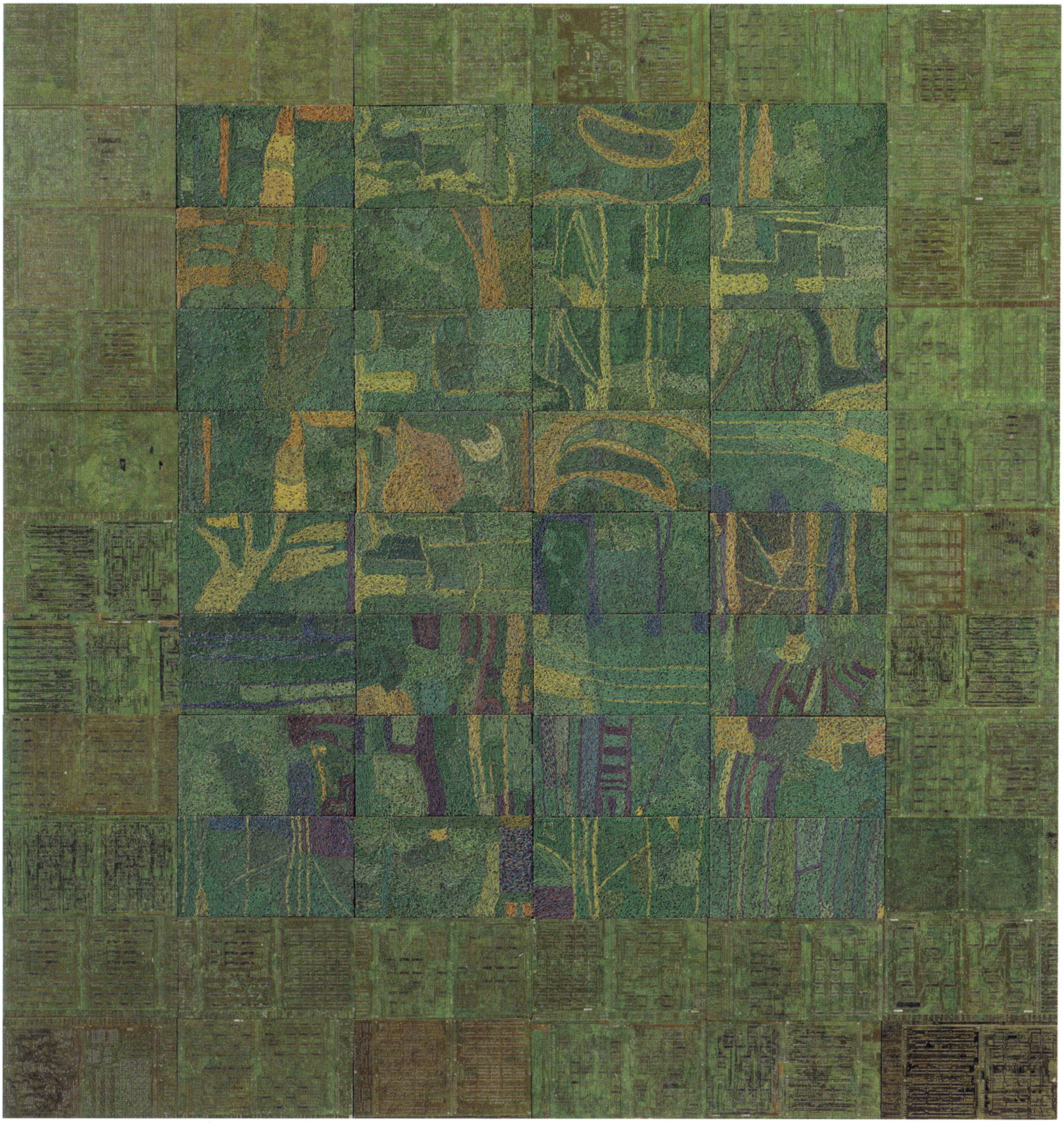

Tightrope: Behind the Processor No.1
2023, reclaimed electrical wires and components
on panel, 276 × 160 × 2 cm

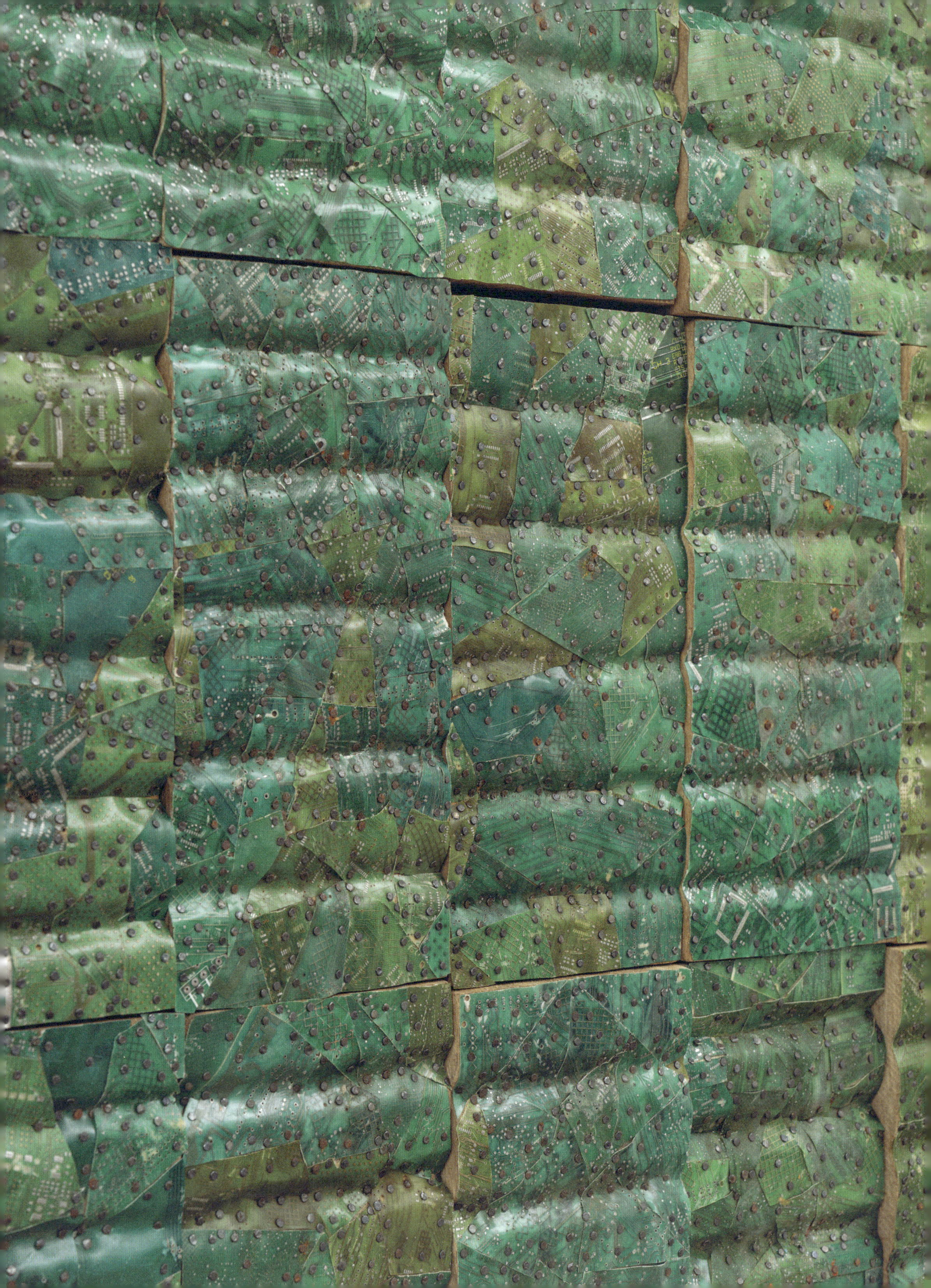

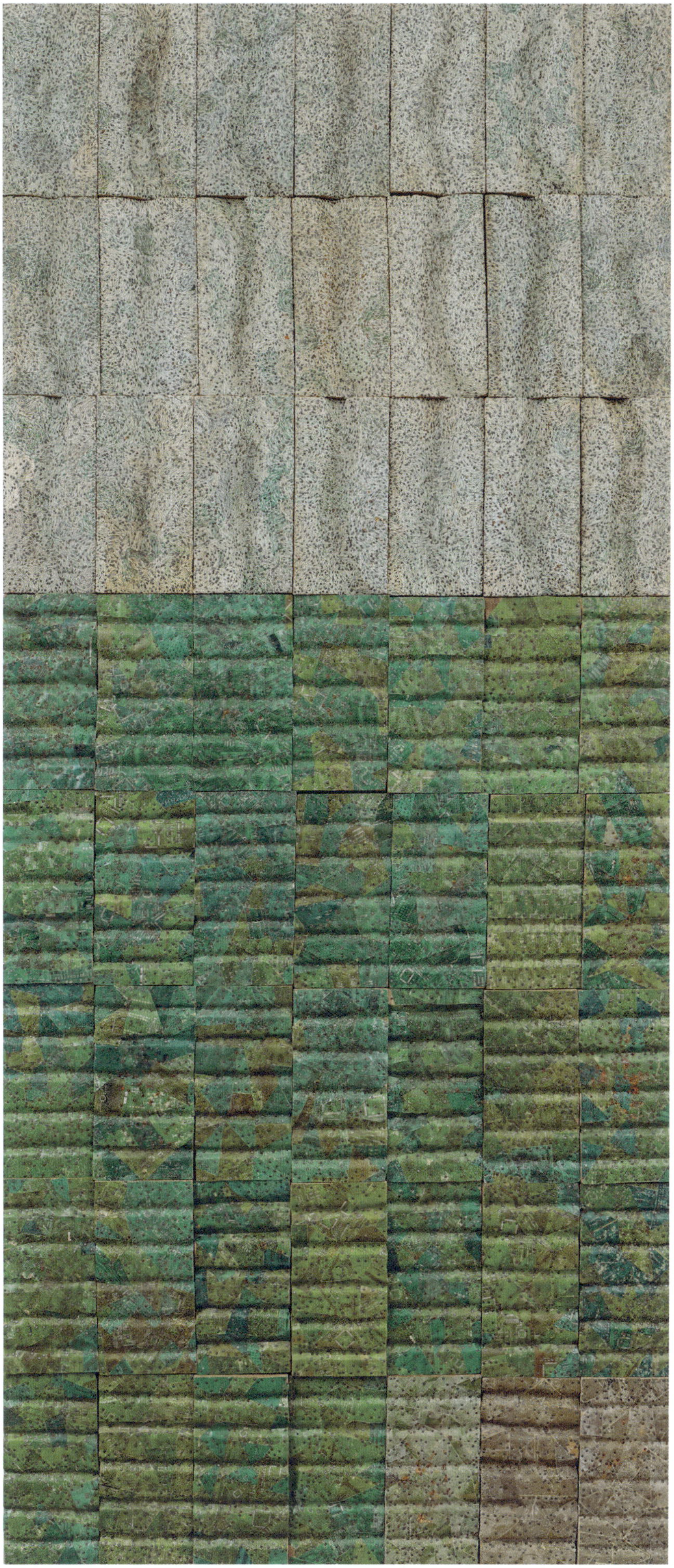

Tightrope: We are all Green: Swollen Waves
2020, reclaimed electrical wires and components on panel, 280 × 120 × 6 cm

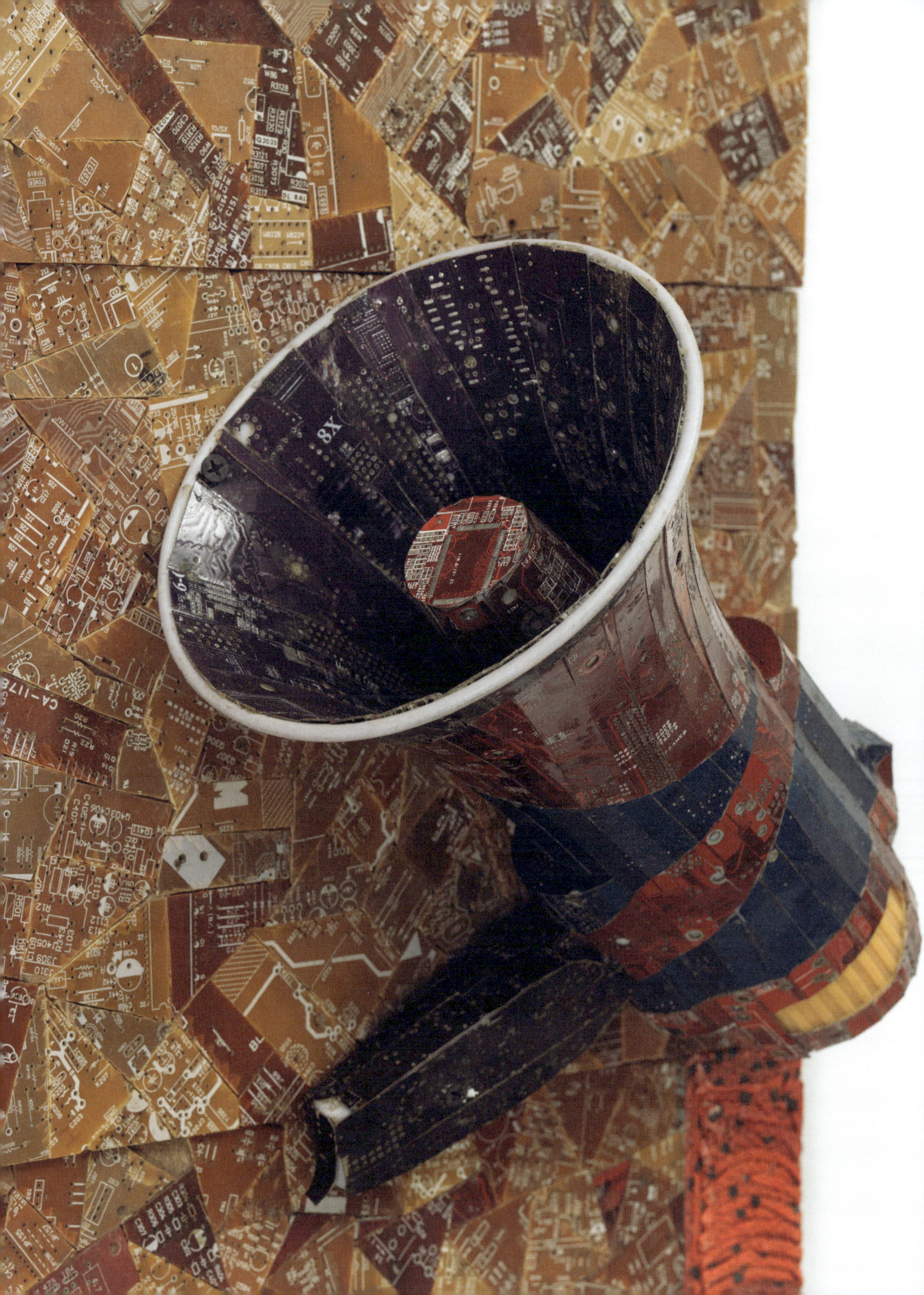

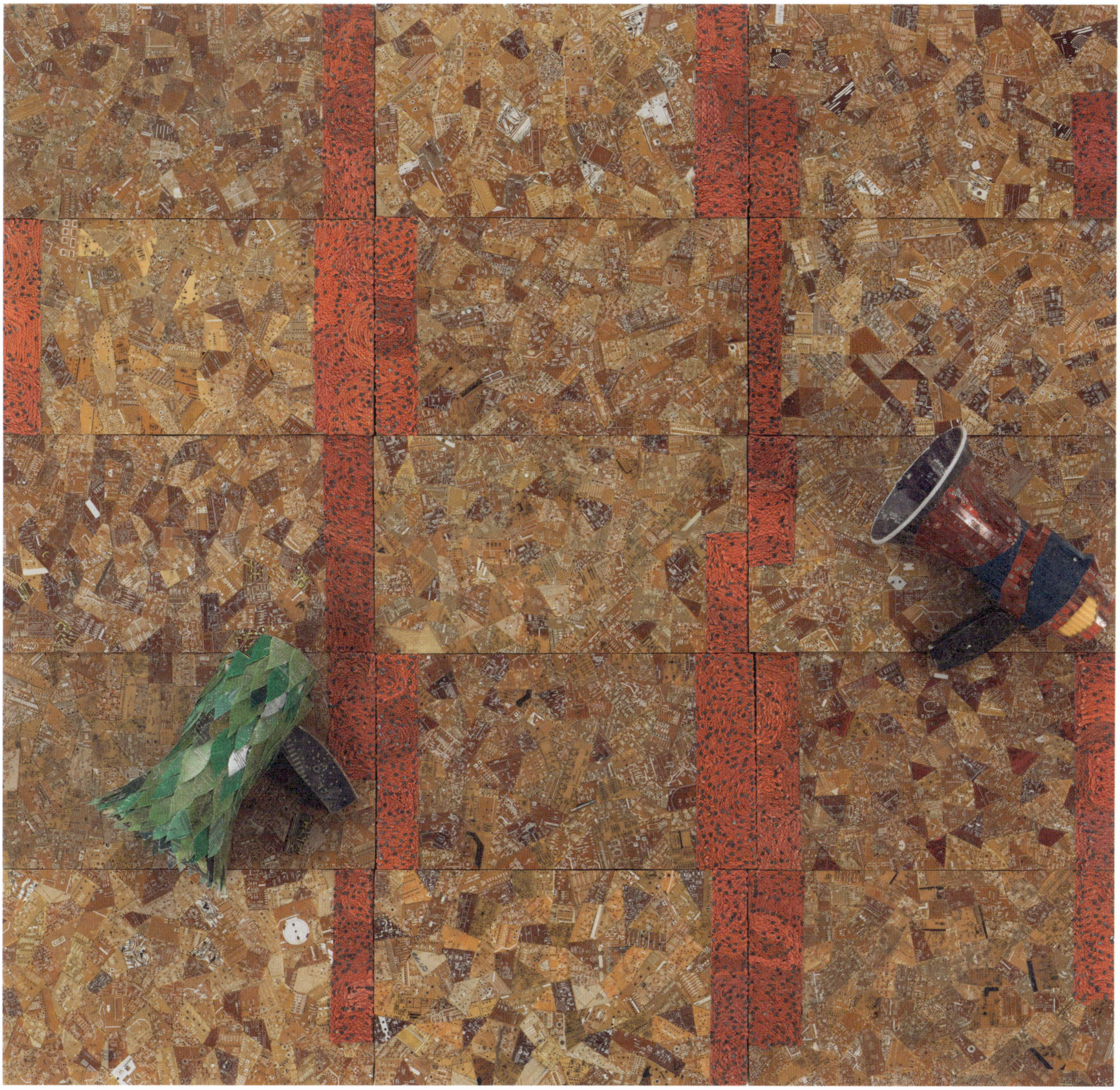

Tightrope: Echo!?
2021, reclaimed electrical wires and components
on panel with two megaphones, 114.9 × 120 × 15.2 cm

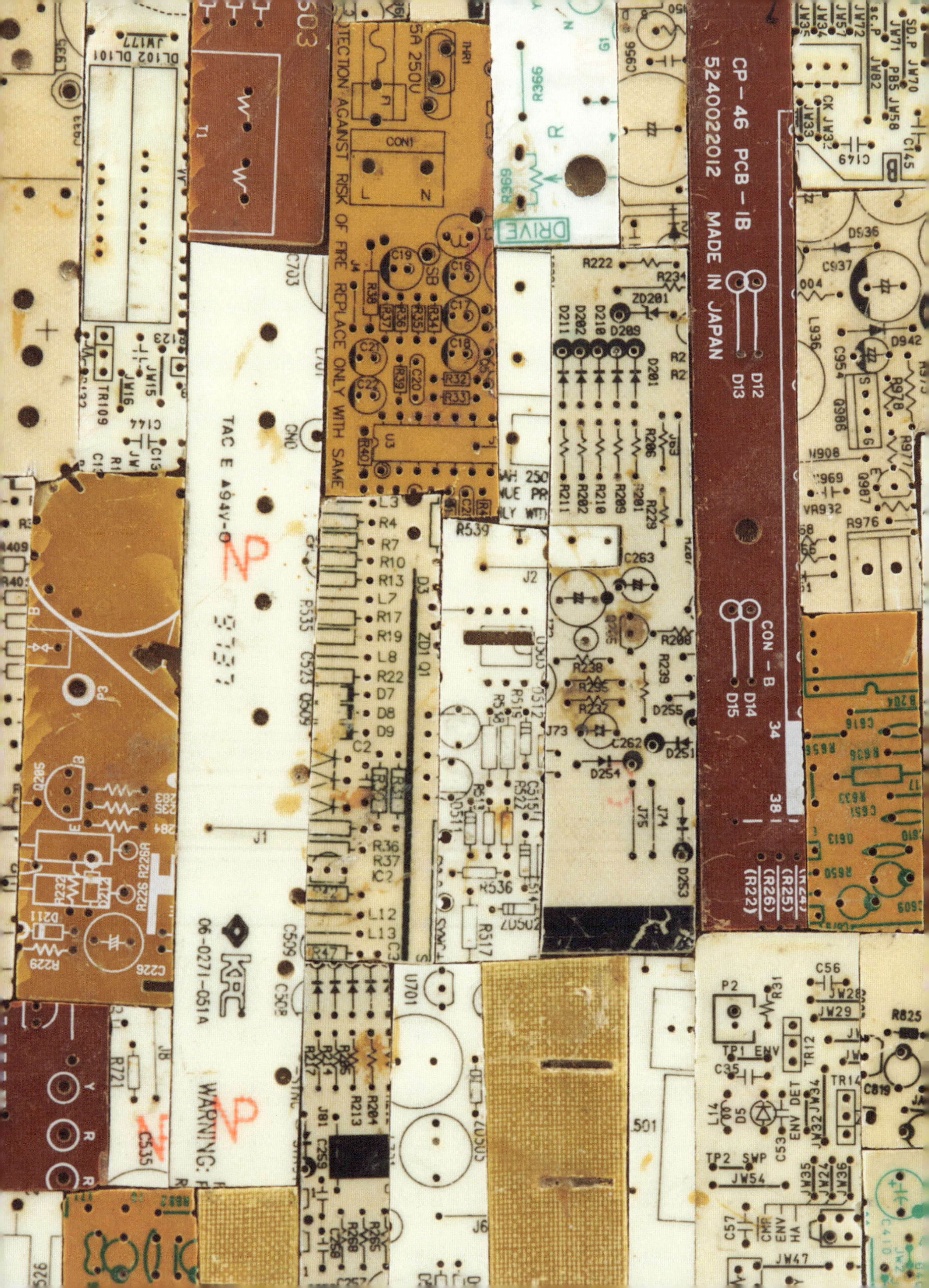

CP-46 PCB-1B
5240022012
MADE IN JAPAN
CON-B
DRIVE
TECTION AGAINST RISK OF FIRE REPLACE ONLY WITH SAME
5A 250V
TAC E 94V-0
06-0271-051A
WARNING:

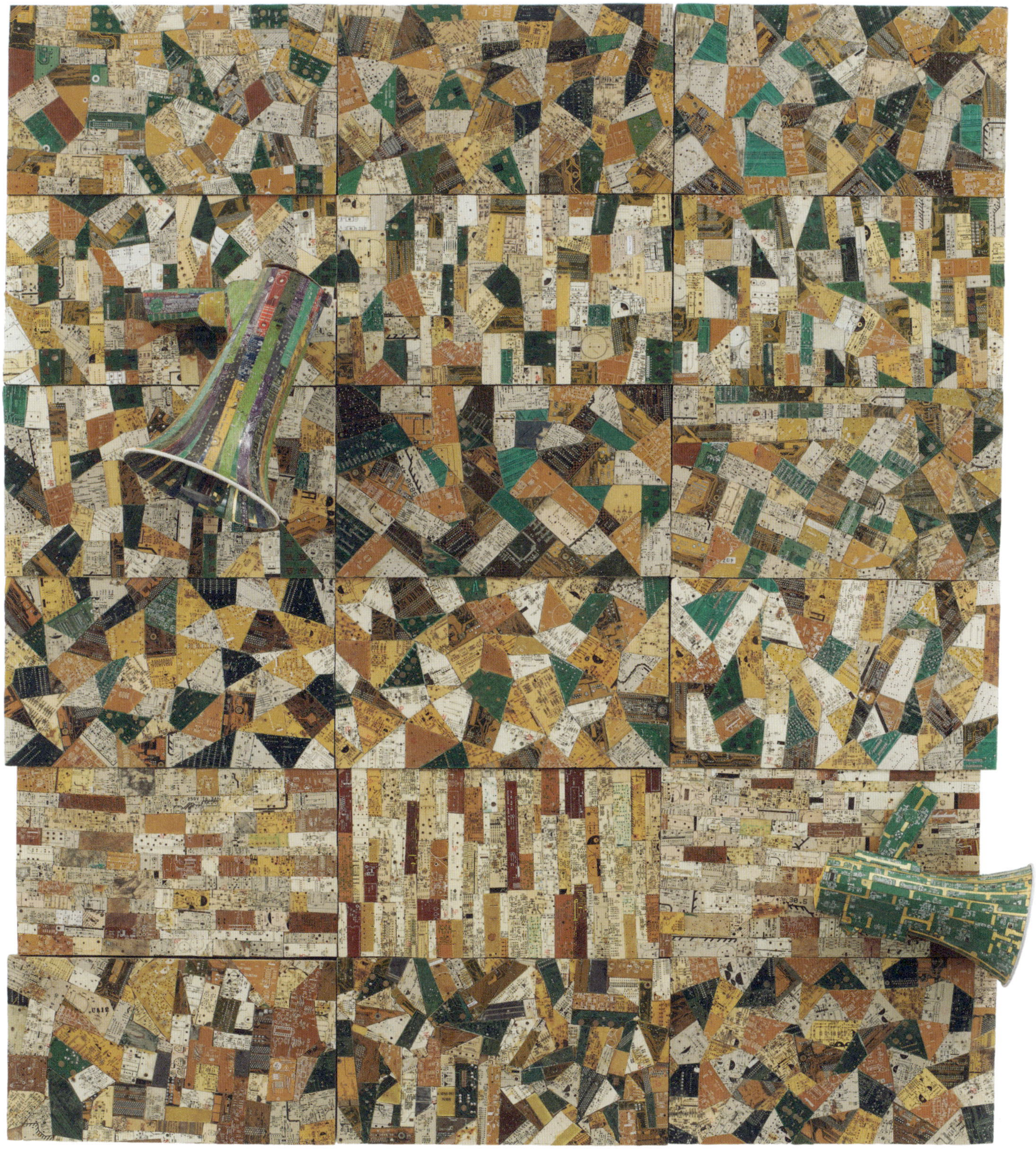

Tightrope: Echo!?
2021, reclaimed electrical components on panel
with two megaphones, 139 × 125 × 23 cm

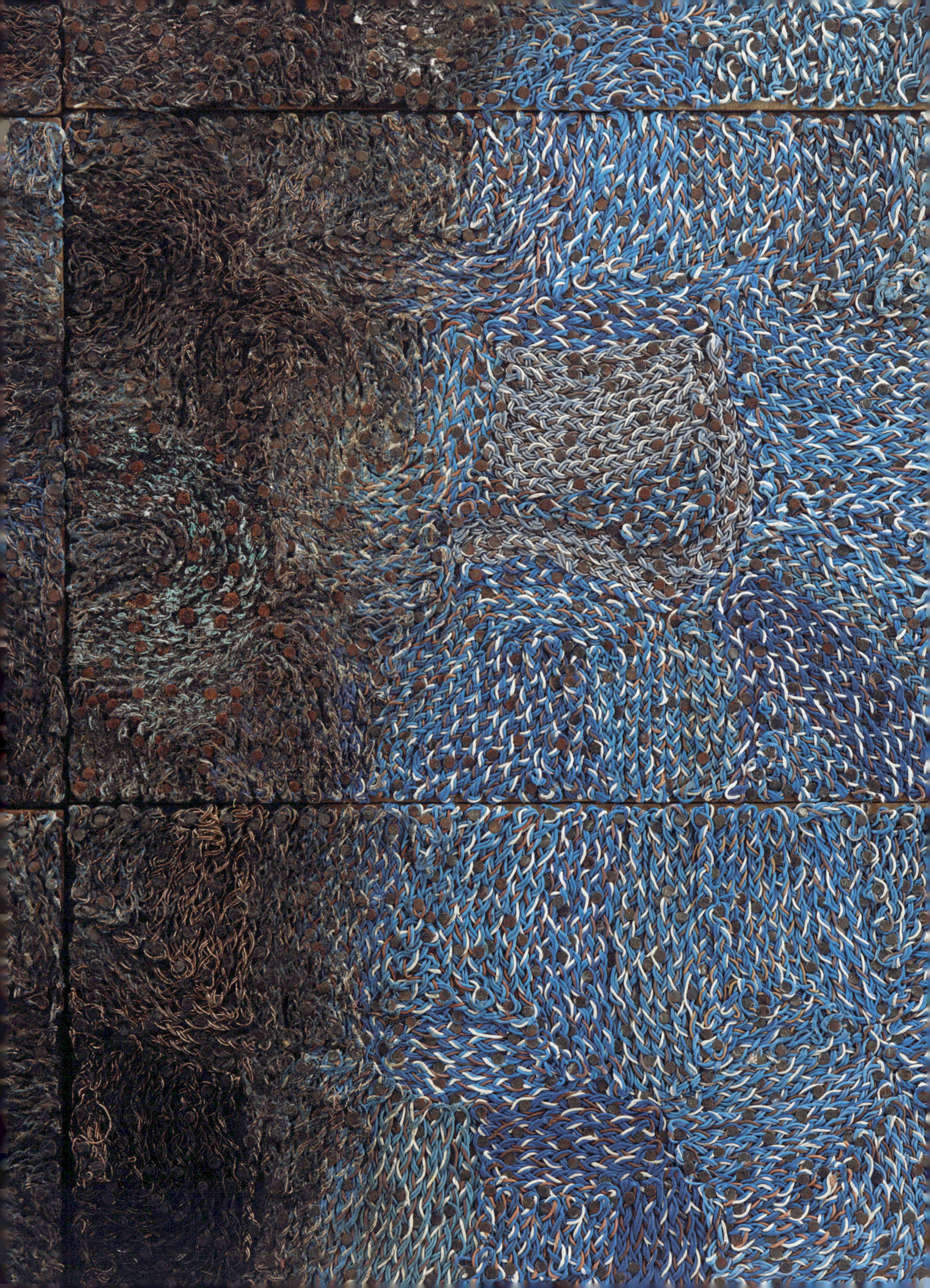

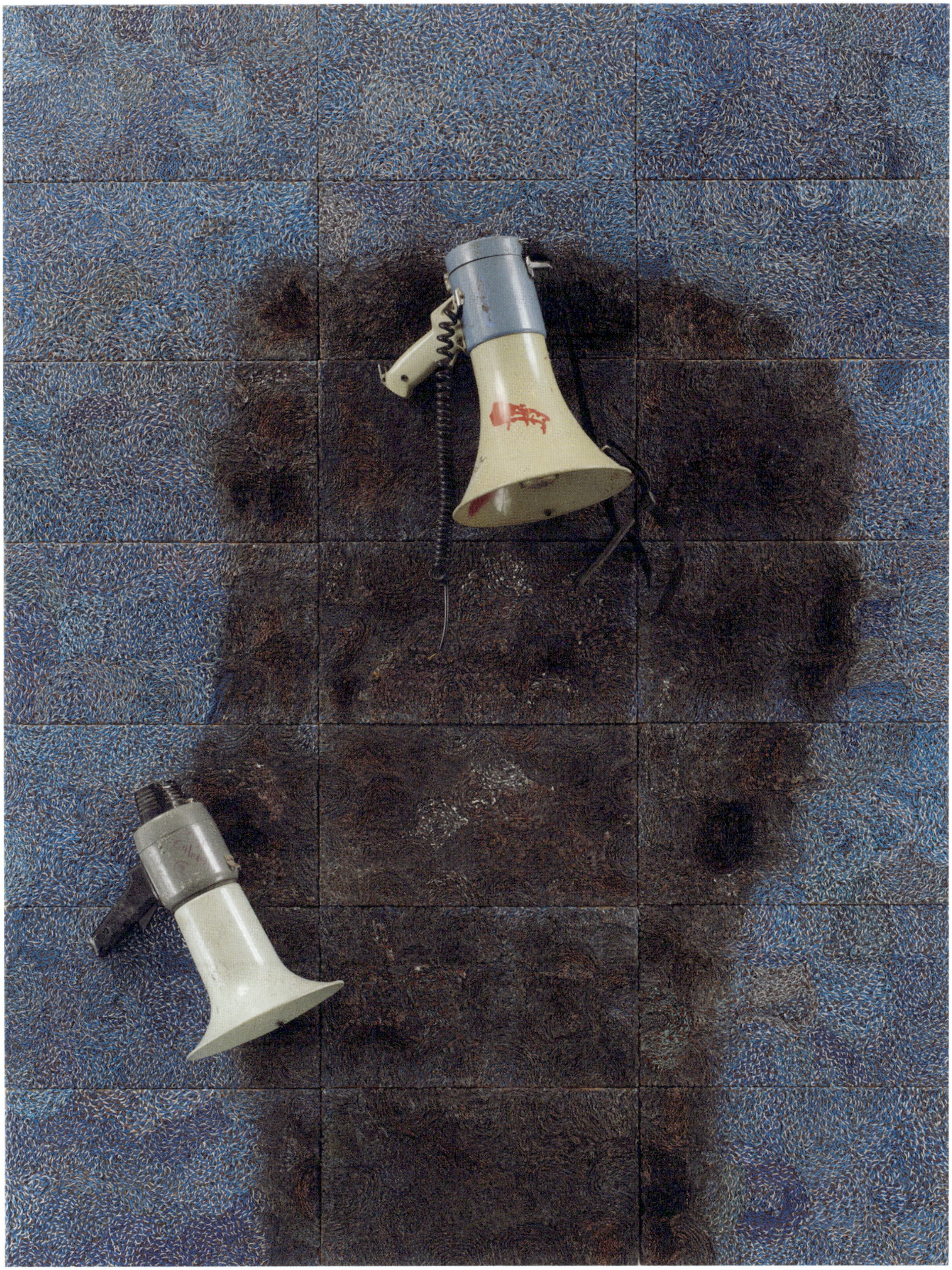

Tightrope: Echo!?
2021, reclaimed electrical wires and components
on panel with two megaphones, 161 × 120 × 24 cm

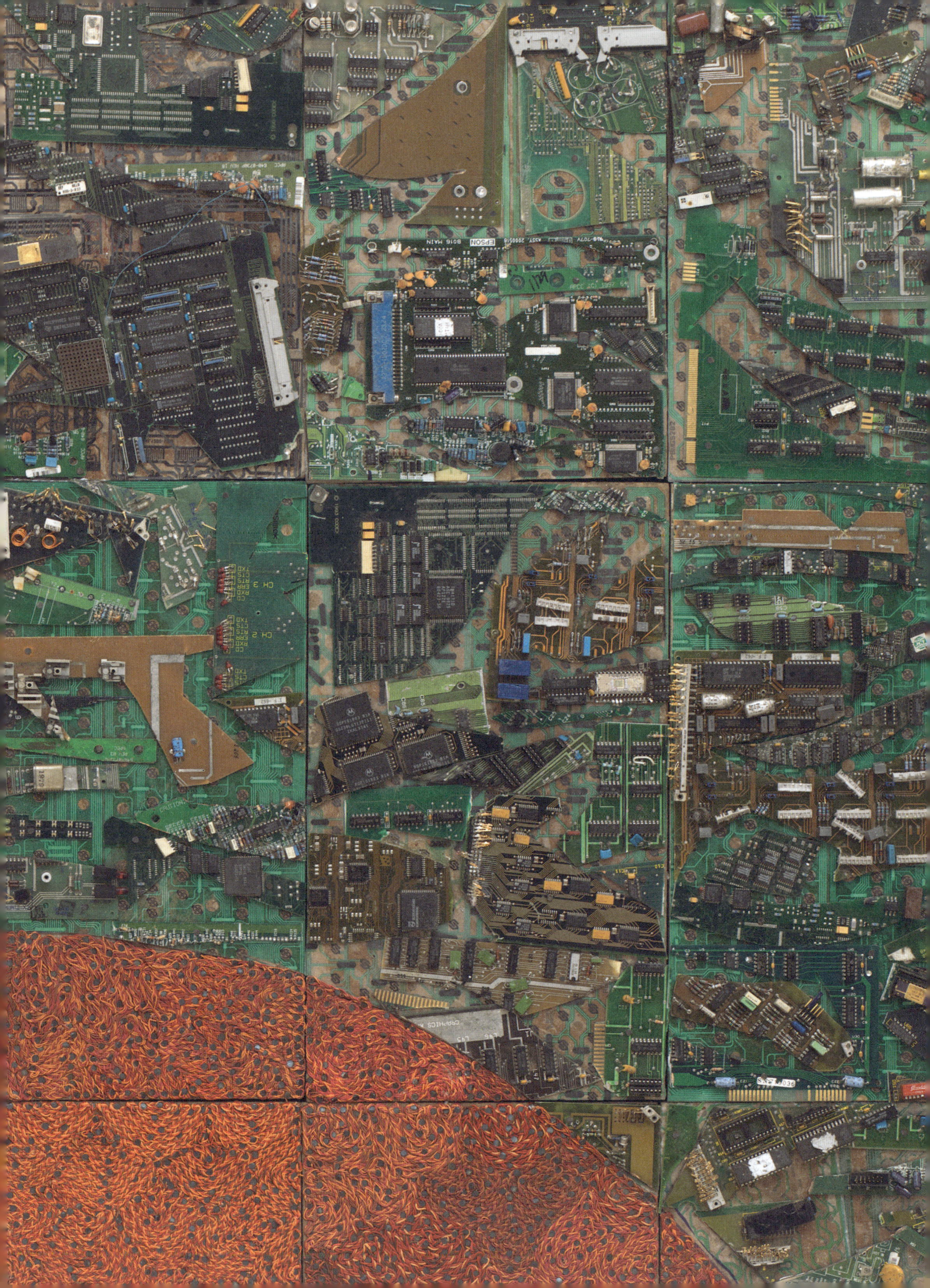

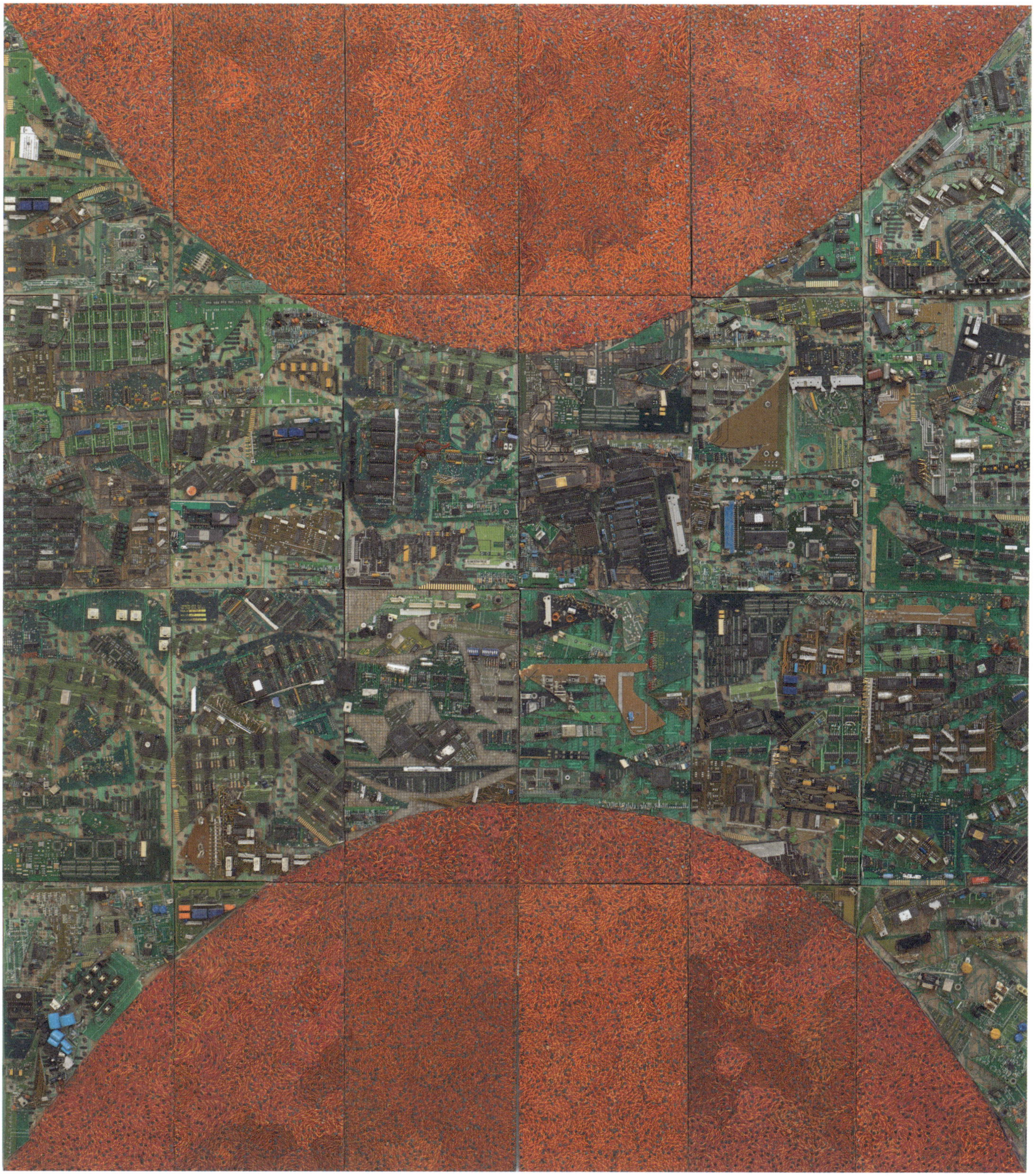

Tightrope: (4) While Observing...
2018, reclaimed electrical wires and components on panel, 160 × 139 cm

LIST OF EXHIBITED WORKS

Tightrope: Behind the Flowers
2017, reclaimed electronic components and wire on panel, 162.6 × 320 cm

—

Tightrope: High Pitch and Low Pitch
2021, reclaimed electrical components on panel, 208.3 × 481.3 cm

—

Tightrope: Evolution (1)
2017, reclaimed electrical wires on panel, 279.4 × 422.3 cm

—

Tightrope: Echo!?
2021, reclaimed electrical wires and components on panel, 365.8 × 480.1 cm
Courtesy of Christen Sveaas Art Collection

—

Tightrope: (20) While Observing…
2018, reclaimed electrical wires on panel, 208.6 × 321.3 cm

—

Tightrope: Noiseless 18
2019, reclaimed electrical wires and components on panel, 254.6 × 160.7 cm
Courtesy of Bill and Christy Gautreaux Collection, Kansas City, Mo., USA

—

Tightrope: 99
2009–2014, reclaimed electronic components on panel, 200 × 481.3 cm

—

Tightrope: Concave Triangle No.2
2020, reclaimed electrical wires and computer keys on wood, 185 × 185 × 60 cm

—

Tightrope: Concave Triangle No.3
2020, reclaimed electrical wires and watch faces on wood, 185 × 185 × 60 cm

—

Tightrope: Concave Triangle No.4
2020, reclaimed electrical wires and computer keys on wood, 185 × 185 × 60 cm

—

Mewezageb
date unknown, metal, cloth and buttons, 96 × 75 cm
Courtesy of the Museum of Everything

Melayo
2003–2004, buttons on hessian, 130 × 163 cm
Courtesy of the Museum of Everything

—

Chenet
2007, clothes, yarn and stitch on canvas, 160 × 119 cm

—

What is Love? (1)
2007, yarn and stitch on canvas, 188 × 132 cm

—

Yemegnot Alem
2001, yarn, stitch and buttons on canvas, 190 × 164 cm

—

Aremoch
2003–2004, yarn, bottlecaps and fabric on burlap mounted on canvas, 104 × 132 cm
Courtesy of private collection

—

Monkeys, Frogs and Televisions
2005, mud and straw, installation, dimensions variable
Courtesy of the Museum of Everything

—

Bareness
2014, ceramics, installation, dimensions variable

—

Untitled
2005–2010, ceramics, installation, dimensions variable

—

Tightrope: Behind the Processor No.6
2022, three-dimensional wall piece with woven electrical wires and other components on wood panels, 253 × 400 × 12 cm
Courtesy of private collection

—

Tightrope: It is Green 8
2023, three-dimensional wall piece with woven electrical wires on panel, 318.8 × 251.5 × 8.9 cm

Veiled Whispers
2022, three-dimensional wall piece with woven electrical wires and other components on wood panels, 200.7 × 571.5 × 20.3 cm

—

Tightrope: Behind the Processor No.1
2023, reclaimed electrical wires and components on panel, 276 × 160 × 2 cm
Courtesy of private collection

—

Tightrope: We are all Green: Swollen Waves
2020, reclaimed electrical wires and components on panel, 280 × 120 × 6 cm

—

Tightrope: Echo!?
2021, reclaimed electrical wires and components on panel with two megaphones, 114.9 × 120 × 15.2 cm

—

Tightrope: Echo!?
2021, reclaimed electrical components on panel with two megaphones, 139 × 125 × 23 cm

—

Tightrope: Echo!?
2021, reclaimed electrical wires and components on panel with two megaphones, 161 × 120 × 24 cm

—

Tightrope: (4) While Observing…
2018, reclaimed electrical wires and components on panel, 160 × 139 cm
Courtesy of private collection, New York

All works courtesy of the Artist, James Cohan, New York, and GRIMM, Amsterdam | London | New York unless otherwise noted.

The following non-exhibited works have also been featured in the publication: *Messil 3 (self portrait)*, courtesy of private collection; *Migueb 1, Min Neber (what is it)*, courtesy of private collection; *Tightrope: Noiseless 20*, courtesy of collection of Lisa and Steven Tananbaum.

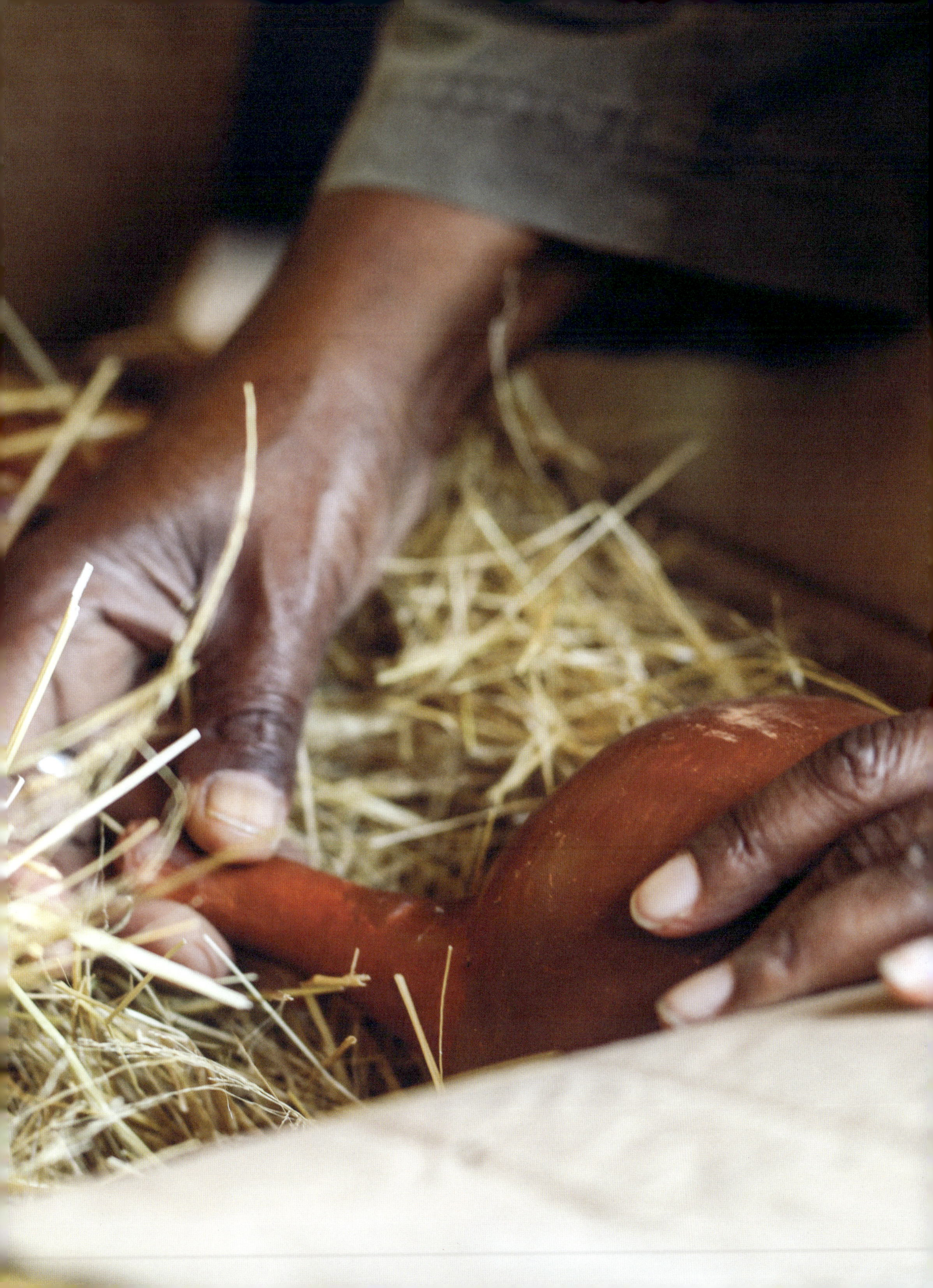

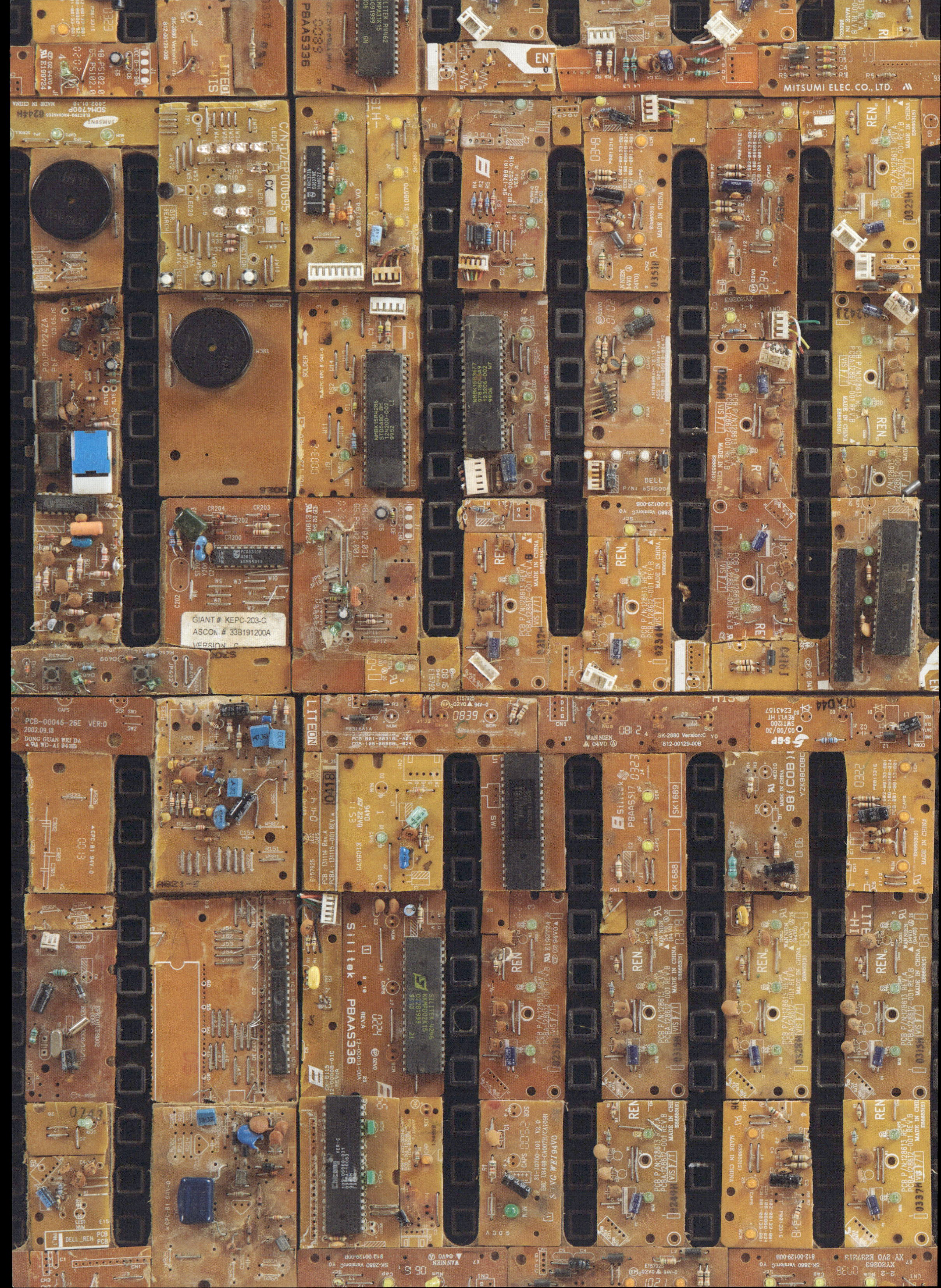

MITSUMI ELEC. CO., LTD.
GIANT # KEPC-203-C
ASCON # 33B191200A
VERSION C
PBAAS336
LITEON
DELL

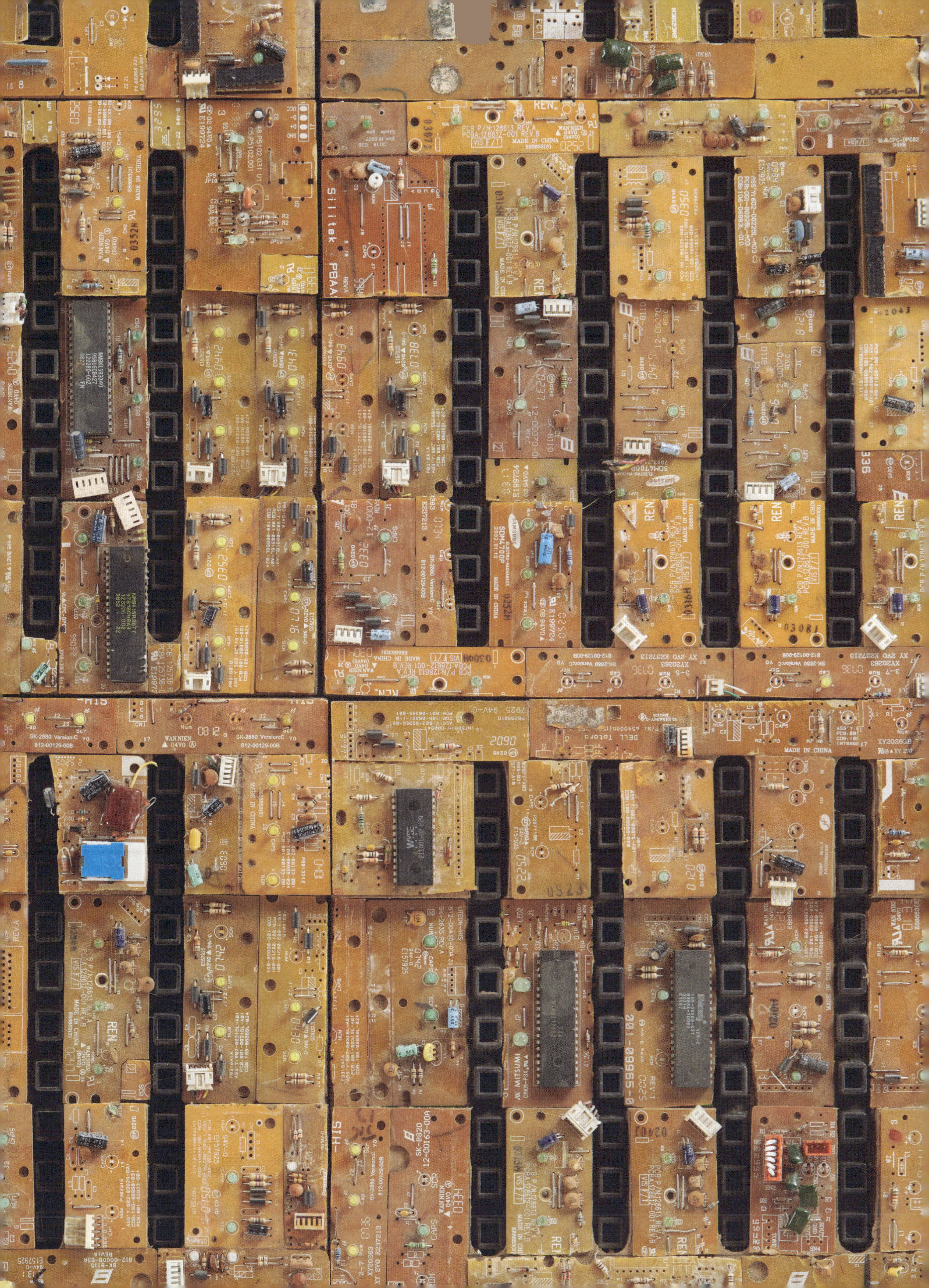

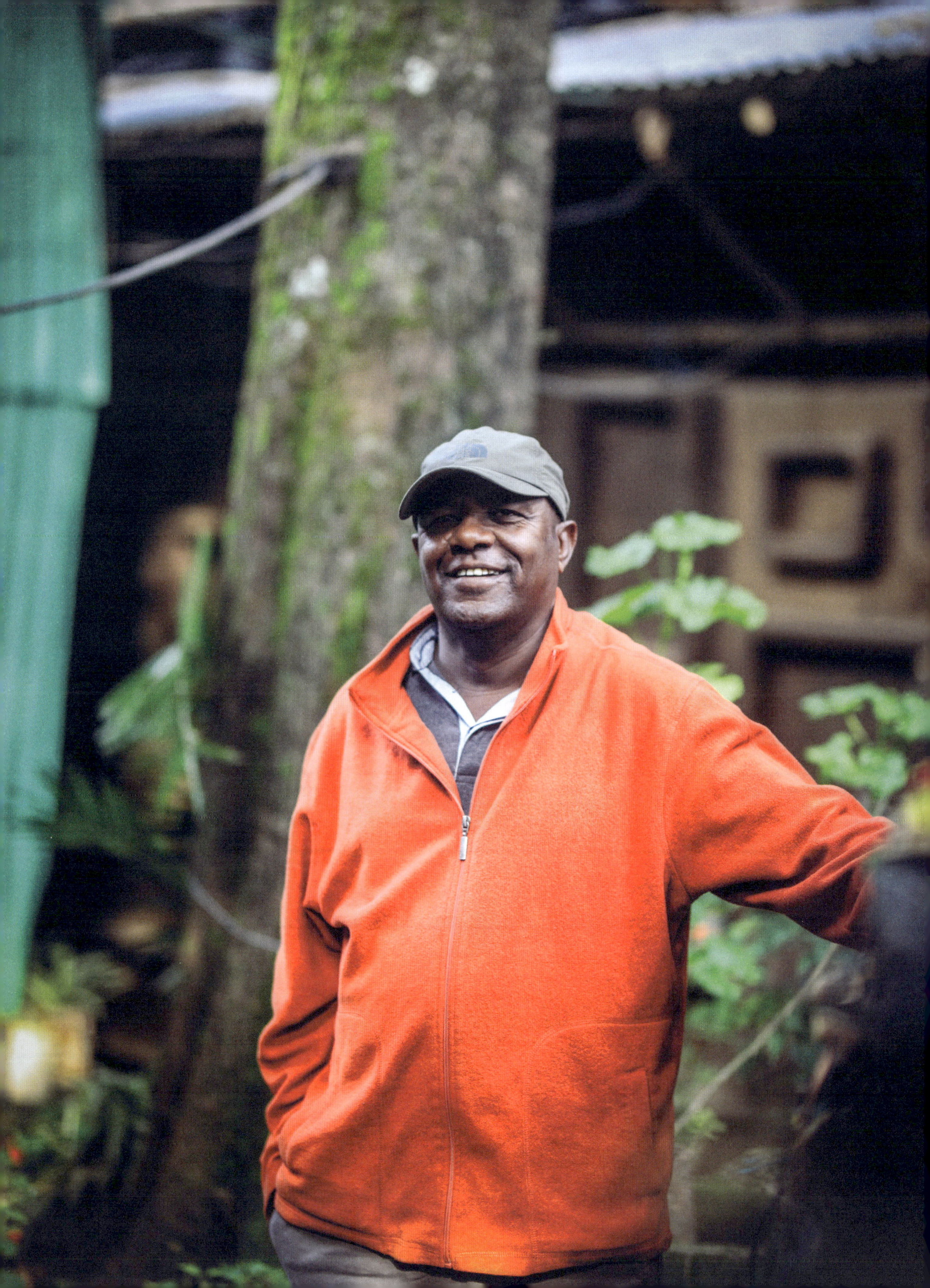

EXHIBITIONS, AWARDS & COLLECTIONS

ELIAS SIME

Born in 1968 in Addis Ababa, Ethiopia
Lives and works in Addis Ababa, Ethiopia

EDUCATION

1990
BFA in Graphic Art from School of Fine Arts and Design at Addis Ababa University, Addis Ababa, Ethiopia

AWARDS

2019
Shortlisted for Hugo Boss Prize, Solomon R. Guggenheim Foundation, New York, NY, USA
—
African Art Award, National Museum of African Art, Smithsonian Institution, Washington, D.C., USA

COMMISSIONS

2019
National Museum of African Art, Smithsonian Institution, Washington, D.C., USA
—
2018
Facebook Artist-in-Residence Program, Menlo Park, CA, USA

SOLO EXHIBITIONS

2023
Elias Sime: Eregata እርጋታ, Arnolfini, Bristol, UK
TIGHTROPE: አረንጓዴ ነው (IT IS GREEN), James Cohan, New York, NY, USA
Tightrope: Behind the Processor, GRIMM, Amsterdam, Netherlands
—
2021
TIGHTROPE: ECHO!?, James Cohan, New York, NY, USA

2020
Tightrope: Concave Triangles, GRIMM, Amsterdam, Netherlands
Currents 118: Elias Sime, St. Louis Art Museum, St. Louis, MO, USA
—
2019
Elias Sime: Tightrope, Ruth and Elmer Wellin Museum of Art, Hamilton College, Clinton, NY, USA, travelling to Akron Art Museum, Akron, OH, USA; Kemper Museum of Contemporary Art, Kansas City, MO, USA; Royal Ontario Museum, Toronto, Canada
Elias Sime: NOISELESS, James Cohan, New York, NY, USA
Elias Sime, Zoma Museum, Addis Ababa, Ethiopia
—
2018
Tightrope, GRIMM, Amsterdam, Netherlands
—
2017
Elias Sime: Twisted & Hidden, James Cohan, New York, NY, USA
—
2015
Elias Sime, James Cohan, New York, NY, USA
—
2013
Tightrope, British Council, Goethe-Institut, Istituto Italiano di Cultura, and Alliance Ethio-française, Addis Ababa, Ethiopia
—
2012
Eye of the Needle, Eye of the Heart, North Dakota Museum of Art, Grand Forks, ND, USA
—
2011
Ants and Ceramicists, British Council, Goethe-Institut, Istituto Italiano di Cultura and Alliance Ethio-française, Addis Ababa, Ethiopia
—
2010
Oedipus-Rex Opera, Sydney Opera House, Sydney, Australia

2009
Täarät-Täarät, Haunch of Venison, London, UK
Oedipus-Rex Opera, Walt Disney Concert Hall, Los Angeles, CA, USA
Eye of the Needle, Eye of the Heart, Santa Monica Museum of Art, Santa Monica, CA, USA
—
2008
What is Love?, Alliance Ethio-française, Addis Ababa, Ethiopia
—
2006
Metamorphosis, public mosaic sponsored by European Union and Zoma Contemporary Art Center, Addis Ababa, Ethiopia
GOTA Täarät-Täarät, Alliance Ethio-française, Addis Ababa, Ethiopia
—
2004
Min Neber, Istituto Italiano di Cultura, Addis Ababa, Ethiopia
—
2002
Retrospect Part 1, part of *Giziawi #1*, Jara Park, Addis Ababa, Ethiopia
—
1999
Hilton Addis Ababa, Addis Ababa, Ethiopia
—
1998
Addis Ababa University, Addis Ababa, Ethiopia
—
1996
United Nations Economic Commission for Africa, Addis Ababa, Ethiopia
—
1995
Organization of African Unity, Addis Ababa, Ethiopia
—
1993
Alliance Ethio-française, Addis Ababa, Ethiopia

GROUP EXHIBITIONS

2023
The Stuff of Life / The Life of Stuff, Sainsbury Centre, Norwich, UK
The Changing Landscape, Museum de Fundatie, Zwolle, Netherlands
Plastic World, Schirn Kunsthalle, Frankfurt am Main, Germany
Together…, Arkansas Museum of Fine Arts, Little Rock, AR, USA
I'll Be Your Mirror: Art and the Digital Screen, Modern Art Museum of Fort Worth, Forth Worth, TX, USA
—
2022
Life Altering: Selections from a Kansas City Collection, Faye G., Jo and James Stone Gallery, Boston University, Boston, MA, USA
The Milk of Dreams, Venice Biennale, curated by Cecilia Alemani, Venice, Italy
—
2021
Reclaiming Magic, Royal Academy of Arts, London, UK
Portals, NEON, Athens, Greece
Experience & Expression, Permanent Installation, Detroit Institute of the Arts, Detroit, MI, USA
Butterflies Frolicking on the Mud: Engendering Sensible Capital, Thailand Biennale 2021, Korat, Thailand
Networked Nature, Art Vault, Thoma Foundation, Santa Fe, NM, USA
—
2020
Allied with Power: African and Africa Diaspora Art from the Jorge M. Pérez Collection, Pérez Art Museum Miami, Miami, FL, USA
Recent Acquisitions by the Homestead Collection, Norval Foundation, Cape Town, South Africa
RELATIONS: Diaspora and Painting, PHI Foundation, Montreal, Canada
15th Anniversary Exhibition Where We Now Stand—In Order to Map the Future, 21st Century Museum of Contemporary Art, Kanazawa, Ishikawa, Japan
Second Careers: Two Tributaries in African Art, curated by Ugochukwu-Smooth C. Nzewi, Cleveland Museum of Art, Cleveland, OH, USA
Matereality—a testament to the challenge of tradition, curated by Andrea Lewis, Iziko South African National Gallery, Cape Town, South Africa
—
2019
Borders, James Cohan, New York, NY, USA
—
2018
I Was Raised on the Internet, Museum of Contemporary Art Chicago, Chicago, IL, USA
Grids, James Cohan, New York, NY, USA
—
2017
Abstract Minded: Works by Six Contemporary African Artists, N'Namdi Center for Contemporary Art, Detroit, MI, USA
Innovative Approaches, Honored Traditions: The Ruth and Elmer Wellin Museum of Art at Five Years; Highlights from the Permanent Collection, Ruth and Elmer Wellin Museum of Art, Hamilton College, Clinton, NY, USA
THE ART SHOW—Art of the New Millennium in Taguchi Art Collection, Museum of Modern Art Gunma, Gunma, Japan
—
2016
The Distance of a Day, Israel Museum, Jerusalem, Israel
Festival International d'Art Lyrique with Peter Sellars, Aix-en-Provence, France
—
2010
Stitches, Armory Center for the Arts, Pasadena, CA, USA
—
2008
The Essential Art of African Textiles: Design Without End, Metropolitan Museum of Art, New York, NY, USA
Flow, Studio Museum in Harlem, New York, NY, USA

2006
Green Flame, New Crowned Hope Festival, directed by Peter Sellars, Vienna, Austria
Goethe-Institut — Addis Wubet and Zoma Contemporary Art Center, Addis Ababa, Ethiopia
—
2005
Hidden Talent, European Union and Zoma Contemporary Art Center, Addis Ababa, Ethiopia
Addis Abeba Zare, Addis Ababa University School of Fine Arts and Design, Addis Ababa, Ethiopia
—
2004
Dak'Art 2004, the 6th Biennale of Contemporary African Art, Dakar, Senegal
—
2003
Min Neber, Istituto Italiano di Cultura, Addis Ababa, Ethiopia
—
2002
Giziawi #1, Meskel Square, Addis Ababa, Ethiopia
—
2000
Istituto Italiano di Cultura, Addis Ababa, Ethiopia
—
1999
Alliance Ethio-française, Addis Ababa, Ethiopia
—
1997
Goshu Gallery, Addis Ababa, Ethiopia
Joint Exhibition of Dutch-Ethiopian Artists in the Netherlands and in Addis Ababa Fine Arts School, Ethiopia
—
1995
National Museum of Ethiopia, Addis Ababa, Ethiopia

PUBLIC COLLECTIONS

The Ahmanson Foundation, Los Angeles, CA, USA
Arkansas Museum of Fine Arts, Little Rock, AR, USA
Chrysler Museum of Art, Norfolk, VA, USA
Denning House, Stanford University, Stanford, CA, USA
Denver Art Museum, Denver, CO, USA
Des Moines Art Center, Des Moines, IA, USA
Detroit Institute of Arts, Detroit, MI, USA
Fondation H, Madagascar
Samuel P. Harn Museum of Art, University of Florida, Gainesville, FL, USA
Hood Museum of Art, Dartmouth College, Hanover, NH, USA
Israel Museum, Jerusalem, Israel
Kemper Museum of Contemporary Art, Kansas City, MO, USA
Kistefos Museum, Jevnaker, Norway
Metropolitan Museum of Art, New York, NY, USA
Newark Museum, Newark, NJ, USA
N'Namdi Center for Contemporary Art, Detroit, MI, USA
North Carolina Museum of Art, Raleigh, NC, USA
North Dakota Museum of Art, Grand Forks, ND, USA
Norval Foundation, Cape Town, South Africa
Pérez Art Museum Miami, Miami, FL, USA
The Phillips Collection, Washington, D.C., USA
Pizzuti Collection at the Columbus Museum of Art, Columbus, OH, USA
Princeton University Art Museum, Princeton, NJ, USA
Rollins Museum of Art, Rollins College, Orlando, FL
Royal Ontario Museum, Toronto, Canada
Saint Louis Art Museum, St. Louis, MO, USA
Toledo Museum of Art, Toledo, OH, USA
Utah Museum of Fine Arts, Salt Lake City, UT, USA
Virginia Museum of Fine Arts, Richmond, VA, USA
Ruth and Elmer Wellin Museum of Art, Hamilton College, Clinton, NY, USA
21st Century Museum of Contemporary Art, Kanazawa, Japan

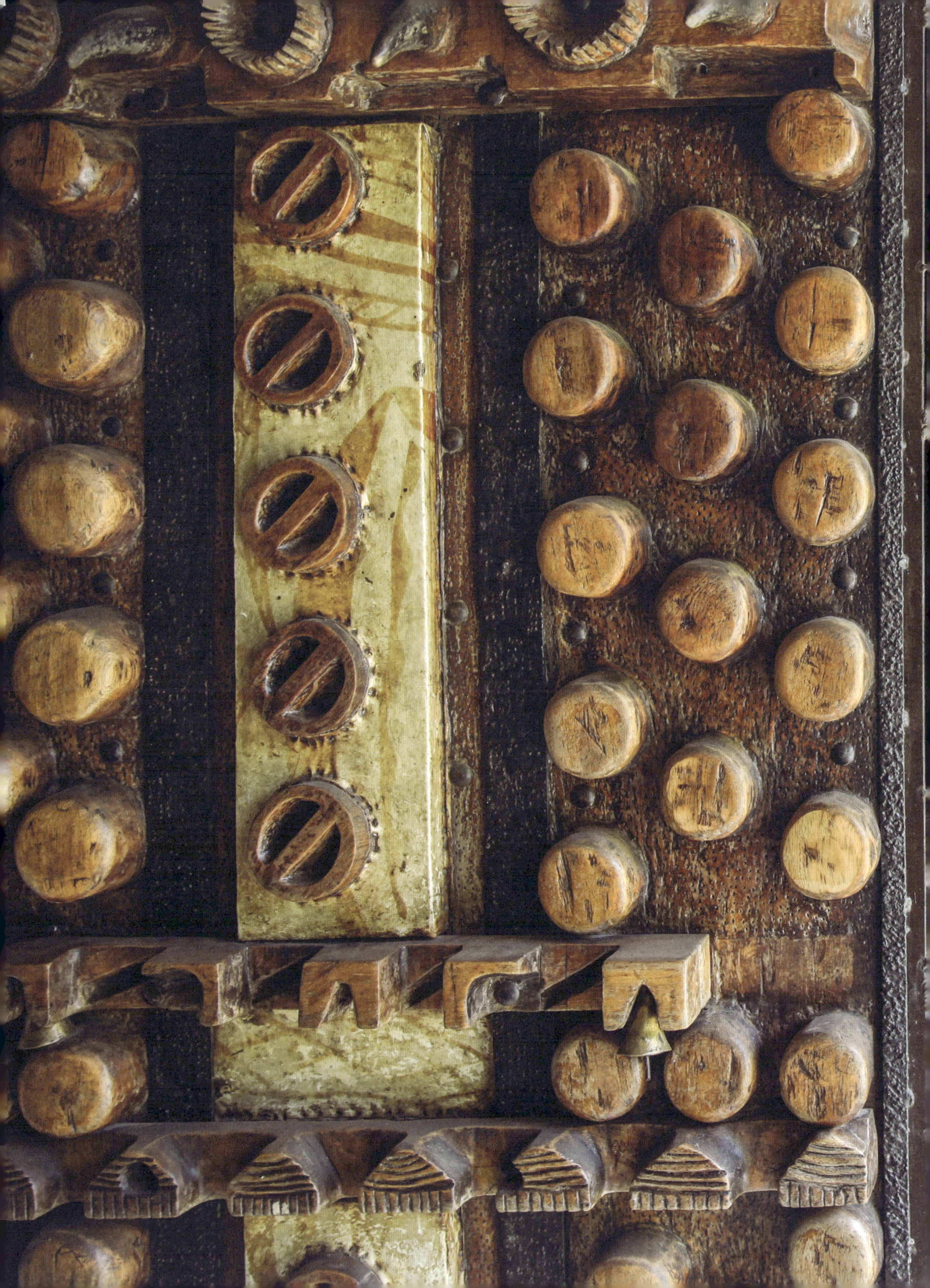

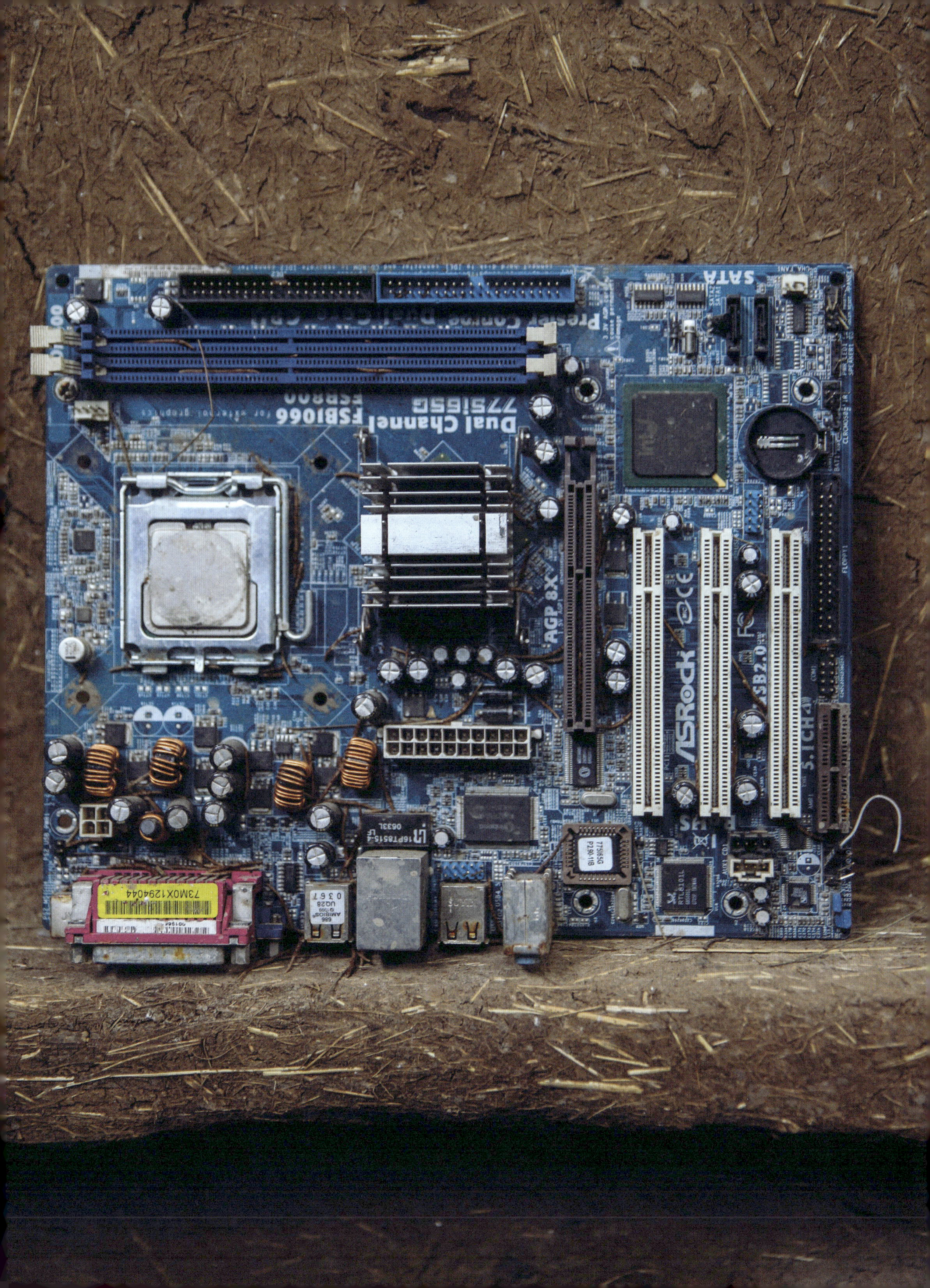
Dual Channel FSB1066
775i65G
AGP 8X
ASRock
SATA
USB2.0
73MOX1294044

ENDNOTES

Looking slowly

1 — Elias Sime quoted in 'Elias Sime: Elias Sime on living and working with technology' by Zach Hatfield in *Art Forum*, 3 September 2019, www.artforum.com/interviews/elias-sime-80540 [accessed 9 May 2023]

2 — Elias Sime in conversation with author and Meskerem Assegued, 21 June 2023

3 — Sime, 21 June 2023

4 — Meskerem Assegued, *Tightrope: ECHO!? Elias Sime*, 2021, www.jamescohan.com/exhibitions/elias-sime4 [accessed 9 May 2023]

5 — Elias Sime quoted in 'A retrospective observation of Elias Sime' by Meskerem Assegued in *African Identities*, Volume 6, 2008, Issue 4: *Ethiopia The New Millennium*, p477

6 — Katy Donoghue, 'Elias Sime: The Story of Globalization and Connection Technology Tells' in *Whitewall*, Issue 53, Spring 2019, www.jamescohan.com/artists/elias-sime [accessed 9 May 2023]

7 — Sime, *African Identities*, 2008, p492

8 — Meskerem Assegued in 'Interview with Elias Sime and Meskerem Assegued' by Tracy L. Adler in *Elias Sime — Tightrope*, Ed. Tracy L. Adler (New York: Wellin Museum of Art and DelMonico Books • Prestel, 2020), p179

9 — Assegued, *African Identities*, 2008, p495

10 — Adler, *Elias Sime — Tightrope*, 2020, p30

11 — Sime, *Art Forum*, 2019

12 — Ugochukwu-Smooth C. Nzewi, 'Art, Life and Emotion: Elias Sime's Affective Objects' in *Elias Sime — Tightrope*, Ed. Tracy L. Adler (New York: Wellin Museum of Art and DelMonico Books • Prestel, 2020), p52

13 — Sime, *Art Forum*, 2019

14 — Ibid

15 — Ibid

16 — Kate Cowcher, 'Exhibition Review, Tightrope: Elias Sime' in *African Arts*, Winter 2014, Vol.47, No.4, p90

17 — Sime, *Whitewall*, 2019

18 — Nzewi, *Elias Sime — Tightrope*, 2020, p53

19 — Karen E. Milbourne, 'Personal Touch: Vital Materialism in the work of Elias Sime' in *Elias Sime — Tightrope*, Ed. Tracy L. Adler (New York: Wellin Museum of Art and DelMonico Books • Prestel, 2020), p66

20 — Sime, *Whitewall*, 2019

21 — Sime, *Tightrope: ECHO!?*, 2021

22 — Sime, *Elias Sime — Tightrope*, 2020, p31

—

Collaboration and care

1 — Hans Ulrich Obrist, 'Feature: Elias Sime'; *Pin-Up*, Spring-Summer 2016, www.jamescohan.com/artists/elias-sime [accessed 9 May 2023]

—

A tapestry for humanity

1 — Ursula K. Le Guin, 'The Carrier Bag Theory of Fiction', 1988, republished in *The Carrier Bag Theory of Fiction* (London: Terra Ignota, 2019), p33

2 — Katy Donoghue, 'Elias Sime: The Story of Globalization and Connection Technology Tells' in *Whitewall*, Issue 53, Spring 2019, www.jamescohan.com/artists/elias-sime [accessed 10 June 2023]

3 — 'Interview with Elias Sime and Meskerem Assegued' by Tracy L. Adler in *Elias Sime — Tightrope*, Ed. Tracy L. Adler (New York: Wellin Museum of Art and DelMonico Books • Prestel, 2020), p175

4 — Donoghue, *Whitewall*, 2019

5 — Ibid

6 — Conversation with Elias Sime, 6 July 2023

7 — Adler, *Elias Sime — Tightrope*, 2020, p30

8 — Donoghue, *Whitewall*, 2019

9 — Ugochukwu-Smooth C. Nzewi, 'Art, Life and Emotions: Elias Sime's Affective Objects' in *Elias Sime — Tightrope* (New York: Wellin Museum of Art and DelMonico Books • Prestel, 2020), p56

10 — Conversation with Elias Sime, 6 July 2023

—

Building with love

1 — Zoma Museum has another centre in Harla, a small historic village in the Dire Dawa region of Southeastern Ethiopia.

2 — Sime and Assegued often speak of their practice as 'building with love'. Interview with the author, Addis Ababa, June 2023

3 — Katy Donoghue, 'Elias Sime: The Story of Globalization and Connection Technology Tells' in *Whitewall*, Issue 53, Spring 2019, www.jamescohan.com/artists/elias-sime [accessed 1 July 2023]

4 — Translated from Amharic, *Menyalesh*, means 'what do you have?' The naming of this place, the source of some of Sime's materials, is significant to his practice. Like Menyalesh, Sime's work can also be read as what we have as a society. The collected and reassembled materials tell our collective story — what we have.

5 — Sime, *Whitewall*, 2019

6 — The author visited Sime and Assegued in Addis Ababa in June 2023. She spent time observing them in their everyday work, activities and rituals. Through informal conversations as well as recorded interviews, a clear image of their practice and concerns emerged.

7 — Meskerem Assegued, 'A retrospective observation of Elias Sime' in *African Identities*, Volume 6, 2008, Issue 4: *Ethiopia The New Millennium*, p480–481

8 — Assegued in 'A retrospective observation of Elias Sime' describes a pivotal moment in Sime's practice. In 2005, Sime was invited to participate in a live art installation in the gallery of the Addis Ababa University School of Fine Art and Design in response to the rapidly changing city. In this work, Sime spent a week mixing mud and straw in the centre of the exhibition space. At the end of the week, dressed in a suit and tie and dress shoes, he walked into the mud and straw mixture and spoke about how its chemistry makes it strong enough to build a house to last over a hundred years. Connecting himself to the earth by calmly sifting the mud mixture, Sime talked about how even his outfit, with its Eurocentric appearance, still came from the earth — the same place as the mud and straw. Finally, he walked out of the exhibition barefoot, leaving his footprints on the ground.

9 — Assegued, *African Identities*, 2008, p489–490

10 — Hans Ulrich Obrist, 'Feature: Elias Sime', *Pin-Up*, Spring-Summer 2016, www.jamescohan.com/artists/elias-sime [accessed 19 June 2023]

11 — Renate Bornberg, 'Vernacular Ethiopian Homes' in *Architectural Guide Volume 4: Eastern Africa. From the Sahel to the Horn of Africa*, DOM Publishers, 2022, p284

12 — David Hammons visited Addis Ababa in October 2003 after meeting Assegued at the African Museum Professionals and Curators workshop at the Museum of Modern Art in New York. The exhibition *Divine Light* was curated by Assegued and held at Zoma that year. Similarly, Assegued met Ernesto Novelo, at the time a young emerging artist, in Yucatan in 2004. Novelo subsequently visited Zoma and, inspired by the centre, opened Zoma Contemporary Art Centre in Yucatan as an extension of Zoma in Ethiopia.

13 — Ginanne Brownell Mitic, 'Arts Centre in Ethiopia Links Local and Global' in *The New York Times*, 16 June 2016, www.nytimes.com/2016/06/16/arts/international/arts-center-in-ethiopia-links-local-and-global.html [accessed 7 July 2023]

14 — A film by Jonathan Dayton and Valerie Faris, which was presented at *Eye of the Needle, Eye of the Heart* at Santa Monica Museum of Art, documents the construction process. In this film, Sime, barefoot and dressed in workman overalls, mixes the mud and straw mixture on the ground, with his feet. He then takes handfuls of the mixture and weaves and kneads it into malleable strands which can be moulded, carved and imprinted to create these elaborate mud walls.

15 — Susan Morgan in 'The Talk; Hut Couture' in *The New York Times*, 19 April 2019, describes the house as a 'voluptuous dream, a swirl of ancient techniques and ecstatic imagination.' https://archive.nytimes.com/query.nytimes.com/gst/fullpage-9C03EFDA1538F93AA25757C0A96F9C8B63.html [accessed 7 July 2023]

16 — Assegued in conversation with the author, Addis Ababa, June 2023

17 — Morgan, 'The Talk; Hut Couture', 2019

18 — The theatre and festival director Peter Sellars, a collaborator of Sime's, has described his practice as a combination of modesty and grandeur. Ibid.

19 — Elias Sime in *Elias Sime: Tightrope* https://www.youtube.com/watch?v=K7Vm8JXYQ3E [accessed 7 July 2023]

20 — Peter Sellars describes Sime and Assegued's building practice as a 'devotional act ... alive and breathing.' in Morgan, 'The Talk; Hut Couture', 2019

ABOUT THE AUTHORS

Meskerem Assegued
Meskerem Assegued is an anthropologist, curator and writer. In 2002, she co-founded ZCAC (Zoma Contemporary Art Center), an artist residency located in Addis Ababa and Harla, a small village south of Dire Dawa, Ethiopia. She is also the co-founder of Zoma Museum, Addis Ababa, and a variety of architectural projects including Zoma Village Entoto. Over the last 16 years, Assegued has curated numerous exhibitions both in Ethiopia and abroad. These include *Giziawi #1*, an art happening in Addis Ababa (2002); *Divine Light* by David Hammons at ZCAC (2003); *Green Flame* (2006), with Elias Sime, Ernesto Novelo and Julie Mehretu; and the co-curated *Eye of the Needle, Eye of the Heart* by Elias Sime with Peter Sellars (2009). She was a member of the selection committee for the 2004 Dak'Art Biennale and the 2007 Venice Biennale African Pavilion.

Nana Biamah-Ofosu
Nana Biamah-Ofosu is an architect and director of YAA Projects, an architecture, design and research practice dedicated to exploring counter-histories, material and diasporic culture, through making, speaking and writing architecture. Alongside her architectural practice, she has lectured widely in the UK and internationally. Her research interests include questions on diaspora cultures and identities, hybridity, and communality, and particularly how these subjects encounter, align and manifest through architecture and space. She is currently working on a publication focused on the African compound house as a communal housing typology. As a writer, she has contributed to several art, architecture and design publications, engaging with leading practitioners in contemporary practice.

Gemma Brace
Gemma Brace is Head of Exhibitions at the Arnolfini, Bristol, and a freelance writer and curator. Recent curatorial projects include *Threads: 'Breathing stories into materials'* (2023); *Garry Fabian Miller: Adore* (2023); *Bharti Kher: The Body is a Place* (2022); *Donna Huanca: CUEVA DE COPAL* (2022); *Paula Rego: Subversive Stories* (2022); *Frank Bowling: Land of Many Waters* (2021); *Chantal Joffe: For Esme—with Love and Squalor* (2020); and *Franko B: The Body is Not Here* (2019). She has edited and co-authored publications on Bharti Kher, Frank Bowling and Chantal Joffe, and is a prior recipient of a Paul Mellon Curatorial Research Support Grant, the Art Fund's Jonathan Ruffer Curatorial Grant and an Arvon and Visual Arts South West Critical Writing for the Visual Arts Award.

Andria Hickey
Andria Hickey is a curator and writer based in New York. She is currently Curator-at-Large at The Shed, New York. Previously, she was the founding Senior Curator and Director of Pace Gallery's global curatorial department. Before joining Pace in 2018, Hickey was Senior Curator at MOCA Cleveland, where she oversaw the artistic vision of the institution, curated numerous exhibitions and launched the museum's inaugural Toby Devan Lewis Prize for emerging artists. Hailing from Newfoundland, Canada, Hickey began her curatorial work in the United States as a Curatorial Fellow in the Visual Arts Department at the Walker Art Center. Moving on to serve as Curator at Art in General in New York, she was appointed Curator at Public Art Fund in 2011, where she organised public projects throughout New York City until 2016. She has lectured broadly and her written work has been published in a wide variety of journals and exhibition catalogues.

Elias Sime
Elias Sime deftly weaves, layers and assembles carefully selected everyday materials, transforming commonplace items into lyrical abstract compositions that suggest topography, figuration and colour fields. He often creates intricate works from electronic components —including circuit boards, computer keys and telecommunications wires. For Sime, the history of these materials holds meaning and their significance emerges after thorough consideration. They suggest the tenuousness of our interconnected world, alluding to the frictions between tradition and progress, human contact and social networks, nature and the man-made, and physical presence and the virtual.

As an extension of his art-making, Sime is involved in the exploration of vernacular architecture. Working with his longtime collaborator, Meskerem Assegued, Sime co-founded, designed and built the award-winning Zoma Museum in Addis Ababa, an environmentally conscious international art centre described by *The New York Times* in 2009 as 'a voluptuous dream, a swirl of ancient technique and ecstatic imagination.' Zoma Museum celebrated its grand opening in its new location in March 2019, with expanded facilities that include a gallery space, library, children's centre, edible garden, elementary school, art and vernacular school, amphitheatre, cafe and museum shop.

ABOUT ARNOLFINI

Woven into the fabric of Bristol since 1961, Arnolfini is an international centre of interdisciplinary contemporary arts, presenting an ambitious and wide-ranging programme of visual art, performance, dance, film and music.

Housed in Bush House, a prominent nineteenth-century former warehouse on the city's harbourside, Arnolfini is a pioneering, inspiring public space for arts and learning, offering an innovative, inclusive and engaging experience for all.

Arnolfini has welcomed artists from around the world throughout its history —sharing works by Paula Rego, Jannis Kounellis, John Akomfrah, Grayson Perry, Rachel Whiteread, Peter Doig, Richard Long, Veronica Ryan, Chantal Joffe, Sonia Boyce, Garry Fabian Miller, Alice Kettle and Frank Bowling, to name just a few—as well as supporting talent from in and around Bristol.

Alongside its main programme, Arnolfini is a centre of everyday creativity and learning, working with a wide range of community and artistic partners, while continuing to explore and develop new collaborations across the city and beyond. Spaces are used regularly by families, schools and colleges and health and wellbeing groups.

Through sharing a 62-plus year archive of exhibition slides, publications and an extensive artist book collection, Arnolfini celebrates its heritage and the wide-reaching impact the organisation has had since its foundation.

From 2019, Director Gary Topp and the team have sought to honour Arnolfini's founder Jeremy Rees's principle to 'enjoy yourself', welcoming everyone into the accessible space and inviting engagement in any number of ways. Arnolfini is part of the University of the West of England and a key element of their City Campus.

An independent charity (CIO), Arnolfini is supported by Arts Council England and the Ashley Clinton Barker-Mill Trust.

—

The University of the West of England (UWE Bristol) has a global and inclusive outlook, with approximately 36,000 students and strong industry networks and connections with over 1,000 employers. Research at UWE Bristol focuses on real-world problems and the University plays a pivotal role in the regional economy. With over £300 million invested in infrastructure, buildings and facilities across all campuses, UWE Bristol is creating a place for learning that is innovative, ambitious, connected, enabling and inclusive. UWE Bristol is ranked 43rd out of 122 institutions in *The Guardian* university league table. www.uwe.ac.uk

ACKNOWLEDGEMENTS

Arnolfini would like to warmly thank Elias Sime and Meskerem Assegued for working with us from afar (and at times less far afield), in what proved to be a powerful time for us all over the last two years to realise *Eregata* (the book and exhibition) at Arnolfini. Their shared dreams and collaborative spirit have inspired this project from start to finish.

We would also like to thank writers Andria Hickey and Nana Biamah-Ofosu for exploring Sime's work and the collaborative practice behind the Zoma Museum, bringing both to life for our readers and generating new conversations in the publication alongside those brought to the fore in the exhibition.

A similar heartfelt thank you to Alice Hendy for her always colourful and sensitive photography, allowing readers and audiences to appreciate the magic of Zoma as also experienced by Keiko Higashi, Mian Ng, Sado Jirde, Angelique Retief and Andy Francis in July 2023.

Our greatest thanks to Jim Cohan and Annie Stuart of James Cohan, New York, who have tirelessly supported the project from the start, working with us on the exhibition and the publication, and inspiring and sharing our passion to introduce new audiences to Sime's work.

To Jorg Grimm and Jorien de Vries of GRIMM gallery for welcoming us so warmly to Amsterdam on a cold day in January and working with us to show as wide a selection of Sime's work as possible.

To Stephanie Camu and Southern & Partners for introducing us to Sime's work and endlessly supporting our ambitions to tour the exhibition from the very beginning.

To the many private lenders of Sime's work for allowing us to share it with our audiences for both the duration of the exhibition at Arnolfini and beyond.

To Stefanie Schulz-Klingauf and Felicity Korn at Kunstpalast Düsseldorf for sharing our enthusiasm and helping to grow audiences for Sime's work across Europe.

To our many collaborative partners who have had input into the wider project, including Jo Midgley and Mian Ng at UWE, Sado Jirde and the Black South West Network and Let's Make Art, some of whom accompanied us on a trip to Zoma in July 2023.

To Wilf Whitty at Ratiotype for his thoughtful and playful design, and Taylor Brothers (especially Shaun Cooper) for their care and attention to detail in bringing the book to life in print.

And to our team at Arnolfini who have helped to realise the exhibition and publication in numerous ways, including creating an accompanying programme of engagement, installing the work and sharing the journey with our audiences.

Arnolfini would also like to thank their Board of Trustees for their vital guidance, Arts Council England for their ongoing support, the University of the West of England, whom we are proud to be a part of, and the Ashley Clinton Barker-Mill Trust, who have supported the Arnolfini over many years, including helping us to realise our new Arnolfini and ACBMT International Artist Residency Award, of which both Elias and Meskerem are recipients for 2023.

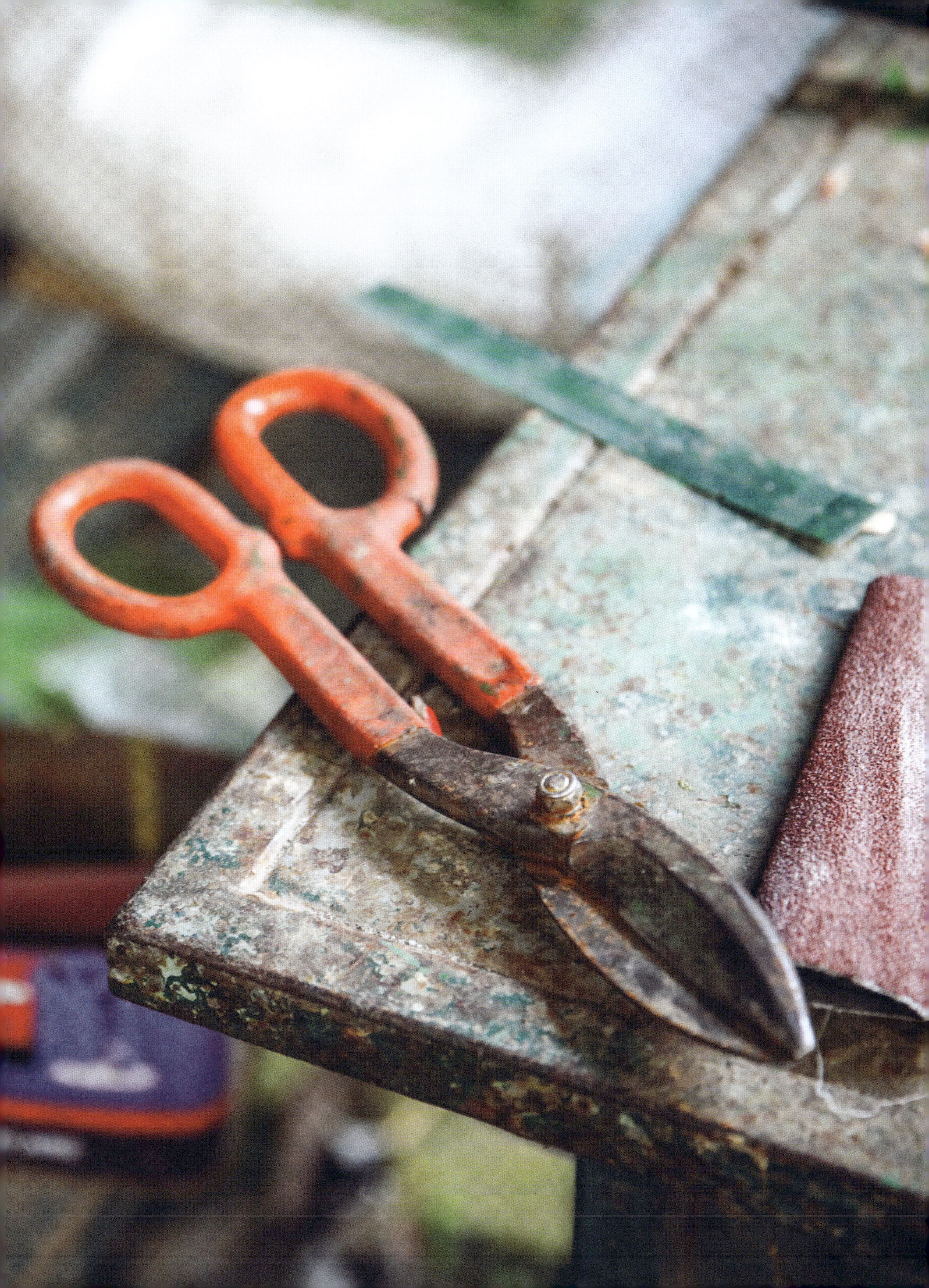

Published by Arnolfini to
accompany the exhibition:
Elias Sime: Eregata እርጋታ
Autumn 2023

Arnolfini, 16 Narrow Quay,
Bristol, BS1 4QA
www.arnolfini.org.uk

Edited by Gemma Brace
Design by Ratiotype
Printed by Taylor Brothers
Printed on FSC® certified paper

Cover image: *Tightrope: It is Green 8*
2023, three-dimensional wall piece
with woven electrical wires on panel,
318.8 × 251.5 × 8.9 cm
Courtesy of the Artist and James Cohan,
New York.

Arnolfini is a registered charity
(number 311504)

This publication has been kindly
supported by James Cohan, New York.

ISBN 978-1-399963-85-5

Image credits
Front and back cover, inside covers,
14, 16, 57, 82, 83, 86, 87, 88, 89, 90, 91,
108, 109, 118, 119, 120, 121, 126–127
Phoebe d'Heurle. Courtesy of the Artist
and James Cohan, New York.

Pages 2, 4–5, 10–11, 12, 19, 22, 23, 24,
25, 26–27, 31, 32, 35, 41, 42–43, 44–45,
46, 49, 53, 58–59, 60–61, 65, 66, 69, 70,
72, 73, 74, 75, 76, 77, 78–79, 125, 128, 132,
133, 139, 141, 142–143
Alice Hendy © Alice Hendy.
Courtesy of Arnolfini.

Pages 6–7, 54, 110, 111
Thomas Barratt. Courtesy of the Artist
and James Cohan, New York.

Pages 8–9, 50, 62, 94, 95, 96, 97, 106,
107, 112, 113
Jonathan de Waart. Courtesy of the
Artist and GRIMM, Amsterdam | London |
New York and James Cohan, New York.

Page 17
Jonathan Bentham. Courtesy of Ruth and
Elmer Wellin Museum of Art.

Pages 21, 28, 38, 116, 117, 122, 123
Christopher Burke Studios. Courtesy of
the Artist and James Cohan, New York.

Pages 36, 102, 103, 104, 105
Izzy Leung. Courtesy of the Artist and
James Cohan, New York.

Pages 80, 84, 85
Adam Reich. Courtesy of the Artist and
James Cohan, New York.

Pages 92, 93
Charles Benton. Courtesy of the Artist
and James Cohan, New York.

Pages 98, 99, 100, 101
Courtesy of Museum of Everything.

Pages 114, 115
Brett Moen. Courtesy of the Artist and
James Cohan, New York.

MIX
Paper from responsible sources
FSC® C002762

ARNOLFINI EST. 1961
James Cohan
Supported using public funding by ARTS COUNCIL ENGLAND
ACBMT Ashley Clinton Barker Mills Trust
UWE Bristol University of the West of England

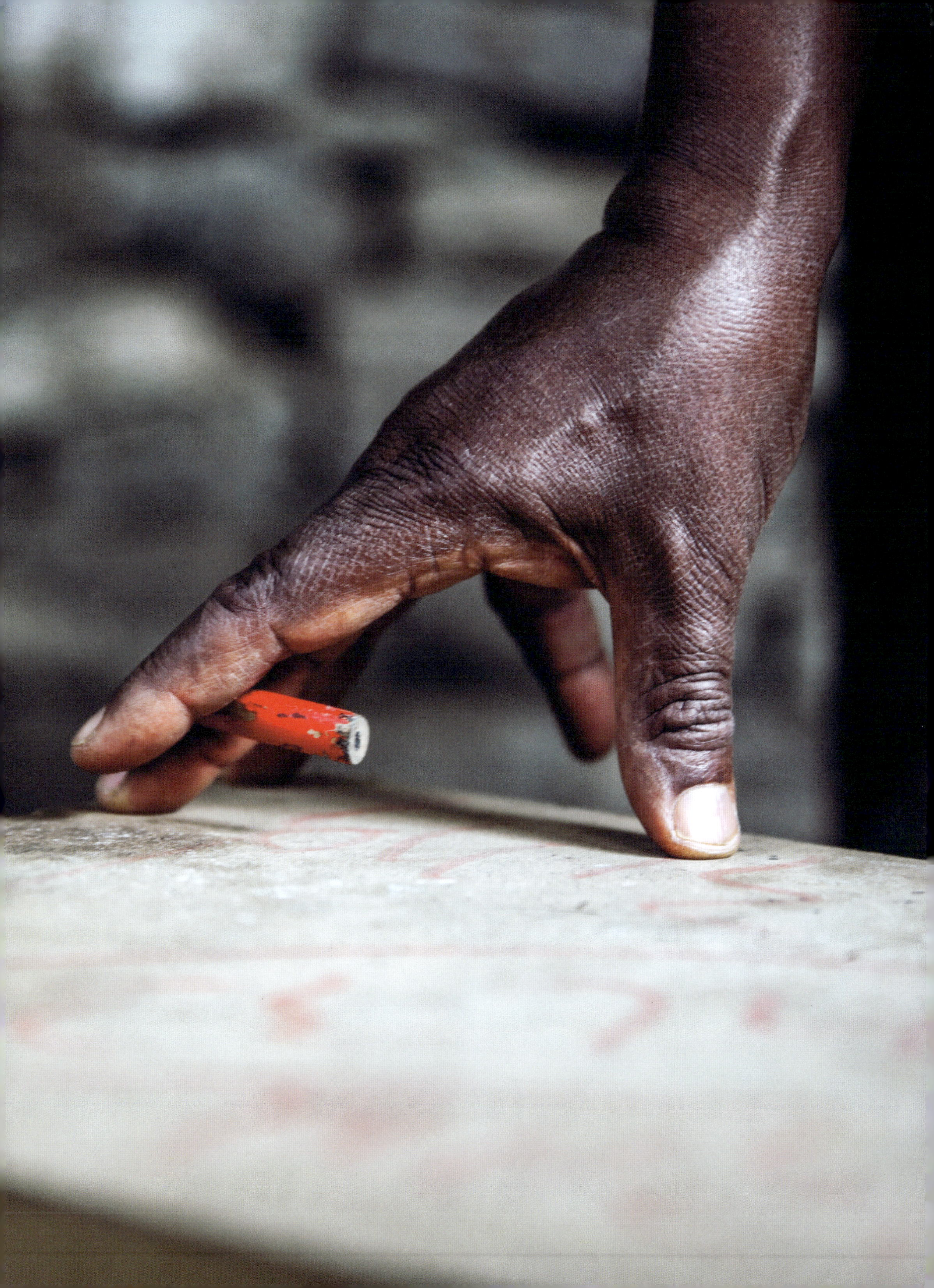

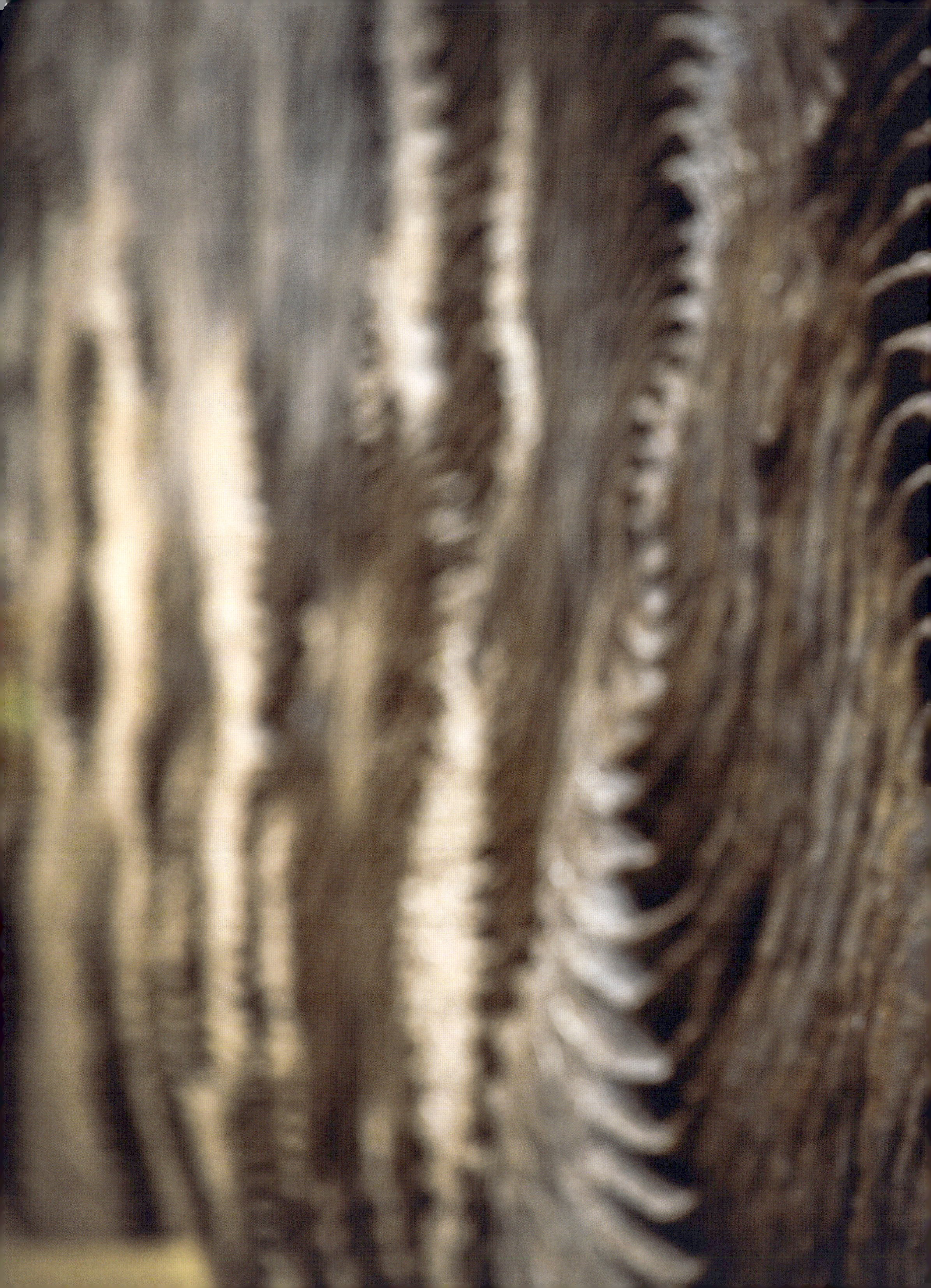

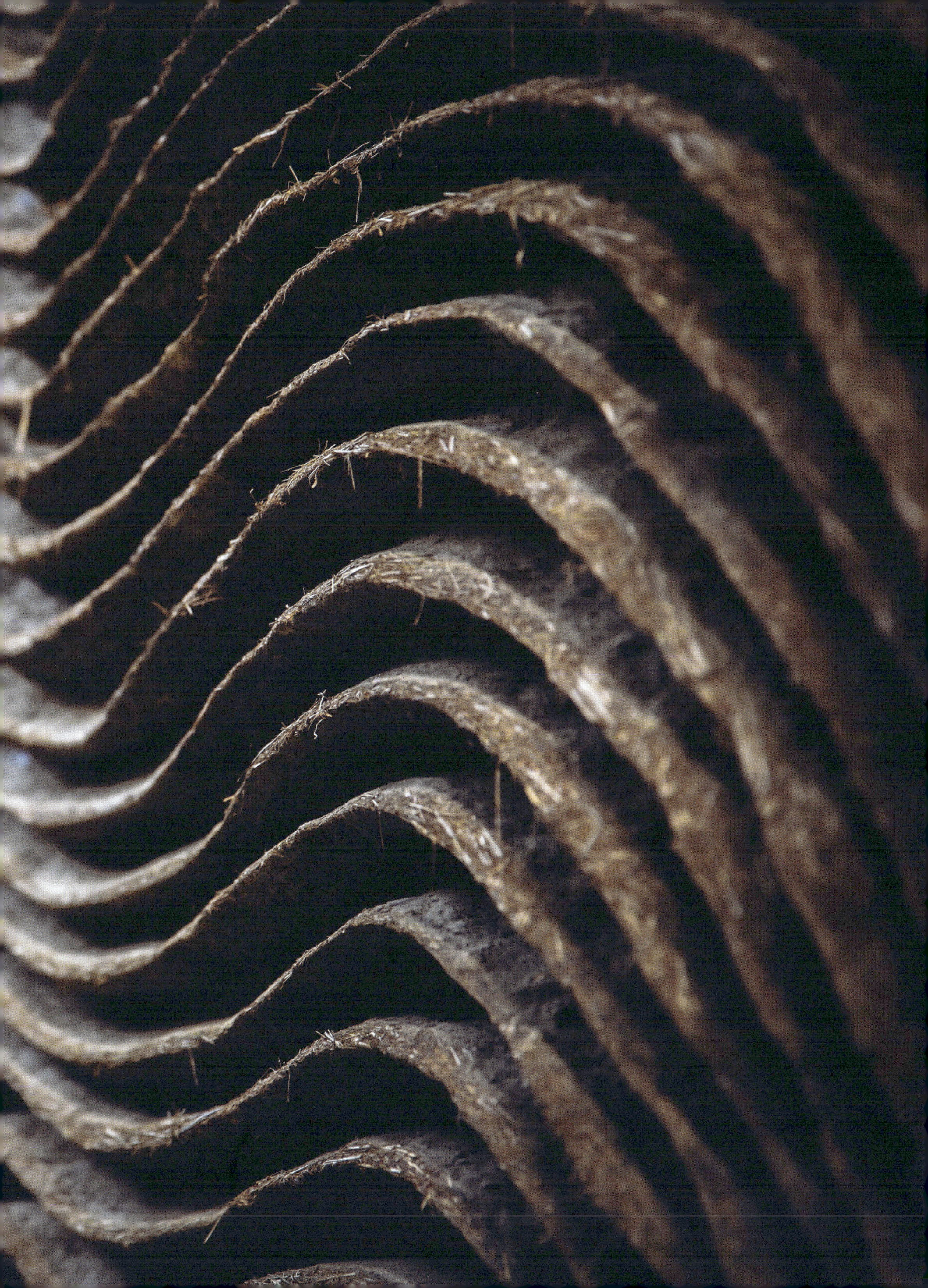